D1635111

Ireland's Revolutionary Tradition

Kieran Allen

PlutoPress
www.plutobooks.com

First published 2016 by Pluto Press
345 Archway Road, London N6 5AA

www.plutobooks.com

British Library Cataloguing in Publication Data
A catalogue record for this book is available from the British Library

ISBN   978 0 7453 3637 4   Hardback
ISBN   978 0 7453 3632 9   Paperback
ISBN   978 1 7837 1743 9   PDF eBook
ISBN   978 1 7837 1745 3   Kindle eBook
ISBN   978 1 7837 1744 6   EPUB eBook

This book is printed on paper suitable for recycling and made from fully managed
and sustained forest sources. Logging, pulping and manufacturing processes are
expected to conform to the environmental standards of the country of origin.

Typeset by Stanford DTP Services, Northampton, England
Simultaneously printed in the European Union and United States of America

Contents

Preface

The commemoration of the 1916 Rising takes place against a background of tremendous change in Irish society. Who would have imagined even a decade ago that Ireland would be the first country in the world to introduce marriage equality by a popular referendum? The image of a conservative backwater has finally been put to rest.

But even though there is a new discourse of equality, there are many outstanding issues to be resolved. In modern Ireland, you can still wait for three years for a hip operation even if you are in agony. Care and treatment is still determined by the size of one's wallet. You can live in cramped conditions and wait for years for social housing. By contrast, wealthy individuals can declare themselves to be 'non-resident' for tax purposes and not contribute to the public purse. It is still a cruel country for some and a paradise for others.

One hundred years after the Rising, there is much reflection on where Irish society is going. Many want to honour the rebels but they also question how the current Irish state matches up to their ideals. This book is written as a contribution to that debate. It is not simply a description of historical events. It looks at how the 1916 Rising led to a revolutionary tradition that still haunts the political establishment.

My thanks to Willie Cumming and Eamonn McCann for their comments. The book is dedicated to those who want to see a new Rising in Ireland.

CHAPTER ONE

Ireland Turned Upside Down

Who fears to speak of the 1916 Easter Rising? A year before the hundredth anniversary of the Rising, the Irish government issued a video, *Ireland Inspires 2016*. It did not mention the executions of the signatories of Ireland's proclamation and instead the camera focused on such luminaries as Ian Paisley, Queen Elizabeth and Bob Geldof. The appearance of Elizabeth Windsor rather than, say, Patrick Pearse or James Connolly was highly unusual. 1916, the video proclaimed, was 'where we came from' but Reconciliation was 'where we are now'. Somebody, somewhere, it appeared was worried about the commemoration and they covered their fears with slick public relations banalities. The video provoked such outrage that it had to be withdrawn.

The 1916 rebellion set off a chain of events which expelled British rule from the 26 counties. It was the beginning of a phase of revolution that is commonly – but rather narrowly – called the 'War of Independence'. What started as an insurrection of the few became a revolt of the many. The current political elite owe their positions to the series of violent events that followed the Rising. Yet they do not like to be reminded of how their ancestors came to power through a revolution that culminated in a bloody counter-revolution, preferring to think of themselves as self-made men or women who rose through the ranks by their own merits. They are embarrassed by connections that are often made between the modern IRA, who fought the Northern state, and the 'old IRA', who fought the British. So they want to put all that behind them – except, of course, for a heritage-linked tourist opportunity. Major, earth-shaking events are supposed to belong to a distant past and need to be packaged up purely for cultural memories. Moreover, too much talk of revolution can be dangerous. There are many angry people suffering from the policies of austerity in modern Ireland and you don't want to give them too many ideas. If the population became too fired up by the 1916 commemorations, some malcontents might even be tempted to do a repeat today. Hence all the talk of reconciliation and cultural memory.

Yet, despite their unease, few of the elite will openly disown the Rising. They know that generations of Irish people have been brought up to regard the 1916 leaders as heroes, and that it is politically dangerous to attack them. An exception, however, is John Bruton, the former Fine Gael Taoiseach who denounced the Rising for starting a period of armed struggle that has damaged the Irish psyche to this day. 'If the 1916 leaders had had more patience', he declared, 'a lot of destruction could have been avoided, and I believe we would still have achieved the independence we enjoy today.'[1] The rebels should not have attacked the British Army and should have supported the peaceful, moderate tactics of Bruton's hero, John Redmond, the leader of the Irish Parliamentary Party, who, he argued, was on the verge of winning Home Rule for Ireland. Why, Bruton asked, was there no commemoration of the hundredth anniversary of the passage into law of Home Rule for Ireland on 18 September 1914?

Although separated by a hundred years, there is an affinity of social class between Bruton and Redmond. Both came from respectable farming stock, Bruton growing up on a large 400-acre farm in Meath, and Redmond turning Parnell's ancestral home at Aughavanagh into his landed estate and permanent Irish residence. Both were Clongowes boys, attending the legendary private school which did so much to instil self-confidence into the Irish elite. Both bestrode the nerve centres of the respective empires. Redmond was a power broker and 'the best dressed man' of the House of Commons. Bruton became the EU Ambassador to the United States before taking up a post of paid lobbyist for Ireland's financial industry. Both lived a life of immense privilege without the slightest embarrassment about their wealth.

Redmond lived the life of a country squire while Bruton retired on a €150,000 Ministerial pension while receiving another 'six-figure' sum as lobbyist of the Irish Financial Services Centre. Small wonder that a finance industry lobbyist finds his hero in the figure of Catholic landlord and squire.

Class ties can be thicker than ones formed around nationality, which perhaps explains why John Bruton's arguments against the 1916 Rising show a remarkable amnesia. While attacking the 'violent separatism' of the Rising, he conveniently forgets or ignores the far greater shedding of blood of the First World War. Consider for a moment the disparity in the figures for those killed. The rebellion costs of the lives of 116 British soldiers, 16 policemen and 318 rebels and civilians. In the Battle of the Somme – which occurred within weeks of the Rising – over 300,000 soldiers from the opposing armies died, including 3,500 Irishmen. Yet nowhere does Bruton assign any responsibility to John Redmond for urging men to enlist in this pointless war. Redmond argued that Catholics and Protestants should die side by side in defence of the British Empire so that 'their blood may be the seal that will bring all Ireland together in one nation.'[2] Presenting revolutionaries as violent fanatics while staying silent about Redmond's vigorous support for war is, to say the least, a little inconsistent. Yet there is a point to it. Bruton wants to pretend that constitutional politicians are peaceful individuals while revolutionaries are effectively 'terrorists'.

However, if logic is not Bruton's strongest point, his intervention has still one redeeming feature: it focuses attention on the nearly forgotten figure of John Redmond. One of the great effects of Irish nationalism has been its power to rewrite the past, so that it appears as one long, 700-year struggle. There is a historical narrative that the Irish all hailed from a common stock of dispossessed peasants who resisted a British landlord class that had stolen their land. Each uprising against British rule was only the latest instalment of a longer story. The Irish world before 1916 is virtually unknown and figures like John Redmond appear as an aberration – a sort of bumbling interlude between the Fenian rebellion of 1867 and the Rising.

This is, however, a caricature because John Redmond had more support than modern Irish political leaders. His party was so dominant in elections that nationalist Ireland was virtually a one-party state. In the 1910 election, for example, two-thirds of the Irish Parliamentary Party candidates were returned unopposed. He led a mass political party of more than a hundred thousand members scattered across a thousand branches.[3] Its tentacles stretched into every aspect of society and for most of his political life Redmond was known as the 'leader of the Irish race'.[4] In other words, Ireland before 1916 was seen as a rock of conservative stability.

But in 1918, Redmond died and his party melted away. The elaborate network of power and patronage that had been created around him was dismantled. What was remarkable about the Rising and the revolution that followed was not just the way it overthrew the British Empire, but also the manner in which it destroyed an Irish political caste. How this occurred is an intriguing story in itself, because it can lead to a more general understanding of how revolutions happen. Revolutions are like unexpected thunderbolts, that come out of the blue. Someone writing about the need for a revolution in Redmond's Ireland would have been regarded as a political lunatic. Redmondism was the only game in town and the Irish Parliamentary Party held all the cards. Talk of revolution could only come from a dreamer or a madman. And yet it happened.

The magnitude of the change can be illustrated by comparing two events. The first took place in Dublin, just one year before the Easter Rising. On the first Sunday in April, the National Volunteers – followers of John Redmond who were willing to enlist in Britain's war effort – staged what the London *Times* correspondent called the 'largest military display Dublin has ever seen'.[5] Nearly 30,000 uniformed volunteers, many with rifles, assembled in Phoenix Park and then marched through the streets of Dublin to be reviewed by

Redmond. They were brought to the city by fifty special trains from all over the country and somewhere between 100,000 and 200,000 people witnessed this display.

The second event took place in Galway a few months before. The Irish Volunteers, as those opposed to involvement in Britain's war were called, planned to hold a meeting in the city centre. But the twenty or thirty members who turned up were confronted by a number of soldiers and sailors who were on leave. When they tried to march out of their drill hall, they were met by an angry crowd who attacked and wrenched their rifles from them. They were chased through the city and subsequently the windows smashed of anyone professing sympathies for Sinn Féin. With some exaggeration, one writer has described it as 'Galway's Kristallnacht'.[6] No wonder then that the Redmondites could look down on the revolutionaries as 'a little group of obscure persons with ridiculous pretensions'.[7] Yet within a short period, all of this was turned upside down.

How did such a turn-about happen? The conventional answer is that the sacrifice of 1916 pricked the conscience of a nation and re-awakened its national instincts. As the saying goes, the leaders of 1916 'gave their lives so that Ireland might be free'. Unfortunately, this rather simplistic explanation leads to mistaken conclusions. It suggests that revolutions occur because a tiny minority of revolutionaries are organised, determined and, above all, willing to sacrifice their own lives. The mass of the people, it appears, are governed only by their emotions and spring to life when their sympathies are aroused. If that were true, martyrdom would be the key to change. Yet throughout history, there have been countless examples of people giving their lives to a cause – and little has followed. In the case of the 1916 rebellion, there were other reasons besides the horror at the executions of its leaders for why Irish people chose a revolutionary road.

Revolutions, therefore, are more complex affairs. Their roots lie deep in society and do not spring simply from the imagination or bravery of the few. To understand why the Irish revolution occurred, it is first necessary to look at what kept Irish society in the thrall of conservatism for decades – and how its own internal contradictions blew it apart.

The Defeat of Fenianism

Redmondism can be described as an imperial mindset of the respectable elements of Irish society before 1916. Its origins lay in the enormous social changes that overtook Ireland in the wake of the Famine and the crushing of an earlier revolutionary tradition of Fenianism.

In the years of the Great Famine, between 1846 and 1851, 1 million people out of a population of 8 million lost their lives and a further million emigrants fled. Despite attempts by 'revisionist' historians to absolve the British government of responsibility, there can be no avoiding their guilt. Roy Foster, for example, has claimed that Britain operated no differently than the Belgian government when they confronted their famine by providing a similar amount of relief. The problem, he suggested, was that 'local differentiation' meant that the British government 'underestimated what faced them.'[8] His implication was that the tragedy arose from a misunderstanding and poor administration. Yet the reality was that Britain only provided £10 million in relief and much of this was spent on an ill-administered public works scheme. That amounted to just 0.2 percent of its GNP and was a good deal less than the £89 million spent on the Crimean War a few years later.[9]

The British elite's approach to the Famine was conditioned both by their racism and their free market fundamentalism. The Famine coincided with the rise of the Whigs who were committed to market forces and free trade, and who opposed any ban on the export of food, a measure that could have saved many lives. They also ended food relief schemes and put the burden of paying for public works programmes onto ratepayers who were already devastated by the famine. Assistant Secretary to the Treasury Charles Trevelyan explained the reasoning behind restricting the supply of free food in a letter to Lord Mount Eagle in 1846, stating that he wished to dispel all doubts about the 'magnitude of the existing calamity and its danger not being fully known and appreciated in Downing Street'. However,

> The ability even of the most powerful government is extremely limited in dealing with a social evil of this description. It forms no part of the functions of government to provide supplies of food or to increase the productive powers of the land. In the great institutions of the business of society, it falls to the share of government to protect the merchant and the agriculturist in the free exercise of their respective employments, but not itself to carry on these employments.[10]

He added that it was part of 'the defective part of the national character' of the Irish that they demanded such intervention.[11] The famine, Trevelyan hinted, provided a God-sent opportunity to remove the surplus population. 'The real evil with which we have to contend', he later claimed, 'is not the physical evil of the Famine, but the moral evil of the selfish, perverse and turbulent character of the people.'[12]

The horrors of the Famine left an indelible impression on a generation of survivors. John Mitchell gave expression to this blinding rage in his *Jail Journal* where he described how 'husbands and wives fought like wolves for the last morsel of food in the house ... how the "laws" [were] vindicated all this time ... how starving wretches were transported for stealing vegetables at night.'[13] Mitchell had called for uprising in the midst of the Famine, but he was working with a Young Ireland movement led by upper-class gentlemen such as William Smith O'Brien and Gavan Duffy, who appeared to be more concerned about the rights of private property than in actually pursuing an insurrection. As James Connolly later recounted it, the crowning absurdity of their efforts was the sight of William Smith O'Brien telling the peasants of Mullinahone that they should not fell trees to build barricades until they first asked permission of the landlord.[14]

However, despite this fiasco, the flame of revolution was passed on. It was taken up by poorer Irish men and women, who had been driven into emigration or left smouldering with resentment at the state of their country. The Irish Revolutionary Brotherhood – later renamed the Irish Republican Brotherhood and known as the Fenians – was formed by James Stephens in a woodyard in Dublin in 1858. Modelled on Irish secret societies such as the Ribbonmen – peasant groups which attacked landlords – and also the Continental revolutionary conspiracies in which Stephens had participated, the aim of the Fenians was the overthrow of British rule in Ireland by means of an insurrection. Despite being organised in secret revolutionary circles, the Fenians grew into a mass movement with a membership variously estimated at between 50,000 and 80,000. They were particularly strong among Irish emigrants in Britain, who co-operated actively with radical British workers. When, in 1867, they mustered for an attack on Chester, they could mobilise a thousand members. The Fenians even had many members serving in the British Army in Ireland and it took over a hundred court martials to break up their network.[15] Overall, the Fenians' main base in Dublin came from skilled workers and shop assistants, while in the countryside, agricultural labourers often formed the backbone of the organisation.

Fenianism became a wider revolutionary attitude of opposition and rebellion. As one historian described it:

> ... they were losing the 'tug-of-the-forelock' mentality that traditionally pervaded Irish society. The Fenians came mainly from the lower classes – artisans, town and country labourers, small farmers. Some of them, at least instinctively, resented the place delegated to them in Irish society by social betters. Lack of deference became almost a physical characteristic in the eyes of the authorities.[16]

The Fenian tradition was based on older notions of revolution as a conspiracy fomented by an organised minority. The Fenians were to infiltrate movements, create provocations and name the time and date for revolution. They – and not mood or determination of the wider mass of the people – were to decide when to make the call for insurrection. The uprising was seen as a technical issue to be determined by the inner readiness of their organisation and by opportunities inadvertently presented by the state. Revolution was not seen as a social upheaval, but was reduced to a purely military operation. It was divorced from wider developments in society and sprung only from the fact of British domination. There was no social programme in Fenianism – its focus was purely on the political separation of Ireland and Britain. While the Fenians continually attacked the general evil of landlordism, they believed that nothing could be done about it until Ireland was free. The Fenian leader, James Stephens, noted that while the movement sometimes advocated peasant ownership of land, 'national independence was put forward as the point to be gained first.'[17] There was no discussion on what *type* of republic might emerge from separation. One result of this was that the Fenian movement went through long periods of inactivity as it simply waited for the great day of the Rising.

The Catholic Church hated the Fenians. Led by the influential Cardinal Manning in Westminster, the Catholic hierarchy wanted to keep an Irish representation in the House of Commons as leverage to gain some advantage in a largely Protestant society. They also feared the republican ethos that proclaimed solidarity between Catholic and Protestant and a common citizenship based on nationality rather than religion. They preferred continuing British rule over Ireland – albeit with discrimination against their own church – to outright revolutionary politics. As Cardinal Cullen, the leader of the Irish Catholic Church put it:

For thirty years I have studied the Revolution on the Continent; and for nearly thirty years I have watched the Nationalist movement in Ireland. It is tainted at its sources with the Revolutionary spirit. If ever an attempt is made to abridge the rights and liberties of the Catholic Church in Ireland, it will not be the English government, nor by a 'No Popery' cry in England but by the revolutionary and irreligious nationalists in Ireland.[18]

Much to the delight of the bishops, the Fenian uprising of 5 March 1867 was a disaster. A Fenian provisional government, based in London, had appointed an Irish-American officer, Godfrey Massey, to organise the uprising. Instead of embarking on a guerrilla-style action, he went for a full-scale insurrection, even though the movement had been weakened by previous arrests. The crushing of the uprising discredited the purely 'physical force' strategy for a generation and helped to bolster the bishops' condemnation of revolutionary secret societies.

From Land Reform to Redmondism

The defeat of the Fenian revolt led to splits and divisions. Some, led by Jeremiah O'Leary, wanted to wait until the time was ripe for another insurrection and did not want their movement sullied by any engagement with social issues. But others looked in a different direction. After the defeat, a number of Fenian revolutionaries began to grasp the connection between social issues and the fight for independence. Led by John Devoy in the US and Michael Davitt in Ireland, they embarked on a strategy of land agitation to win mass support for a national revolt against British rule. To facilitate this, they formed an informal 'broad front' with the rising star of the Irish Parliamentary Party, Charles Stewart Parnell. The 'New Departure' as it became known, was to play a decisive role in the reshaping of Irish society. However, in the bitterest of ironies, it produced the opposite to what both the revolutionaries and Parnell expected.

Davitt and Devoy thought they could mobilise the population around a set of economic issues that would bring them into confrontation with the Empire. They promoted social demands that, they thought, the British government could not concede. Instead of just calling for the traditional demands of fair rent and fixity of tenure, they demanded peasant proprietorship; in other words, the euthanasia of the landlord class. (As a declared socialist, Davitt favoured land nationalisation but this was not to feature in the immediate practical programme.) Devoy and Davitt believed that the British government would never allow Irish peasants to own their own land and so the struggle would 'spill over' into a struggle for a separate Irish parliament.[19] This strategy justified an alliance with constitutional politicians who would champion a national parliament and self-government.

Parnell, by contrast, thought that the Anglo-Irish gentry could play a leadership role in Irish society. He thought that the class war in the Irish countryside had forced the gentry to look for the protection of the British garrison and so they turned their back on the Irish nation. If a peasant purchase scheme could be devised, he thought, the former landlords could assume their natural role as leaders of society. With the money they would receive from the purchase of their land, they might even help to stimulate Irish industry. Parnell was bold enough to form an alliance with the Fenians and was willing to use their networks to gain control over the Irish nationalist movement. But his aims were different, because he hoped that after the peasants bought out their land, 'There would remain no class in Ireland interested in the maintenance of English supremacy there; and we would in a rational and peaceful way, without any violent revolution, in my opinion and without jingle of arms, but by the union of all classes in Ireland obtain the restoration of our legislative independence.'[20]

The alliance between the Fenians and Parnell laid the basis for the Land League; the subsequent land war that the League fought was to reshape Ireland. And, in one of the strangest ironies, the struggle created the social conditions out of which Redmondism grew. A number of factors worked together to bring about this unexpected development.

Even before the Land League was formed, the devastation of the Famine had cleared the way for more capitalist forms of agriculture. In its aftermath, there was a huge number of evictions, the main victims being the large class of farm labourers who often cultivated small plots of land of less than one acre. Their numbers fell by two-thirds between 1841 and 1911.[21] This in turn led to a growth of the 'middle peasantry', but this was a somewhat vague description of an amorphous mass, which was divided between graziers such as the cattle king Valentine McDonnell, who held over 1,200 acres in Roscommon, and smaller tenant farmers. The improved living standards in British cities created new demands for meat and dairy which coincided with a shift in Irish agriculture from tillage to pasture. The national cattle herd increased from 1.9 million to 3.1 million between 1854 and 1901 and the proportion being shipped to Britain rose by 25 per cent.[22] In brief, there was a growing reliance on the market and a shift away from subsistence farming. However, as Marx pointed out, this was still a 'caricature' of the type of capitalist re-organisation that had occurred in Britain, because it produced few farmers who invested heavily in land improvement.[23]

The Land League was originally formed amongst the poorer farmers in Connaught, where 83 per cent of the holdings were less than 30 acres.[24] They campaigned for a reduction in rents and resisted all evictions through the famous boycott tactic. But they also wanted a re-distribution of land and a break-up of the graziers' holdings. However, the big farmers belonging to the farmers' clubs of Leinster also joined the Land League, because they were in the throes of a crisis in agricultural prices. Their interests differed from those of poorer farmers and they focused on rent reductions *rather than* land redistribution. The *Roscommon Herald,* which supported the poorest peasants, described how the 'ranchers' 'wormed themselves into the Land League; they have had poor men fighting for rent reductions which were practically worthless to struggling tenants but great boons to the owners of bullock-walks.'[25] The group that lost out most were the landless labourers who had nothing to gain from rent reductions.[26] These class divisions within the League came to a head after Parnell concluded the Kilmainham Treaty with the British government in 1881. In effect, the principles of co-ownership between tenant and landlord were established and rents were reduced.[27] But the calls for land redistribution were neglected.

Finally, contrary to the expectations of Devoy and Davitt, the landlord class and the British government agreed to a scheme for peasant proprietorship in the Wyndham Act of 1903. This transfer of ownership from landlord to peasants was exceptional because nowhere else in the world had a state subsidised the buying-out of landlords on such a scale. In other countries, it took a combination of an agrarian and national revolution to break the grip of landlordism and divide out land. But the sheer wealth and power of the British Empire – which at that point commanded over 25 per cent of the land mass of the world – made this distribution possible. As a result of successive Land Acts, over 316,000 holdings, comprising an area of 11 million acres were purchased for £100 million.[28] The landlords also benefited as they received a cash bonus and payment for their estates spread over 68 years.[29]

The settlement of Ireland's land question was by no means complete, and soon an anti-grazier campaign was launched to call for redistribution. Nevertheless, relative social peace was created in the Irish countryside and a new class of more comfortable farmers emerged, who were serviced by small-time capitalists and traders. This section of society became the principle base for Redmondism. They had no time for the revolutionary doctrines of Fenianism and wanted only to gain a niche for themselves within the Empire. This development also coincided with a shift in Britain's own interest in

Ireland. Its ruling elite were no longer intimately tied to a landed aristocracy which drew rent from Ireland. By the early twentieth century, Britain also found that Ireland was no longer contributing to the imperial exchequer, but was instead draining funds from it. It therefore suited the British state to grant more autonomy to their province, in the form of Home Rule. And this created the social conditions from which Redmondism emerged.

Clericalism and Redmondism

There is a particular type of Irish liberal who seems to think that praising Britain's involvement in Ireland is the highest form of critical thinking. They get a frisson of excitement in challenging nationalist stories about the 1916 Rising and British skulduggery. The former left winger, Lord Bew, is a good example. In his youth, he pioneered an important Marxist study of the Land League, but in his later years he settled comfortably into the establishment. In a short study, he once presented John Redmond as an advocate of 'cultural diversity'.[30] If only Redmond had been allowed to progress on the peaceful road to Home Rule, there would have been a more tolerant Ireland, built on a greater respect between Protestant and Catholic.

This entirely mythological reading of the past suits an establishment that feels threatened by a revolutionary tradition. The reality, however, is that there was no contradiction between a British Empire, which imagined itself to be a bastion of liberal progress, and a colony which it reshaped into a conservative, sectarian society. Empires often present themselves as more modern and liberal than the 'backward' societies they colonise. They claim that their 'leadership' is necessary to promote better equality for women, or tolerance between different religious creeds. This 'liberalism' is really a mark of their own sense of superiority over the colonised population. The implicit suggestion is that the imperial rulers can resort to reason while the natives are mired in 'fanatical' emotion. However, the reality is that empires tend to foster backwardness and conservatism as a bulwark of support for their rule. They seek out the most traditional leaders and the more privileged layers of society to create a social base for their control. In imperial Ireland, this took place through a deadly alliance of Redmondism and Clericalism.

The land settlement led to the growth of a more secure farming class, whose members saw their incomes and savings increase. Between 1850 and 1900, the value of combined bank deposits in Ireland grew sixfold and banks sprung up all around the country. In 1851, there was one bank for every 37,600 people; by 1891, the number had grown to one for every 8,200 people.[31] The sons and daughters of the wealthier farming class also moved into the towns, buying up pubs and property. Others joined the professions, and the proportion of Catholic doctors and lawyers rose dramatically.[32] This expansion of the professional strata was also reflected in the re-organisation of the Catholic Church, as the ambition of every comfortable farmer was to have a son who would become a doctor, a lawyer, or a priest. Whereas before the Famine, Irish Catholicism had a much looser structure and a greater mixture of religious and superstitious beliefs, in its aftermath, this changed dramatically. The number of priests rose by 150 per cent at the very time the population was shrinking. In 1861, there was one priest for every 755 Catholics, but by 1911 there was one for every 210.[33]

The growth of the organised Catholic Church led to a new morality of sexual repression and a downgrading of the status of women. The more comfortable farmers who owned their land were terrified at the thought of 'illegitimate' births and so preferred pre-marital celibacy to any risk to dividing out their land. Traumatised by the recent history of the Famine, they listened avidly to priests who warned of the dangers of fornication. The Virgin Mary was promoted as the ideal image for Irish woman whose 'reward' was to be the mistress of the kitchen, bringing up her children in the doctrinal purities of the Church. Irish Catholicism began its obsession with controlling sexuality that lasted for decades, primarily because its priests were drawn from the class of farmers who had acquired land. Truly, the Irish Catholic Church became the property-owning farmer at prayer.[34]

From another side of the country emerged the muscle for the Catholic lay movement. The Ancient Order of Hibernians (AOH) was founded as a Catholic version of the Orange Order and was eventually taken over by the nationalist MP Joe Devlin, who declared himself the Order's grand master. It was a secret society, committed to providing physical defence for priests, and fighting 'freemasonry, socialism, atheism, proselytism and all other combinations which collectively are doing considerable injury to the church'.[35] By the start of the twentieth century, it had spread rapidly to every part of Ireland, growing from 5,000 members in 1900 to 64,000 nine years later. Its aim was to impose Catholic fundamentalism on those parts of Ireland that it could control. When James Connolly, for example, tried to speak in Cobh, he was driven out of town by AOH thugs. He later wrote that they brought 'religious terrorism with it into quarters hitherto known for their broad mindedness and discernment'.[36]

Redmond's social base lay in the countryside but the AOH acted as his muscle men. In 1909, for example, an attempt was made by William O'Brien MP, the leader of the anti-grazier movement, to gain greater influence over the Irish Parliamentary Party. In what became known as the 'Baton convention', his supporters were attacked by an AOH contingent from Longford and Westmeath, 'who arrived with "hazels" hitherto reserved for use on the flank of bullocks'.[37] Amidst cries of 'Down with the Russian Jewess' – a reference to O'Brien's wife – he was actually driven out of the party. The Irish parliamentary apparatus was, in reality, an alliance between wealthy farmers and the more conservative urban professionals, but holding it together in a tight organisation was the semi-secretive AOH.

Redmond's central vision was to make Ireland a junior partner within the British Empire. He saw the Empire as 'an instrument of civilisation and progress whose existence was not incompatible with national freedom.'[38] 'We want', he proclaimed 'to have our Imperial patriotism as well as our local patriotism.'[39] He forged an alliance with the Liberal Party to achieve the goal of Home Rule within that empire. The Liberals in turn bolstered Redmond's organisation by giving the AOH an opportunity to dispense patronage and gain greater control. After Lloyd George pushed through the National Insurance Act in 1911, the AOH was allowed to staff many of the insurance departments. They, and the Irish Parliamentary Party more generally, were appointed as judges or justices of the peace. And just as in modern Irish society, this political caste knew how to play the 'jobs-for-the-boys' game. Relatives and supporters of prominent nationalists, such as Joseph Devlin, John Dillon and Redmond gained plum jobs in the Irish Administration.[40] It was a clear attempt by the Empire to develop a controlling apparatus over the Irish people, in the event of Home Rule.

Redmond's alliance with British Liberalism was combined with reactionary policies at home. Far from being a 'progressive', Redmond was a deeply conservative politician who defended privilege in almost every sphere of life. He opposed the suffragette movement and stayed quiet when AOH thugs broke up their meetings. Women were often excluded from Irish Parliamentary Party meetings and were banned from involvement in its youth wing.[41] Redmond denounced labourers who wanted to form their own union and urged them to vote for nationalist landlords. He opposed the extension of the Feeding of School Children Act to Ireland – even though he accepted it for England. He wanted a Catholic university to be established, but then backed the bishops when they reached a compromise with the British state and gained a university with 'substantial Catholic influence'. Women, of course, were excluded from this university. Overall, then, Redmondism promoted Ireland as a conservative backwater within the Empire. Supporters of the Irish Parliamentary Party stressed their Irish heritage and sometimes even proclaimed a need to 'de-Anglicise' Ireland. But even while wearing their badge of cultural identity, their eyes were set on posts in the Indian civil service or in the patronage system controlled by the AOH. Their allegiance hovered between the arch-imperialist 'Rudyard Kipling and Kathleen Ni Houlihan'.[42]

On the Margins

There were, however, two groups who were marginalised in Redmond's constitutional nationalist movement. Foremost was the urban working class. In Belfast, workers were divided on sectarian lines but, on occasion, would unite to mount a vigorous class war. In 1907, Jim Larkin made his first appearance in Ireland during a massive dock strike and, for a brief period, Devlin's AOH and the Orange Order lost control.[43] But it was in Dublin that the struggles of the working class caused the greatest danger to the Irish Parliamentary Party. Although a relative social peace had descended on the countryside, the stunted nature of Irish capitalism created great pools of poverty in the capital. Arnold Wright, although hostile to the workers' movement, had to admit that 'the degradation of human kind is carried to a point of abjectness beyond that reached in any city of the Western world, save perhaps Naples.'[44] The huge numbers of unemployed and casual workers made any sort of conventional trade unionism impossible and only the most militant form of class struggle and revolutionary socialism stood any chance of making an impact. Larkinism provided this potent mix and from 1908 until 1913, there were a series of battles that put the Dublin employers on the defensive. Larkin's paper, the *Irish Worker*, which had a circulation of 20,000 a week, repeatedly condemned the Home Rule party for not being concerned with the material welfare of Irish workers because the party voted against extending social legislation to Ireland.

In 1913, the titanic battle between Dublin workers and the leaders of native Irish capitalism commenced. It seemed that Home Rule was about to be won and the leaders of corporate Ireland decided to 'celebrate their maturity in "affairs of state" by declaring war to [the] death on the Irish labour movement.'[45] William Martin Murphy, the owner of the *Independent* newspapers and the Dublin Tram Company, carefully planned an employers' lockout to break Larkin's Irish Transport and General Workers Union. Though they adopted a pose of neutrality in the conflict, the activities of the AOH showed where the Redmondites actually stood. They attacked a scheme to temporarily move the children of strikers to England by claiming it was a plot to undermine Irish Catholicism. The close association of the prominent nationalist MP Tim Healy with the employers' leader, William Martin Murphy, was further evidence of where the sympathies of the Redmondite party lay. Certainly James Connolly did not mince his words. The Irish Parliamentary Party stood for 'naked, unashamed reaction stirring up the blackest passions in the lowest depths of human nature – the line of the obscurantist and the bigot.'[46]

The other groups marginalised in Redmond's project were the lower strata of the intelligentsia. The term 'intelligentsia' does not refer solely to a handful of intellectuals but rather to a wider social group who earned their living through mental labour. While the Catholic upper-class professionals made considerable advances within the structures of the Empire, those at the lower rungs experienced greater status frustration. The expansion of the British state led to a greater recruitment of the intelligentsia. The Irish civil service increased tenfold between 1861 and 1911. The numbers of teachers, postal clerks and local authority clerks also grew considerably. Those who left university and joined these occupations often had a distinctly modern outlook. They wanted Ireland to move beyond its agrarian past and believed firmly in the possibility of self-improvement through education. Many thought that the Empire opened up new vistas for progress and prided themselves on being part of its liberal culture. Some even thought that women should have equal opportunities to men.

They found, however, that their avenues for advance were blocked because the Protestant Ascendancy still controlled access to the top positions in the civil service. As one young writer wrote, in an essay entitled 'A plague of BAs', many brilliant Catholic graduates had to content themselves with 'wretched clerkships'.[47] Those who became teachers found that there were no set wages in Catholic schools and they were often badly paid. Despite an official ideology of social mobility through education and merit, the reality of discrimination against the 'natives' was all too apparent. The result was that many of the intelligentsia became 'doubly isolated': their modern outlook alienated them from their rural communities, but their secular ambitions were frustrated by exclusion from power and status. A minority began to interpret this dilemma in terms of the suffering of the nation itself, believing that they, as individuals, and Ireland, as a nation, had been humiliated. A Gaelic revival movement became attractive for this intelligentsia. It was a means both to reconnect with their roots and to wield together a force that would remove their humiliation.

Conradh na Gaeilge, or the Gaelic League, became a crucial vehicle for this sentiment, combining demands for progress with a revival of the national culture. It supported an industrial revival, temperance, technical education, agricultural cooperation and the teaching of the Irish language in schools and universities. By 1906, it had grown to 75,000 members.[48] An earlier Celtic Revival movement, led by Lady Gregory and William Butler Yeats, was dismissed as one populated by aristocratic romantics, and the new movement took on the task of de-Anglicising Ireland. On its edges, it shaded off into a harder anti-imperialism. The visits of two British monarchs to Dublin – Queen Victoria in 1900 and King Edward VII in 1903 – provided useful markers for the shift from Gaelic revivalism to a growth of republican sentiment. Relatively small numbers had protested against Queen Victoria but by the time of Edward VII's visit there were, according to *The Times*, 'half as many threats' as well wishers.[49] The

Irish Parliamentary Party had refused to condemn Edward's visit and so a considerable number of cultural nationalists were drawn towards Arthur Griffith's National Council movement and later Sinn Féin. They demanded political freedom *from* the empire rather than *within* it, but they were still very much a minority movement.

Aside from activist minorities within these two marginalised groups, the domination of Redmondism over Irish life in the early twentieth century was all pervasive. The number of committed revolutionaries was tiny and one participant has claimed that the strength of the Irish Republican Brotherhood, even as late as 1914, was only around two hundred.[50] However, underneath the iceberg of conformity, a number of contradictions were growing that would eventually blow apart Redmond's Ireland. These developed at the heart of the Empire itself.

Splits and Crisis of Empire

To understand how Redmondism broke apart, it is necessary to shift focus to the centre of the Empire. Redmondism was all about creating an 'imperial Ireland' – a country where a distinct national and Catholic identity would be subsumed within the wider empire. But the imperialist world had entered a period of crisis and this had dramatic effects on the British ruling class.

By the early twentieth century, the leaders of British imperialism had to confront three major issues. The first was the growing military costs of maintaining the empire. This became evident during the Boer War, when the British state had to mobilise 450,000 troops and intern a quarter of the Boer population in concentration camps to suppress the rebellion. The second related difficulty was Britain's economic decline in relation to its main rivals. The ruling class feared the growing economic might of Germany, and some supporters of the politician Joseph Chamberlain started to talk of tariffs to protect British industry. The third issue was how to involve the working class in the political system while defending the elite in an age that was moving towards mass democracy. The Liberals tended to favour a policy of incorporation, in order to woo the British trade union movement into a Liberal-Labour alliance. The Tories favoured a policy of whipping up jingoism and chauvinism so that the British masses could be led by their betters. These conflicts about how best to manage the empire led to more intense clashes within the British ruling elite.

Matters came to a head when the Liberal Chancellor of the Exchequer, Lloyd George, introduced a 'people's budget' to pay for growing military expenditure and welfare payments. This proposed a super tax on incomes above £5,000, an increase in death duties, and a special tax on undeveloped land. The landed aristocracy and their traditional spokesmen in the Tory Party were outraged and in an unprecedented move, they used their majority in the House of Lords to veto a budget from the House of Commons. The result was a constitutional crisis which exposed the deep divisions inside the British ruling class. The initial beneficiary was John Redmond and the Irish Parliamentary Party because the Liberals had to rely on their votes to push through an Act in 1911 which removed a House of Lords veto. In return, Redmond got a promise of Home Rule legislation.

The Home Rule Bill of 1912 was really no more than an extended form of local government. The imperial Parliament in London would continue to control foreign affairs, as well as the army and navy. It would have the power to repeal Acts of the Irish Parliament and Irish members would continue to attend Westminster. The Dublin Parliament could not vary taxes set in London by more than 10 per cent.[51] The Bill was regarded by some of Redmond's own supporters as 'a poor and paltry thing as to be an almost insult to Irish intelligence and patriotism'.[52] But even this mild measure was too much for Irish Unionism. The Unionist leader, Edward Carson, who acted as prosecutor of Land League activists and, most famously, of Oscar Wilde, whipped up Protestant workers' fears that Home Rule would lead to protectionism and the destruction of Belfast industry. These fears were translated into a sectarian bigotry as Catholics and 'rotten Prods' were driven from their jobs in Belfast. Carson made no secret of the fact that they fully intended to resist Home Rule – and by extension the British Parliament – by force of arms. The Ulster Covenant, which was signed by 218,000 Ulstermen, pledged to resist Home Rule by 'all means' and to 'refuse to recognise the authority of such a parliament'.[53] A week later, Carson declared 'I do not care two pence whether it is treason or not. I do not shrink from the horrors of civil commotion.'[54] Nor was this idle rhetoric, because a provisional Ulster government was formed and a 'business' committee, chaired by a leading shipbuilder, was charged with procuring arms. Thirty thousand rifles and three million rounds of ammunition were subsequently landed.

The Tory Party saw the Unionist rebellion as their opportunity to get their revenge on the Liberals. They responded to their loss of veto in the House of Lords by forging a tight alliance with Edward Carson and the Unionists. Such were the divisions at the heart of the British ruling class, that the Tories tore apart the facade of parliamentary rule and supported naked physical force to destroy their opponents. In brief, they favoured the use of armed force against their own elected government. In April 2012, the Tory leader, Bonar Law reviewed a march of thousands of Ulster Volunteers who marched in military formation. He told them 'you hold the pass for the Empire' and that 'even though the Government had erected the Parliament Act, as a boom against you, to shut you off from the British people, you will burst that boom.'[55] Some months later, he declared that if Ulster resists, 'there are stronger things than parliamentary majorities.'[56] At a mass rally held at the Duke of Marlborough's residence at Blenheim in England, Bonar Law made his most audacious speech:

> We regard the Government as a revolutionary committee which has seized power by fraud upon despotic power. In our opposition to them we shall not be guided by considerations ... which would influence us in ordinary political struggle ... We shall use any means to deprive them of the power they have usurped ... I can

imagine no length of resistance to which Ulster will go in which I will not be ready to support them.[57]

This rhetoric encouraged British Army officers to mutiny when they received orders to move against the Ulster Volunteers. In March 1914, 58 officers in the British Army stationed in the Curragh resigned their commissions rather than move against the Tories' allies. Their leader, Brigadier General Gough, even added that if it came to a civil war, 'I would fight for Ulster rather than against her.'[58] The mutineers were summoned to London but instead of being dismissed, they were assured that 'under no circumstances shall we be used to force Home Rule on the Ulster people.'[59]

The response of Redmond and the Irish Parliamentary Party exposed all their weakness. They had pinned their hopes on the 'progressive' aspect of the Empire and assumed that their friends in the Liberal Party would deliver Home Rule. At no point had they even contemplated the prospect of partition. They wanted Home Rule for the whole island and rejected the 'two nations theory' – which was being advocated by Carson. This was, Redmond claimed, 'an abomination and a blasphemy'.[60] But under pressure from Asquith and the Liberals, he agreed to a three-year temporary exclusion of Ulster. Four days later, the exclusion period was doubled to six years. Redmond then insisted on automatic inclusion of Ulster after six years but the Liberals did a deal with the Tories to grant Ulster a plebiscite. Both agreed that it would be the prerogative of the British Parliament to decide whether or not the excluded province would come under a Dublin Parliament. As the Tories were likely to have a majority at that point, the partition of Ireland had become a reality.

Redmond's compromises showed that the Irish Parliamentary Party had more faith in the democratic pretensions of the British state than the Tories had. They had soaked up the atmosphere of Westminster and sought only to ascend 'the ladder of high society, to become drawing room favourites or secure the social attention of dukes and duchesses'. [61] Living on a comfortable salary of £400 a year, they spent a considerable amount of time in London and were often out of touch with their constituents. However, some of their own supporters, who were watching the behaviour of Carson and the Tories, began to realise that a purely constitutional solution to the Irish question was no longer possible. Eoin MacNéill, a vice president of the Gaelic League, wrote a famous article for its paper entitled 'The North began'. It drew attention to how Unionist arms were used to overthrow parliamentary majorities and called for a nationalist response. The prominent scholar was still fully supportive of Redmond, but his call led to the formation of the Irish Volunteers in October 1913. Those who answered his call were predominantly 'moderate' constitutionalists who believed that they had to redress the balance against Carson and not rely on British officers to advance their interests. As Thomas Kettle, a moderate Home Ruler, put it, 'we are not going to rely for our national security upon the whims or fancies of some tall fellow with gold braid down the sides of his breeches.'[62]

The Irish Volunteers grew rapidly despite the initial refusal of the Irish Parliamentary Party to support them but within ten days of their formation, a Royal Proclamation was issued which outlawed the importation of weaponry. Carson and the Ulster Volunteers had been drilling for a year, but as soon as nationalists began to acquire weapons, the British state cracked down. This discrepancy only added to the growth of nationalist sentiment, but worse was to follow. When the Irish Volunteers imported 900 rifles at Howth in July 1914, the King's Own Scottish Borderers were sent to suppress them. When they failed, they shot dead three civilians and injured three dozen more. The effect on Irish society was electric. Thousands more joined the Volunteers and, even though Redmond's supporters had insinuated themselves into the Volunteers' ranks, many began to look with contempt at the Irish Parliamentary Party.

In many ways, Redmond's support for the British Empire in the First World War was his last throw of the dice. He had wagered everything on embracing the traditions of British Liberalism but he had gained little. The war, however, gave him cover to explain why Home Rule had to be postponed. More crucially, he was able to regain support from the intense chauvinist atmosphere that accompanied the outbreak of war. This mood prevailed across many European countries – war was seen as a break from the humdrum of everyday life. Fighting for your country meant being treated as an equal and being accorded an element of respect. The First World War was initially marked by an 'August madness', whereby masses of people were caught up in a feeling that they had entered a 'time of greatness' as national community was reborn. Imperial Ireland participated fully in this mood, as the plight of poor little Catholic Belgium became the rallying cry to recruit for the war effort.

However, the initial political advantages that came with supporting the war soon evaporated as its full horror became known. As the war progressed, Redmond, however, gradually upped his rhetoric. He initially suggested that people should enlist in the British Army to defend Ireland against the 'despotism' of Germany. Then, he suggested, that Irish recruits should join the British forces wherever the battle lines were drawn. He urged the volunteers to go 'wherever the front line stretched' and 'to come together in the trenches and spill their blood together'.[63] But later when it became clear that the Unionists were still insisting on Partition, he argued that the number of Irish Catholic recruits had to keep up with the numbers of Unionists, lest Britain favour the latter after the war. Even worse was to follow when in May 1915, the British Liberal government fell and was replaced by a Coalition government which included none other than Bonar Law and Edward Carson, the two figures who had fomented armed rebellion to stop Home Rule. The strategy of looking to British Liberals to grant Home Rule by constitutional means was in tatters.

The contradictions of Redmondism were now in full view. It remained only for severe disillusionment with war and a determined Rising to tear down the edifice of Redmondism and Imperial Ireland.

CHAPTER TWO

1916: Armed Insurrection

On the fiftieth anniversary of the 1916 Rising, the Irish television network, RTE, showed an eight-part series called *Insurrection*, which used Irish troops and a host of actors to re-enact the story of the week-long rebellion. Its purpose, according to the RTE Controller of Programmes Roibéárd Ó Faracháin, was to pay homage to 'the high emotion and daring of that week, which not only aroused the moribund mind of Ireland, but afterwards fired that considerable part of the world which until then was sunk in Colonialism'.[1] For many it was the highlight of the Golden Jubilee but the spirit that animated the series was in evidence all over the country. Copies of the Proclamation were displayed in every school, some unveiled by veterans. Every child was given a copy of a specially produced 1916 Rising booklet. Many towns staged parades, led by a contingent from the Irish Army. The song 'The Merry Ploughboy', which told of a farmer's son who went to Dublin to join the IRA and 'fight for the land that the Saxon stole', went to the top spot on the Irish hit parade. It stayed there for eight weeks.

Five years later, there was radio silence. The Irish government stopped the official commemorations of the 1916 Rising and republican songs were banned from the airwaves. A strict censorship on any form of militant republicanism was imposed through the notorious Section 31 of the Broadcasting Act. The Northern conflict had erupted in 1969 and a new generation of fighters were joining the IRA. The state's elite came to regret the lavish nature of the Golden Jubilee celebrations and thought they had helped inspire the growth of the modern IRA. The commemorations had, according to Conor Cruise O'Brien, popularised the idea of dying for Ireland and so helped produce the mythology of the gun.[2] The mawkish image of the 'merry ploughboy' had now become the 'evil terrorist'.

Most nations use 'myths of origins' to bind their people together into a loyalty to the state. These often tell of heroic battles or warriors who gave birth to the nation. The story of 1916, however, has been described as a 'creation story as good as any' it was 'ever likely to get'.[3] A few hundred brave men and a few women are supposed to have marched into the GPO, knowing that they were going to their deaths. Their sacrifice was thought to have awakened the Irish nation from its slumbers and let flow its vital energies. This 'blood sacrifice' theory was unashamedly trumpeted during the 1966 commemoration. Small wonder then that the state's elite were worried when the myth they had fostered could be turned against them.

However, the 'blood sacrifice' image of the Rising was itself an entirely artificial creation. It was originally popularised by an early writer P.S. O'Hegarty, who was a former member of the IRB Supreme Council. He claimed that 'the insurrection of 1916 was a forlorn hope and a deliberate blood sacrifice … But they [the IRB's leaders] counted on being executed afterwards and knew that that would save Ireland's soul'.[4] O'Hegarty had a particular reason for portraying the Rising in these terms. He was an avid supporter of Arthur Griffith and had long time been a member of the original Sinn Féin party. While he supported the Rising, he was totally opposed to the launching of an IRA guerrilla campaign afterwards. The Rising was necessary to awaken the nation's soul, but he regarded the subsequent War of Independence as 'Frankenstein's monster'.[5] He therefore wanted to draw a sharp distinction between the sacrificial and almost saintly conduct of the 1916 leaders and the subsequent unruly revolutionary activity that he feared. The 'blood sacrifice' image served this purpose.

This mythology has influenced many historians since and, ironically, it tends to unite both traditional defenders of the Rising, who believe it led to Irish freedom and revisionists, who deride it as a dramatic performance of the Redemption story.[6] Even the left-wing historian, John Newsinger, embraced the theory:

> The Easter Rising was a deliberate blood sacrifice whereby the participants hoped to save the soul of Ireland by laying down their lives. The 700 Volunteers and 120 Citizen Army members who seized control of the centre of Dublin on 23 April 1916 never had any hope of success whatsoever. There was no popular support for the rebels, indeed once they had been defeated grateful crowds assembled in the streets to cheer the British troops and shout abuse at the prisoners. It was in every sense of the word a putsch, and, moreover, a putsch where the organisers did not even believe success to be possible.[7]

The idea that 1916 was a blood sacrifice helps to explain why commemorations evoke such controversy and tension. Elites normally have condescending views about how the majority of people think and this leads them to a very crude view of how actual revolutions occur. They assume that plumbers or mechanics prefer to spend most of their time looking at topless women on page 3 of the *Sun* or just discussing the sports results. Big revolts only occur because tiny groups of 'agitators' stir up dark passions and lead the ignorant masses into conflict. They fear that the blood sacrifice of 1916 could be repeated again if enough fanatics got together and stormed the GPO.

Ironically, a parallel view is popular among republican activists. These do not share the elite's condescending view of the people, because the activists mainly come the lower social classes in society. But their own nationalism and their despair about the passivity of ordinary people in normal times leads to a deep cynicism about mass action. They believe that the actions of a few brave guerrillas are the 'cutting edge' which brings about change. Mass demonstrations, strikes, occupations are at best a sideshow or supporting chorus to the main action. The image of 1916 as a blood sacrifice is, therefore, a potent narrative because it helps sustain republican organisations through periods of unpopularity. When condemnations mounted after the bombings or military actions during the armed conflict in Northern Ireland, republicans comforted themselves with the thought that the leaders of 1916 went through similar opprobrium before finally changing history. No doubt 'dissident' republicans will do the same in the future.

However, almost every element of the blood sacrifice myth can be challenged. Most of those who fought in 1916 did not set out to deliberately die for Ireland. Nor were they as isolated from the wider population as some historians sometimes assert. And while their bravery cannot be disputed, it was not their actions alone which changed Ireland forever. Or to put it differently, those who fought in 1916 deserve to be honoured as decent human beings who challenged the greatest empire of the day. They were fighters, not saintly martyrs.

The Rising

At the outbreak of World War, the Supreme Council of the Irish Republican Brotherhood made a momentous decision. They decided to prepare for a rising and formed a Military Council to draw up plans. The date for the rising would be determined by three possible scenarios: an attempt to arrest Volunteers, the imposition of conscription, or an early termination of the war.[8] The last point was crucial in their thinking. The World War between the major powers presented a major opportunity for Irish freedom. If an armed uprising succeeded in holding even part of the country for a limited period, Ireland's demands could be presented to an eventual peace conference. Britain, it was thought, might not win an outright victory and this could be an opportunity to advance Irish demands.

However, behind the appearance of unanimity, there were deep divisions within the organisation. An 'activist' group led by the veteran Tom Clarke and the IRB organiser, Séan MacDiarmada, were determined that, come what may, the rising would definitely take place. But a 'passive' group, led by Bulmer Hobson, wanted to continue a defensive, 'wait and see' position.[9] Hobson had previously capitulated to Redmond's ultimatum that he should gain control over the Volunteer movement and was no longer deemed trustworthy by the hardliners.[10] So they kept discussions of their detailed plans within the confines of the Military Council, which alongside Clarke and MacDiarmada included Joseph Plunkett, Eamonn Ceannt and Patrick Pearse. In September 1914, their plans took a step forward when Eoin MacNéill and the original leadership of the Volunteer movement expelled the Redmondites because of their support for Britain's war. There were now two movements: the Redmond-led National Volunteers, who comprised 90 per cent of the original membership and were 180,000 strong, and the Irish Volunteers, who numbered 11,000 but who, crucially, were concentrated in the Dublin area. The IRB strategy was to infiltrate the Irish Volunteers and, accordingly, the Military Council members took up key positions in its leadership.

The Rising broke out on Easter Monday, 24 April 1916 and lasted six days. It was derided by British Chief Secretary for Ireland Augustine Birrell as 'really nothing more than a row in Dublin'[11] but, in reality, it was a serious military operation that struck a blow against the greatest imperial power of its time. In the words of Piers Brendon, the author of *The Decline and Fall of the British Empire*, it 'blasted the widest breach in the ramparts of the British Empire since Yorktown'.[12] The Rising involved approximately 1,300 insurgents, including 152 from the Irish Citizens Army, a workers' militia formed during the great lockout of 1913. British intelligence – which had penetrated every other attempt at an uprising – was completely caught off guard. Birrell had previously boasted that he had all the republican dissidents 'under a microscope'.[13] Yet two days before the Rising his undersecretary, Sir Matthew Nathan was writing that 'I see no indications of a "rising"'.[14]

The rebels seized key buildings to take control of an inner cordon around the centre of Dublin. A unit led by Michael Mallin from the Citizens Army seized hold of St Stephen's Green and the Royal College of Surgeons. Another from the 3rd Battalion of the Irish Volunteers led by Éamon de Valera occupied Boland's Mills in Grand Canal Street, while another smaller unit seized Westland Row railway station. Others from the same 3rd Battalion, led by Michael Malone, seized a number of key buildings at Mount Street and Northumberland Road, a position which commanded a major route into the city centre. When 2,000 British soldiers from the Sherwood Foresters tried to march into the city from Dun Laoghaire, the Volunteers inflicted heavy casualties.

Meanwhile, in the south inner city, Thomas McDonagh's 2nd Battalion seized the Jacob's factory in Bishop Street, while others occupied a house opposite Kevin Street police barracks. Over in James Street, Eamonn Ceannt's 4th Battalion seized a complex of buildings known as the South Dublin Union and attacked a column of British soldiers. Ned Daly's 1st Battalion seized the Four Courts and soon engaged with fifty lancers from the nearby barracks. A smaller contingent from the same battalion, led by Sean Heuston, seized the Mendicity Institution, which had a commanding position on the Liffey quays. Volunteers also took up positions in Church Street and erected barricades on North King Street and North Brunswick Street. Throughout this area, there was extensive urban fighting, and it would become the most hard-fought combat zone of the Rising. British soldiers who tried to bayonet charge a barricade were shot down and others were killed trying to retake the area. General Maxwell, the officer in overall command of the British troops, called on all civilians to leave the area but some did not. When British forces eventually swept through North King Street, they massacred some of the remaining civilians.

The focal point of the Rising was the seizure of the General Post Office, where Pearse read out the proclamation declaring an Irish republic. Shortly after its seizure, a contingent of lancers from Marlborough Barracks charged down Sackville Street – or O'Connell

Street, as it is known today – but were quickly dispersed by Volunteer fire. The rebels seized the Imperial Hotel and Clery's department store opposite the GPO and also the nearby Metropole Hotel. The British, however, took control of Trinity College and erected machine guns on the roof. Liberty Hall, the union headquarters thought to be the centre of the Rising, and Sackville Street were shelled, leading eventually to a firestorm in the GPO. James Connolly, who was the effective commander of the garrison, was forced to call for an evacuation and the Volunteers began tunnelling through buildings on Moore Street to make their escape. However, British firing and bombardment became so intense that Pearse and Connolly decided on an unconditional surrender to save civilian lives. The GPO command sent an emissary around the Volunteer positions to order a surrender, an order obeyed with great reluctance. Eventually, however, the Rising was ended and British law and order restored.

One Volunteer, Jim Ryan, who had spoken to Séan MacDiarmada about the conditions agreed for the surrender, later explained its terms:

> That the signatories [of the proclamation] would be shot and the rest of us set free, he thought. I found it hard to believe this at first but later Tom Clarke and Joseph Plunkett used practically the same words when I asked them. Is one to conclude then that these men had agreed amongst themselves before Pearse went to the castle that they should offer their own lives in an attempt to save those of their followers?[15]

This report provides a different perspective on the 'blood sacrifice' theory. The leaders knew that the punishment for an insurrection in the midst of war was certain death, but they sought assurances that the bulk of their rank and file would be spared. In this at least they mainly succeeded. General Maxwell decided to execute 15 of the organisers of the Rising, even though his own court martials had imposed the death penalty on 90 people. Thousands more were sent to internment camps from which they were subsequently released.

The crushing of the Easter Rising was celebrated by the Irish political caste who supported the Empire. While British soldiers may have pulled the triggers on the executed leaders, the Irish rich egged them on. The pro-Unionist *Irish Times* declared that 'Sedition must be rooted out of Ireland once and for all.'[16] The nationalist *Irish Independent* wrote 'Let the worst of the ringleaders be singled out and dealt with.'[17] The Cork employers federation denounced the Rising as 'a shameful outrage',[18] while in Galway the urban council called for the formation of 'a committee for public safety' and enlistment in a special constabulary.[19] In the House of Commons, it was reported that there was cheering for the suppression of the Rising. A Dublin street ballad included the line 'ye'll not forget the members cheering', telling of the nationalist MPs who joined in.[20] The last to be executed were James Connolly and Séan MacDiarmada. But when cries for clemency began to grow, the *Irish Independent* – owned by the employer's leader of 1913, William Martin Murphy – argued that if they 'were treated with too great a leniency, they would take it as an indication of weakness on the part of the government.'[21]

Blood Sacrifice?

The story of the Rising has been told many times but this brief account indicates the absurdity of dismissing it as a blood sacrifice. Quite simply, if the main purpose was to play out a redemption drama, there would have been little point in the detailed military planning that preceded it. Over the last century, there have been many examples across the world of suicide attacks or dramatic stand-offs, but few have resembled the sheer scale of the Rising. The world's biggest imperial power of the time had to re-deploy about 20,000 troops to suppress the insurrection and were pinned down by the Volunteers for almost a week. Most crucially, this uprising took place in the midst of a great imperial conflict when the British forces in Ireland had been severely diminished. In its sheer scale, the 1916 rising is more similar to the Zapatista uprising of 1 January 1994 in Mexico or the 'final offensive' of the FMLN guerrillas in El Salvador in 1981. In both these cases, the rebels held out for a few days but failed to launch a general uprising.

Moreover, the events of the 1916 Rising were of a much smaller scale than its leaders had planned. Writers who characterise the Rising as a blood sacrifice usually do so by plucking out a few quotes from Patrick Pearse's writings, as if his literary expressions sum up the intentions of all the rebel leadership. However, they neglect his final bulletin from the GPO:

> I am satisfied that we would have accomplished more, that we should have accomplished the task of enthroning, as well as proclaiming the Irish Republic as a Sovereign State, had our arrangements for a simultaneous rising, with a combined plan as sound as the Dublin plan has proved to be, been allowed to go through on Easter Sunday.[22]

Pearse's reference to actually 'enthroning' as well as 'proclaiming' an Irish Republic pointed to far more ambitious plans the leaders had had for the Rising. These had been drawn up by Joseph Plunkett and were detailed in a memorandum written with Roger Casement for presentation to the German government. The aim of the memorandum – which was neglected by some historians – was to convince the Germans to provide military aid. In these plans, German arms and troops were to be landed in Ireland. They would be joined by rebels from Kerry, Clare and Limerick who would seize parts of the south-west of the country. German U-boats were also to cut off British warships bringing troop reinforcements, to allow the rebels to take on a weakened garrison. Volunteers from the north of County Dublin were then to join mobile relief columns coming from Athlone to the assistance of Dublin. The seizure of buildings in the inner city of

Dublin must, therefore, be viewed in the context of wider nationwide plans. It was supposed to be a trap to lure in the British soldiers until they were squeezed between rebel strongholds in the city and the advancing rebel columns coming from the south and west.[23]

These plans came apart for two reasons. First, the German ship, the *Aud*, was sighted by the British Navy off the coast of Cork and had to be scuttled to prevent the capture of its arms. It had been carrying 20,000 rifles and a million rounds of ammunition for the Rising. The second failure stemmed from the conspiratorial methods of the IRB itself. It had distributed a forged letter, purporting to come from the British authorities, indicating plans to intern the leaders of the Irish Volunteers. This was designed to bounce the MacNéill-Hobson faction into an uprising but these plans went astray when MacNéill issued a countermanding order, instructing volunteers to avoid manoeuvres on Easter Sunday. James Connolly had previously warned of the need to depose this conservative element within the Irish Volunteers, but his advice went unheeded. The confusion caused by the counter-manded order meant many Volunteers did not mobilise for the Rising on Easter Sunday, and it then had to be moved to Easter Monday.

Once these mishaps occurred, the scope for manoeuvre of the IRB Military Council was very limited. They could call off the Rising and face the tender mercies of British justice which would eventually become aware of their detailed plans. The Military Council knew that instigating a rebellion in wartime and co-operating with an enemy power meant certain death. Or they could go ahead, even though the odds were stacked against them. James Connolly's statement that we are 'going out to be slaughtered' must be read in this context.[24] It was an acknowledgement by a socialist revolutionary, that as a consequence of his earlier decisions in accepting the IRB method of insurrection, he was joining a rising in unfortunate circumstances. It certainly does not indicate that Connolly had any thought of conducting a blood sacrifice – he had previously dismissed such talk as that of a 'blithering idiot'.[25] In reference to ideas that the shedding of blood could somehow cleanse a nation, he added 'we are sick of such teaching and the world is sick of such teaching.'[26] It is also abundantly evident that the vast bulk of the fighters in the Rising were not deliberately marching out to die. They were fighting to free their country and thought they stood a chance of doing so. This explains the reluctance of many to surrender and the testimony of one Volunteer, Robert Holland, about the attitude of his leader, Con Colbert. Colbert, he recounted, said that 'we must win and said to me that we must come in at the peace negotiations when the war had finished.'[27]

Those who see the Rising as a blood sacrifice also suggest that it was lacking popular support entirely. This myth arose for different reasons. It suited the elite of Catholic Ireland to turn the leaders of the Rising into martyrs so that they could present the insurrection as an event led by almost saintly individuals. Patriotism and Catholicism were provided with a powerful set of icons that could be used to enforce control. Revisionist historians who see the rebels as fanatics also tended to dismiss it as a mere putsch lacking in any popular support. More recent research, however, indicates that hostility to the rebels came mainly from two sources. The wealthier people had an instinctive class hatred for 'the rabble' and tended to support the Empire. There were also a large number of soldiers' wives who benefited from separation allowances, who were also hostile. In the aftermath of the Rising, the mainstream press highlighted this combined opposition while those who favoured it kept their heads down for fear of arrest. There is enough evidence to show that the reaction was more mixed.

The Canadian journalist, F.A. Kenzie, challenged reports that the majority of people supported the British troops, stating 'what I myself saw in the poorer districts did not confirm this. It rather indicated a vast amount of sympathy with the rebels.'[28] Reports from Volunteers also confirm a variation in responses. Whereas Michael Mallin's group met with considerable hostility in the wealthier neighbour-hood of Stephen's Green, the local working-class population in Grand

Canal Street and Hogan Place gave the Volunteers who surrendered an ovation.[29] Thomas McDonagh's contingent encountered hostility from the 'separation women', but Eamonn Ceannt's group were 'met with marked enthusiasm by a great crowd of people. All along St Patrick's we were greeted with great jubilation, particularly in the poorer districts.'[30] Frank Thornton, a rebel who was on the surrender march from Sackville Street to Kilmainham Jail noted that people shouted support and saluted, 'despite being pushed around'.[31] Another, J.J. Walsh, stated that people cheered even under the noses of British bayonets and that 'it was grand to feel that already the populace was responding to the latest and one of the greatest bids for liberty.'[32]

The reason why there was considerable sympathy for the rebels was that the actions of the British Empire had undermined constitutional nationalism – even before the execution of the 1916 leaders. The Rising was the tipping point in shifting allegiances to republicanism but it was a tipping point precisely because it took place when the British Empire was fighting for its life. As it did so, all the facades of 'civilisation' and respect for the diverse 'Celtic' cultures were swept aside and replaced by the iron fist of militarism. Like much of the rest of Europe, the population of Ireland were initially caught up in a war fever. The excitement of going to the front and defending little Catholic Belgium offered a relief from the mundane world of poverty and boredom. Moreover, they were told that the sacrifices were to be awarded by the final granting of Home Rule. So initially when Redmond called on the Volunteer movement to defend Ireland, he won considerable support. Yet most people expected that the war would last only a few months or at most a year. When it did not, the futility of Redmond's politics became clearer.

The progress of the war and the imperial mindset of the British ruling class undermined Redmond at almost every step. When he called for the formation for an Irish division, the War Office deemed the Irish too untrustworthy to be allowed to command themselves. When the Home Bill was finally put on the statute book, it came with an amending Act that gave Ulster Unionists an effective veto on their inclusion. While Redmond's supporters in the Ancient Order of Hibernians celebrated with bonfires, the Home Rule MP, William O'Brien noted that a 'silence of death' engulfed the country.[33] To add to Redmond's difficulties, news of the horrors of war began to filter back home and Redmond's National Volunteer movement began to decline. Police reports often indicated that their membership was 'merely nominal' and that 'activity ceased'.[34] Recruitment to the British Army fell off dramatically, even as Redmond urged a competitive enlistment to show that Catholic Ireland was just as loyal as Unionist Ireland as a way of finally guaranteeing Home Rule. In the first year of the war, 75,342 Irishmen enlisted but from August 1915 the numbers dropped to 15,902 a year.[35] This was far below the 1,100 recruits needed each week to maintain Irish battalions' reserves.[36] Those who joined came predominantly from the urban poor, driven into the army to escape poverty. Rural Ireland – the main base of Redmond's party – supplied only a quarter of the recruits. The war produced a mini-boom in food prices and most farmers wanted to profit at home rather than to gain glory abroad. Rising food prices, however, added to discontent of city-dwellers, whose already low wages were then subjected to a wage freeze.[37]

By the end of 1915, the discontent reached new heights. Military defeat at Gallipoli had brought down Asquith's Liberal government and he was forced to form a coalition government with the Tories. The inclusion of Edward Carson in the Cabinet, even though he had previously called for armed defiance of his own Parliament, infuriated much of the nationalist population. While the formal structures of Redmond's party stood as solid as a glacier, support at the base was melting away. When the funeral of the old Fenian, O'Donovan Rossa occurred in August, the republicans were able to mount a huge display of strength. British Undersecretary Nathan stated that 'I have the uncomfortable feeling that the Nationalists are losing ground to the Sinn Féiners.'[38]

When, on top of all this, the threat of conscription appeared, Redmond was in real trouble. The decline in recruitment and military defeats meant that new reserves of manpower were required. Yet the prospect of young Irishmen being dragooned into the army caused panic. A particularly nasty incident had occurred in Liverpool in November 1915 when Irishmen who were fleeing to America were attacked by a chauvinist mob as 'shirkers'.[39] Stokers on the ship refused to set sail with the Irish passengers and they were praised for their actions in the British press. Redmond offered little support,[40] claiming only that it was 'very cowardly of them to try to emigrate'. After the incident, emigration from Ireland was banned. The republican wit, Liam De Roiste, noted that hitherto it was English policy to banish the 'Celts' from Ireland, but it now suited their policy to keep the 'Celts' in Ireland. In December 1915, however, there was a huge anti-conscription meeting in Dublin and the stage was set for massive opposition and even a possible insurrection if it were forced through. In the face of this opposition, the London government retreated. The Irish were exempted from the Conscription Act passed in January 1916, but few believed that its imposition in Ireland was far off.[41]

All of these issues meant that a storm was brewing for the Irish Parliamentary Party – even before the 1916 Rising. They had pinned their hopes on an alliance with the Liberal Party and supported an imperialist war on a vague promise of Home Rule. Yet the British state treated them like lapdogs. This was by no means lost on the wider population and a shift in the popular mood was underway. This helps to explain why there was a more mixed reaction to the Rising than the traditional stereotype of a brave but isolated rebellion. The tremendous bravery of the Irish Volunteers who took on an empire with badly equipped weapons was awesome. Yet brave as their actions were, the Rising cannot stand out as a singular event that by itself changed Irish history. It became the focal point of change – precisely because change was already underway, silently and on the margin of official power structures. Ironically, John Dillon, one of the leaders of the Redmondite party gave a perceptive summary after the event: 'The fact is that since the formation of the Coalition government in June 1915, we had been steadily and rather rapidly losing our hold on the people and the rebellion and the negotiations only brought out in an aggravated form what had been beneath the surface for a year.'[42]

Undersecretary Nathan held a similar view, noting that 'Redmond had been honestly Imperial in the war, but by going so far as he has done, he has lost his position in the country.'[43] If the blood sacrifice theory is discounted, we can look a little more closely at exactly what type of Ireland the leaders of the Rising were trying to achieve. Clearly, one or two leaders cannot fully articulate the complex motives of all who took part. Nevertheless, if we focus on the ideas of Patrick Pearse and James Connolly, we can get some idea of the deeper policies that motivated the Rising.

Patrick Pearse

There was little in Patrick Pearse's background that marked him out as a revolutionary. It was only in the last four years of his life that he embraced the ideals and methods for which he was eventually to die. He was born into a comfortably well-off family and had an English father who originally came from Birmingham. James Pearse had been a stone mason, who built up a considerable business from a major spate of church building in Ireland in the late nineteenth century. Pearse's mother, Margaret Brady, came from a conventional rural background although Pearse suggested that her father had joined the Fenians. The young Patrick was trained as a barrister but never practised, as he had to take responsibility for the family business after his father died.

He joined the Gaelic League and eventually became the full-time editor of its newspaper, *Claidheamh Solas*. He described the paper as an 'organ of militant Gaeldom'; it was aimed not simply at the promotion of the Irish language – its purpose was to save 'all the treasures accumulated in the folk-mind during three thousand years.'[44] From an early age, Pearse was a cultural nationalist who wanted the de-Angli-cisation of Ireland. English culture was seen as the binary opposite of Irish culture, corrupting its roots and leading Irish society astray. Irish people had 'lost their soul and were being vulgarised, commer-cialised, anxious only to imitate the material prosperity of England'.[45] This type of cultural nationalism was a common response of the intel-ligentsia in colonised countries when they moved into opposition to imperialism. It contained a contradictory mix of a yearning for the past glories of pre-colonial times, with democratic and modernist ideals. It reflected a desire to reconnect with 'the people' in order to build up an opposition to the humiliations they themselves encountered from the colonisers. In Pearse, this contradictory mix is very clear.

He strongly denounced those elements of Irish cultural life which were conducted through the English language. He denounced as a 'heresy ... which has paralysed the nation's energy and intellect ... the idea that there can be an Ireland, that there can be an Irish literature, an Irish social life whilst the language of Ireland is English'.[46] He criticised as 'West British' any form of cultural expression that did not promote the Irish language – even though only a tiny minority of people spoke Irish at the time. This led to frivolous attacks on some of the key figures of the Irish literary movement. Yeats, he suggested, was 'a mere English poet of the third or fourth rank'.[47] And while he defended the Abbey Theatre's staging of Synge's *Playboy of the Western World*, he attacked the play for propagating a 'monstrous gospel of animalism' that undermined 'the sane and sweet ideals' of Christian and human morality.[48] James Joyce was so incensed by the attacks on the English language that he left Pearse's Irish-language classes in University College Dublin to study Norwegian and Ibsen.[49]

However, there was also a more democratic spirit in Pearse's assertion of cultural separatism. He wanted Irish writing to concern itself with the realities of modern and European life and called on writers to move away from the idealisation of rural life. He attacked the system of education that had been inherited from England. It was a 'murder machine', he claimed, that was 'manufacturing things', that is, preparing students as products that could fit neatly into the civil service system.[50] Against this, Pearse called for greater freedom for teachers to promote the individual development of their students. He denounced the failure to appoint more women to the governing body of universities and proclaimed their right to be eligible for university chairs. His championship of the Irish language also brought him to conflict with the bishops. Their sole aim was to gain control over the universities and they were willing to ditch the Irish language if they could achieve that. Pearse asserted that the language movement was a non-sectarian organisation and that it had the right to criticise the bishops or anyone else.

Ironically, Pearse's cultural nationalism led him to play down a demand for political separation for most of his life. He argued that 'The language movement is not merely more important than the political movement but it is on a different and altogether higher plane ... Political autonomy may be necessary for the continued existence of the Nation ... but it is not, in itself, an essential of nationality.'[51]

In line with this thinking, he supported an Irish Council Bill in 1906 which gave the most limited autonomy to Ireland, even though many in the Irish Parliamentary Party regarded it as inadequate. It was only in 1911 that he began to get politically active – and that was in support of the Home Rule Bill. He praised Redmond for his achievement in bringing the Bill to the House of Commons and called on other parties to stand behind him in seeking a better one. In May 1912, he spoke at a Home Rule rally alongside Redmond where he again called for unity to 'wring a good measure from the Gall'.[52] At this stage, his aim was the creation of a Gaelic party within a Home Rule Parliament.[53]

However, while Pearse's cultural nationalism might seem idiosyncratic, his trajectory to republican separatism was a journey travelled by many. His political transformation was the direct outcome of two major developments: the Tory elite's backing of armed rebellion to stop Home Rule and Redmond's support for Britain's imperialist war. Even while advocating Home Rule, Pearse had warned that if it was not granted, a resort to arms would be required. Prior to 1913, he had little time for the IRB or the republican separatists and they had little time for him. But after the Curragh mutiny, when British Army officers refused to move against the Ulster Volunteers who were threatening military resistance to Home Rule, Pearse took part in forming the Irish Volunteers and spoke at their first mass rally in the Rotunda. After this, he moved more quickly towards republican-ism. As the drums of war grew louder in Britain and Germany, Pearse became convinced not only that Irishmen should take up arms, but also that a rising should be attempted. From then on, three main strands dominated his thinking.

First, he believed that the Irish nation was a living, organic entity. It was as natural as the family unit and was 'knit together by natural ties, ties mystic and spiritual, and ties human and kindly'.[54] He thought that the Irish nation had existed from the beginning of time and was perpetual, undivided and had its own distinct identity. There was a national 'soul', which was seeking its freedom and an open expression of its identity. This nation – rather than any class or grouping within it – was involved in an incessant struggle for its existence. It needed full sovereignty to conserve its spiritual heritage and while that sovereignty started with physical separation of Ireland from Britain, it also encompassed 'material' sovereignty. By this, Pearse meant that the Irish nation had to control the 'soil and all its resources, all wealth and all wealth-producing processes within the nation. In other words, no private right to property is good as against the public right of the nation.'[55] As the reference to material sovereignty indicated, the influence of Fintan Lawlor, who had proclaimed that the land of Ireland must belong to the people of Ireland, was added to Pearse's cultural nationalism.

The idea, however, that the Irish nation was an entity that began thousands of years ago makes little historical sense. It is doubtful, for example, that Irish clans of the sixth or eighth century identified themselves as part of a nation. Nor can it be claimed that in a great battle such as Clontarf in 1014, that an Irish nation lined up against an invader – as many Irish tribesmen actually fought on the side of the Vikings as on the side of the High King, Brian Boru. Contrary to what Pearse thought, the nation is very much an 'imagined community' brought into existence by great changes caused by the spread of the market and growth of state power. As Anderson has pointed out, it is only in modern society where print capitalism has helped to create a common readership and more standardised histories of the past that people begin to imagine themselves part of a nation.[56] In some cases, this national consciousness is actively promoted by a rising bourgeois class which seeks to break free of semi-feudal constraints and remould an area in their image. In the Irish case, it was the most advanced, English-speaking, Protestant industrialists who founded the United Irishmen, a revolutionary movement which in turn promoted a national, republican consciousness.

Pearse's shift to republicanism, however, combined elements of woolly thinking that are common to many nationalists with genuine democratic instincts. He had moved leftwards but could not in any sense be described as anti-capitalist. Rather, he supported a right to private property, but argued that the 'nation' had to decide democratically on how that right should be exercised:

The people, if wise, will choose as the makers and administrators of their laws … the men and women of no property equally with the men and women of property; they will regard such an accident as the possession of 'property', 'capital', 'wealth' in any shape … as conferring no more right to represent the people than would the accident of possessing a red head or the accident of having been born on a Tuesday.[57]

However, while possession of property or capital might be an 'accident' from a democratic perspective, its concentration in a few hands was no accident. Pearse, however, never delved into *why* these inequalities occurred.

Second, despite this, Pearse developed a greater concern for social justice. The immediate trigger was the 1913 lockout and his growing alliance with James Connolly. He supported the workers and called on the 'well fed citizens' to put themselves in 'the shoes of our hungry citizens, just for an experiment'.[58] He deplored the hypocrisy of 'millionaires promoting universal peace' and Irish employers who accepted the aid of 'foreign bayonets to enforce a lockout'. [59] But he stated that 'he was nothing so new fangled as a socialist or a syndicalist. I am old fashioned enough to be both a Catholic and a nationalist.'[60] He thought that poverty and Ireland's woes were caused by foreign intrusion – not capitalism. Once Ireland was free, these problems would end and a free Ireland, Pearse asserted, 'would not and could not have hunger in her fertile vales and squalor in her cities'.[61]

Pearse eventually took up Wolfe Tone's cry to look to the 'men of no property'. He thought that the wealthier elements of Irish society had been willing to bow the knee to their imperial masters while the poor maintained the seeds of rebellion. He stated that 'In Ireland "the gentry" (as they affect to call themselves) have uniformly been corrupted by England, and the merchants and middle-class capitalists have, when not corrupted, been uniformly intimidated, whereas the common people have for the most part remained unbought and unterrified.'[62]

However, as with Tone, this embrace of the 'common people' was both a cry of indignation against the betrayals of the rich and a warning to them to do their national duty. It was not a call for the abolition of their privileges. Rather those privileges had to be, firstly, rooted in the consent of the nation and, secondly, informed by duties to other classes within the nation: 'No class in the nation has rights superior to those of any other class. No class in the nation is entitled to privileges beyond any other class except with the consent of the nation. The right and privilege to make laws or to administer laws does not reside in any class within the nation.'[63]

Pearse's growing social radicalism, therefore, was impressive and deep, but it was limited by a tradition which put nation before class and was unable to question where economic inequality came from. He was not opposed to privileges in themselves, but wanted them limited by the democratic consent of the nation.

The third main theme in Pearse's writings was the need for Irish nationalists to arm themselves, and he returned to this theme repeatedly in the years up to 1916. At first, the call to arms was a bitter reaction to the failure to gain Home Rule by purely parliamentary means. Even at the height of the Home Rule agitation, when he was supporting Redmond, Pearse was warning that 'Let the English understand that if we are betrayed again, there shall be red war throughout Ireland.'[64] The British government's capitulation to armed Unionist opposition only confirmed his view that weapons would be needed to win political freedom. Later, however, the resort to arms became an important ingredient in itself for achieving freedom because a nation that was not willing to fight physically for its freedom almost deserved to be enslaved. 'The lesson of history' he suggested was that 'it was only by strong men with courage and determination with guns in their hands that freedom could be won.'[65] Pearse was deadly serious in this and went to some lengths to ensure that arms were in the hands of Irishmen. He hid guns in his school in St Enda's and he wrote to Clann na nGael in America imploring them for money to buy weapons. He had no time for pub republicans or sentimental old Fenians who dwelt on stories of past glories. He wanted military action to gain national freedom and was determined to bring it about.

Pearse's fascination with weaponry and bloodshed increased as the First World War approached. He continually drew a connection between arming and masculinity. Strong men and strong nations were willing to die for freedom and they complemented each other.

He also, unfortunately, indulged in some of the bombastic rhetoric about war and dying that pervaded society at this time. One result is that the most recent generation of school students have come to see him purely as an advocate of a blood sacrifice. He is often quoted as saying that 'bloodshed is a cleansing and sanctifying thing'[66] and for this, he can, as Connolly put it, rightly be called a 'blithering idiot'. But the essential point that Pearse was making in this most quoted passage is often missed, namely that 'there are many things more horrible than bloodshed, and slavery is one of them.'[67] This argument – rather than an obsession with bloodshed – was the primary reason he urged insurrection: to break the might of the British Empire.

This was really the essence of Pearse's latter-day republicanism. After the failure to win Home Rule, he thought that 'the people' had to be awakened by the military action of the few. It was quite simply the only way to win Irish independence and freedom from the Empire. It never dawned on him that there could be a mass revolution that combined demands for national and social freedom. Like many nationalists, he had limited methods for achieving his objectives. There could either be a gradual cultural change that came through education or armed insurrection when parliamentary action failed. But for all his ambiguities, Patrick Pearse was a principled anti-imperialist who vigorously opposed the idea of Empire.

James Connolly

In many respects, the contrast between James Connolly and Patrick Pearse could not have been sharper. Connolly was born into a working-class family and grew up in an Irish slum in the Cowgate in Edinburgh. Poverty drove him into the British Army at the age of 14 and he was sent to serve in Ireland. When he heard that his regiment was being transferred to India, he deserted and returned to Scotland. There he became active in the socialist movement and from a very early stage stood on its revolutionary wing. When the miners' leader,

Keir Hardie, was forming the British Labour Party, Connolly argued that 'It's not a Labour party the workers need. It's a revolutionary party pledged to overthrow the capitalist class in the only way it can be done by putting up barricades and taking over factories by force. There is no other way.'[68]

When he stood for election in 1894, he dismissed all talk of trying to reform the system from within. Connolly did not favour a slow march to win a majority in Parliament in order to bring gradual change. On the contrary, he wrote that 'the election of a Socialist to any public body is only valuable in so far as it is the return of a disturber of the public peace.'[69] In 1896, he responded to an advertisement seeking a socialist organiser in Dublin and took up the position. He then set about forming the Irish Socialist Republican Party.

Connolly's Marxist politics became a profound source of embarrassment to nationalist Ireland and after his death, efforts were made to hide his beliefs. This began with Countess Markievicz, who wrote a pamphlet, 'James Connolly and Catholic Doctrine', where she stated that 'Socialism is what he stood for but it was the socialism of James Connolly and nobody else.'[70] The union that Connolly founded, the Irish Transport and General Workers Union, also suppressed some of his writings, including those which celebrated British working-class solidarity during 1913. Even as late as 1968, when a new revolutionary wave was sweeping across Europe, the historian Owen Dudley Edwards produced a book to commemorate Connolly's birth. In it he made the astounding claim that Connolly was 'one of the best and most enlightened apologists the Catholic Church had since the industrial revolution.'[71]

In reality, Connolly lived and breathed revolutionary socialism and Marxist politics. At the time, the Marxist movement was organised through the Second International, a grouping of different socialist parties mainly in Europe. Formally, the Second International adhered to Marx's analysis of capitalism but the seeds of a more reformist approach were growing within it. Its outlook was also quite deterministic, believing that changes in the economic base of society made socialism inevitable. Socialist practice was, therefore, primarily about propaganda and preparation for elections rather than instigating militant working-class action. Connolly was an adherent of some of this theoretical framework but he was a rebel who stood on the left of this tradition. He opposed the participation of the French socialist, Alexandre Millerand, in a coalition government with right-wing forces. He also took a more revolutionary attitude towards parliamentary democracy arguing:

> The democracy of Parliament is in short the democracy of capitalism. Capitalism gives the worker the right to choose his master but insists that the fact of mastership shall remain unquestioned: parliamentary democracy gives to the worker the right to a voice in the selection of his rulers but insists that he shall bend as a subject to be ruled.[72]

He insisted that socialism did not simply mean state ownership but suggested that 'it implies above all things the co-operative control of workers of the machinery of production.' Without this grass-roots workers' control, 'the public ownership by the State is not socialism – it is only state capitalism.'[73]

These views initially led Connolly to engage with a narrow-minded version of revolutionary socialism which he encountered in Daniel De Leon's Socialist Labour Party of America, when he emigrated there after the collapse of the small Irish Socialist Republican Party. However, he soon broke with this sectarian organisation and became an organiser with a militant union, the Industrial Workers of the World. This was inspired by syndicalist ideas that had developed in a number of countries in the aftermath of the first Russian Revolution of 1905. At the core of its approach was the idea of a general strike as the best way to end capitalism and usher in socialism. Connolly embraced this outlook and sought to create One Big Union which would impose workers control over the capitalist class in each factory where they gained strength. It would then, he hoped, organise a general strike to lock out the employers. In his 1909 pamphlet, *Socialism Made Easy*, he explained what would happen next:

> Would you confiscate the property of the capitalist class and rob men of that which they have, perhaps, worked a whole life to accumulate?
>
> Yes sir, and certainly not. We would certainly confiscate the property of the capitalist class but we do not propose to rob anyone. On the contrary, we propose to establish honesty once and forever as the basis of our social relations. The socialist movement is indeed worthy to be entitled The Great Anti-Theft Movement of the Twentieth Century.[74]

Connolly was also a rebel within the Second International in his approach to Irish national freedom. The dominant grouping within the International suggested that as the working-class movement in the colonies was very weak – mainly due to the lack of industrial development – they would have to wait until the movement in the metropolitan countries would bring about change. Connolly disputed this and boldly proclaimed that Irish freedom and socialism were interlinked. His classic book, *Labour and Irish History*, illustrates this principle by showing how the wealthy Irish 'were tied by a thousand economic strings in the shape of investments binding them to English capitalism'. The working class, he argued, were the 'incorruptible inheritors of the fight for Irish freedom'.[75]

In a remarkable similarity to the ideas advocated by Trotsky in Russia, Connolly advanced his own version of permanent revolution. He opposed the idea of a 'union of classes' which would come together to bring about the first stage of Irish independence. This would, its nationalist advocates suggested, bring about an Irish republic where socio-economic relations would remain the same.

Instead, Connolly argued that the struggle for Irish freedom needed to culminate in a workers' republic and he advanced two main reasons why this was necessary. If the working class were to really mobilise for Irish independence, Connolly suggested that they would not stop at achieving a capitalist republic. They would go further and fight for social as well as national freedom. To the objection that a fight for a socialist republic would frighten off potential allies, he made the following devastating reply:

> It may be pleaded that the ideal of a Socialist Republic, implying, as it does, a complete political and economic revolution would be sure to alienate all our middle-class and aristocratic supporters, who would dread the loss of their property and privileges.
>
> What does this objection mean? That we must conciliate the privileged classes in Ireland! But you can only disarm their hostility by assuring them that in a *free* Ireland their 'privileges' will not be interfered with. That is to say, you must guarantee that when Ireland is free of foreign domination, the green-coated Irish soldiers will guard the fraudulent gains of capitalist and landlord from 'the thin hands of the poor' just as remorselessly and just as effectually as the scarlet-coated emissaries of England do today.
>
> On no other basis will the classes unite with you. Do you expect the masses to fight for this ideal?[76]

The other reason Connolly advocated a socialist solution to Ireland's national question was because of the sectarian divisions inside the working class. Connolly witnessed these at first hand in July 1912, when Carson's violent opposition to Home Rule led to pogroms in Belfast. Three thousand workers were expelled from their jobs, including six hundred who were dubbed 'rotten Prods' because of their socialist or Liberal sympathies. Connolly vigorously opposed Orange supremacism and was adamant in defending the right of Ireland to Home Rule. He also warned against Partition, arguing that it would produce 'a carnival of reaction' which would help 'the Home Rule and Orange capitalists and clerics to keep their rallying cries before the public as the political watch cries of the day'.[77]

But while opposing loyalism and the partition of Ireland, Connolly wanted to appeal openly to Protestant workers. The way to do this, he thought, was not to placate the reactionary sentiments of the Orange Order but to show how its sectarianism divided workers. He thought that only a bold call for a socialist Ireland could hold any appeal to Protestant workers. There was, quite simply, no future for Protestant workers in a capitalist Ireland under the green flag:

> When the Sinn Féiner speaks to men who are fighting against low wages and tells them that the Sinn Féin body has promised lots of Irish labour at low wages to any foreign capitalist who wished to establish in Ireland, what wonder if they come to believe that a change from Toryism to Sinn Féinism would simply be a change from the devil they do know to the devil they do not.[78]

1916 and the Revolutionary Tradition

These brief outlines of the ideals of Pearse and Connolly show how absurd it is to claim that the fruits of the 1916 Rising are embodied in the 26-county state. Yet this is precisely how the elite want to frame its centenary. With some unease, they present the leaders of 1916 as figures 'who gave their lives' to found our state. They are extremely uneasy with the idea of insurrection and revolution, particularly in an Ireland where discontent is growing in response to permanent austerity. So they try to restrict it to an event that gave rise to 'Irish democracy'.

Yet there is almost no link between the motivation of those who took part in the Rising and the current practices of the 26-county state. The Rising was first and foremost a blow against the greatest empire of the day. It was an anti-imperialist revolt that asserted Ireland's right to full independence. The present state, however, is an active collaborator in maintaining the domination of Anglo-American imperialism. Despite its proclaimed neutrality, Ireland has allowed Shannon Airport to be used as a base for transporting US troops to war zones. Shannon has even been named as one of the hubs used for renditions of prisoners to torture centres.[79] Ireland has also sent a small contingent of troops to support the occupation of Afghanistan and is preparing for future military intervention as part of the EU battle groups. If 1916 was about anti-imperialism, then clearly none of this spirit is evident in the current state.

The 1916 Rising also grew out of opposition to the partition of Ireland and an acceptance of a Unionist veto over the political developments on the island. The current 26-county state, however, accepts partition and to justify this stance, promotes the notion of one island with 'two cultures'. This is why it originally planned to send invitations to Queen Elizabeth of Britain to attend the commemoration ceremonies for the Rising.[80] This apparently would help promote understanding and 'reconciliation' between Ireland's republican and Orange cultures. However, even the British establishment thought better of this silly suggestion and noted that they were 'sensitivities' involved.[81]

Nor is any element of Pearse's vision or, still less Connolly's, evident in the 26-county state. Pearse's cultural nationalism is nowhere to be seen and his demand for full sovereignty has simply disappeared. His claim that the nation had to take full control of its natural resources has simply been ignored, as ownership of oil and gas is handed to major global corporations such as Shell or Statoil. Currently, Ireland has one of the lowest government takes from its oil and gas reserves in the world. The state has gone to great length to support this state of affairs by deploying the police force to break popular resistance in Rossport, Co. Mayo, where Shell was trying to develop a gas pipeline. Connolly's revolutionary socialism is simply an embarrassment to a state that has become a tax haven for multi-national corporations. These use the country as a respectable front to suck in funds from all over the world and then dodge taxes that might be used to redistribute resources to the poor. The embrace of neoliberalism has been so fervent that the right-wing think tank, the Heritage Foundation, ranks Ireland ninth in the world for economic liberty – ahead even of the US and Britain.[82] The Rising may – with some stretch – be framed as giving impetus to a series of events that gave birth to the 26-county state. But it defies all logic to assert that the ideal or politics of its leaders are in any way embodied in the modern Irish state.

1916 may be better understood as giving birth to an altogether different child – a revolutionary tradition that has passed like a thread through subsequent decades. Sometimes this tradition has moved masses of people while at other times it has been confined to the margins. But for many it has been a touchstone which has enabled them to express their anger at policies which produced emigration, poverty, low wages and mass unemployment. Sometimes that anger is confined to grumbles in the pubs, but at other times it flares up into great movements which challenge the status quo. 'Was it for this that the men of 1916 died' is one of the most common sayings of the modern rabble-rouser. And, not entirely accidentally, most large protest movements in Ireland find their way to the GPO, the focal point of the original Rising. Most crucially, it is a living tradition that becomes a reference point in times of social crisis. Official Ireland tries to deal with this subterranean revolutionary tradition by canonising and mummifying the leaders of 1916. Train stations, schools and hospitals are all called after them. Even the former tower blocks of the Ballymun flat complex were named after them. But even while their sacrifices are acknowledged, their actual ideas are gutted of anything resembling a revolutionary thought. One must look elsewhere, outside official commemorations, for the enduring living tradition that came out of the 1916 rebellion.

The very existence of such a tradition gives those who yearn for fundamental change an important asset. It means that the idea of revolution in a contemporary Ireland cannot be so easily dismissed as being entirely fanciful. But there is also a weakness because, at the core of this Irish revolutionary tradition, lies a deep ambiguity which can be traced back to the alliance of Connolly and Pearse's politics. The ambiguity is summed up in the phrase 'socialist republicanism' which suggests that the revolutionary socialist ideals of Connolly can be tacked on to a republican tradition. Yet republicanism has provided *both* an honourable critique of the 'betrayals 'of the 26-county state but also, ironically, a repository for new recruits for the political establishment. Until recently, most Irish governments have included at least one former IRA leader. Included in this roll call are former chiefs of staff of the IRA, such as Frank Aiken and Sean McBride. From the most recent campaign, we may include Martin McGuinness who became a minister in the Northern Ireland Executive. All of these once also pledged allegiance to 'the men of 1916' but equally all of them found more comfortable seats at the cabinet tables of two partitioned states. The tragic history of Irish republicanism sees its participants engage in successive rounds of armed struggle only for its leaders, at a later stage, to make their eventual peace with Irish capitalism. This must at least raise some questions about the easy synthesis of socialism and republicanism.

The marriage that gave birth to Ireland's revolutionary tradition was Connolly's and Pearse's determination to launch the 1916 Rising. In Pearse's case, the motivation was straightforward. An armed insurrection was not only a practical tactic that would take advantage of England's difficulty during war. It was also a moral requirement to re-invigorate the soul of the nation and win real freedom. In Connolly's case, the motivations were far more complex. As a revolutionary socialist, he knew that the carnage of the First World War was the outcome of a system driven by greed and profit. He expected that the international socialist movement would live up to its pre-war resolutions and oppose the war. He even hoped that it would use its outbreak to foment a general strike in belligerent nations and bring down a system that bred war. To his absolute horror, he found that the socialist leaders of Germany, Britain and France lined up behind their rulers and swapped the language of socialism for national chauvinism. Connolly, however, remained steadfast: the only solution to war, he thought was revolution. 'The signal for war', he wrote, 'ought to have been the signal of rebellion ... when the bugle sounded the first note of actual war, their notes should have been taken as the tocsin for social revolution.'[83]

Connolly's problem was that his desire for revolution was not matched by a capacity to bring it about. The working class who fought in 1913 were defeated and many had enlisted in the British Army. The Independent Labour Party, the left-wing organisation he was part of, was tiny and even they were divided. Tom Johnson, for example, who was later to become a future leader of the Irish Labour Party, favoured a victory for the Allies as the best way to secure liberty. Connolly could not even get his own branch in Belfast to speak out against the war and he was forced to do so in a personal capacity. The only organisation that was capable of acting was the Irish Citizens Army but this had been constructed as a military defence unit. These objective weaknesses, coupled with Connolly's own impatience and anger at the betrayals of the Second International, led him towards an alliance with the republicans. If there was ever to be an insurrection, he had to encourage and even goad the republicans into action.

Some saw this as Connolly deserting his socialist principles. Sean O'Casey, for example, argued that 'Jim Connolly had stepped from the narrow byway of Irish Socialism on to the broad and crowded highway of Irish Nationalism. The high creed of Irish Nationalism became his daily rosary ... and Irish Labour lost a Leader.'[84] A similar view was repeated by Connolly's biographer, Austen Morgan, who claimed he ceased to be a socialist in August 1914 and became a collaborator with German imperialism.[85] Both writers ignore the fact that Connolly was first and foremost a revolutionary who thought, quite correctly as it transpired, that the war would only end with the outbreak of revolution.

It was, in fact, the revolutions in Russia in 1917 and in Germany in 1918 that stopped the war. Connolly's critics often assume that the struggle for socialism is only conducted in normal times through the peaceful methods of elections or trade-union struggle. They ignore the fact Connolly had a long-standing commitment to fight against imperialism and never confined himself to simple bread-and-butter issues. They also make no distinction between the nationalism of an anti-colonial movement and the jingoism that arises when an empire goes to war. All are simply lumped together in the single category of nationalism and Connolly is then damned as a deserter from socialism.

However, far from deserting socialism, Connolly remained true to its legacy by seeking to deliver a revolutionary blow in Ireland. A revolt in Ireland, he thought, would be hundred times more effective than elsewhere, because Ireland lay at the heart of the British Empire. He hoped that this would cause a chain reaction abroad, which would re-awaken the socialist movement and lead to new revolts against a system which bred war: 'Starting thus, Ireland may yet set the torch to a European conflagration that will not only burn out until the last throne and last capitalist bond and debenture will be shrivelled on the funeral pyre of the last war lord.'[86]

The contrast between this revolutionary socialist and a modern social democratic approach could not be more marked.

None of this implies that there are no criticisms about the manner in which Connolly joined the rebellion. There is little doubt that he embraced the IRB tradition of an insurrection made by a secret conspiracy. Instead of an insurrection arising out of a working-class mobilisation, it became a purely military operation whose timing was not linked to a wider upsurge amongst workers. The Rising was also, in this sense, 'premature'.[87] The threat of conscription in December 1915 and January 1916 had shown that masses of workers were prepared to mobilise and the British government only retreated because they feared revolt. Yet they were also caught in a bind, as the war would soon demand a new attempt at conscription. If Connolly had waited until another upsurge occurred in response to renewed demands for conscription, more fertile revolutionary conditions might be available. But these are only the speculations that arise from hindsight. While, undoubtedly, Connolly made many concessions to republican politics and methods, he did so in from the best of motives. He also had some inkling that his alliance with the republicans was temporary and that conflicts would develop with them later. 'In the event of victory', he told the Irish Citizens Army, 'hold on to your rifles, as those with whom we are fighting may stop before our goal is reached. We are out for economic as well as political liberty.'[88]

Connolly's tragedy was that he died without having constructed a solid party that could carry through his distinct revolutionary socialist legacy. Nevertheless, from the embers of 1916, was born an Irish revolutionary tradition, with all its strengths and weaknesses.

CHAPTER THREE

The Irish Revolution

From 1918 to 1923, Ireland was in the throes of revolution and the British Empire, which had ruled over much of the world's population, was shaken. It had tried to crush a mass uprising by brutal measures – including assassination and burnings of towns – but its troops were forced to leave Ireland. Revolutionary politics, which were once deemed to be marginal and extreme, won the allegiance of many people. Yet, strangely, the full scale of this revolution is played down in official histories.

The period is normally known as the 'War of Independence' or the 'Anglo-Irish War'. As the historian Peter Hart points out, the term 'Irish revolution' is not commonly in general or scholarly use.[1] This omission occurs because mainstream historians are often deeply sceptical about the ability of the mass of people to reshape their societies and so tend to focus on 'great men' or armed conflicts. John A. Murphy's book, *Ireland in the Twentieth Century*, is a good example. The Irish side consists of a guerrilla army who have 'ambivalent' support from the 'population at large' and are led by the 'indefatigable' Michael Collins, who is adjutant-general of the Volunteers, the director of intelligence and minister of finance.[2] There is no mention of strikes, land seizures, soviets, or mass boycotts and the mass of people simply play a support role for the great leader. This way of writing history seeps into popular consciousness so that the period becomes a drama about personalities and their followers. Thus Lloyd George becomes the wily, cunning politician, Michael Collins the brave soldier and Éamon de Valera, the aloof manipulator who pulled the strings. In fictional form, this version appears in Neil Jordan's film,

Michael Collins, where the romantic Collins becomes the hero of the struggle for independence.

Even when the revolution is defined solely as a guerrilla struggle, it is sanitised to fit modern purposes. In 1984, the Fine Gael politician Michael Noonan spoke at a commemoration ceremony at Béal na Bláth (the site of Collins's assassination), and described him as 'the man who fought the Black and Tans terror' with 'matchless and indomitable will'.[3] Yet he was careful to avoid specifics so that comparisons could not be drawn with the Provisional IRA who were then fighting a guerrilla campaign in Northern Ireland. The Southern elite's defence mechanism was to claim that the good old IRA fought a fair, clean fight unlike the 'terrorists' of the Provos.

This, however, is simply a mythological re-telling to suit modern political purposes. The plain fact is that the old IRA shot police officers in cold blood and executed informers – just as much as their modern equivalents. An unfortunate woman, Kathleen McCormack, from Duffy's Cross just outside Monaghan may serve as just one example. She was executed as an informer for simply reporting illegal drink-trafficking to the Royal Irish Constabulary on 17 April 1921.[4] Early IRA executions of police officers were denounced by church leaders like Cardinal Logue as 'cool, deliberate , wilful murder, pure and simple'[5] – almost precisely the same terms in which the modern IRA was denounced. Nor can it be argued that the old IRA had a democratic mandate. The opening shot of the Anglo-Irish War was fired by a Volunteer company in Soloheadbeg on 21 January 1919 at the exact time the first Dáil was meeting. It was carried out without the sanction of the Sinn Féin leadership and was hastily organised to 'strike a demonstrative blow before the Dáil met'.[6] It was only later that the Dáil even accepted that the Irish Republican Army was the official army of the republic.

But while the political elite present the Irish revolution as a sanitised War of Independence, revisionist intellectuals present it as an unfortunate outbreak that threatened to destabilise Ireland's long constitutional tradition. This approach began with the political scientist and television commentator, Brian Farrell, who thought the very idea of an Irish revolution was 'misleading'.[7] Ireland, he claimed, had a long parliamentary tradition that stretched back to medieval times and this produced a distinct political culture. This culture had produced the 'British style liberal conservatism of the Irish rebel' and the events of 1918–23 merely fitted into a pre-established pattern.[8] Tom Garvin takes a similar dismissive attitude to the revolution, noting that 'anti-democratic elements in Irish political culture' legitimised armed resistance after the Treaty.[9] These elements threatened to destabilise the constitutional tradition and only the pro-treaty leaders, who had a 'Hobbesian sense of the necessity of imposing political order', saved it.[10] Peter Hart goes even further, claiming that there was 'no social revolutionary situation in Ireland' and the main result of the struggle was 'communal violence that resulted in the displacement of minority populations'.[11] These attacks are not motivated purely by academic concerns. They come from intellectuals who think that history moves through slow predetermined paths set by a constitutional tradition. Everything else appears as a disruption or, as the French writers Furet and Richet put it, a *derapage*[12] – a skidding off-course from the liberal road.

The reality, however, is that there is no set constitutional tradition that floats above decades of real history. The supposed liberalism of the British elite which apparently gave birth to a constitutional tradition is much exaggerated. Liberal democracy was forced on them by masses of working people who mobilised to win their right to vote.[13] Even after a parliamentary framework was established, the elite discarded their own rules when their privileges were threatened. Thus, they never showed the slightest respect for the democratically expressed wishes of the Irish people for independence. The Tory element connived openly with an army mutiny and pogroms to shore up the loyalist position. The British elite, as a whole, suspended parliamentary elections for nearly a decade to fight the great imperial war of 1914–18. In other words, the notion that the constitutional tradition was a gift that came to Ireland through participation in the British Empire is a comfortable fairy tale. The revisionists mystify the 'democratic processes' by reducing it to parliamentary debates. Thus, we have the bizarre proposition from Brian Farrell that Ireland had a liberal constitutional tradition – even before the mass of people had the right to vote.

There are, thus, two dominant narratives about the period 1918–23. The conventional story describes it as a War of Independence and defines it as a series of military engagements and subsequent negotiations. The revisionists take a more hostile view, seeing it as a dangerous interlude that almost destroyed Ireland's constitutional tradition. Both, however, play down the attempts by masses of people to intervene in public life. In other words, they ignore its revolutionary dynamic.

The Irish Revolution

In his classic account of revolution, the Russian revolutionary Lenin outlined the main features of a revolutionary situation:

1) When there is a crisis, in one form or another, among the 'upper classes,' ... leading to a fissure through which the discontent and indignation of the oppressed classes burst forth. For a revolution to take place, it is usually insufficient for 'the lower classes not to want' to live in the old way; it is also necessary that 'the upper classes should be unable' to live in the old way; (2) when the suffering and want of the oppressed classes have grown more acute than usual; (3) when, as a consequence of the above causes, there is a considerable increase in the activity of the masses.[14]

A number of these elements can illuminate the nature of the Irish revolution. First, the ruling class were no longer able to rule in the old way. In Ireland, the primary mechanism by which the British elite ruled was by collaborating with Redmondism. However, the rebellion of 1916, the horrors of the First World War and, crucially, the threat to conscript an unwilling population destroyed that mechanism. Second, there was suffering among the masses of people but, contrary to Lenin's conditions, it was not necessarily 'more acute than usual'. Nevertheless, there were some key economic issues which mingled with a desire for national freedom. Over a hundred thousand soldiers were demobilised after the war and many wanted to return as farmers. Land hunger, therefore, swept the countryside when they came back home. There was also high inflation due to wartime prices and this squeezed wages. One result was a strong movement calling for higher pay. Then a major slump in 1920 put many out of work, provoking new battles over wage cuts. The Irish revolution, therefore, saw an intersection of demands for national freedom with calls for land distribution and better conditions for workers.

Third, Lenin suggests that a revolution involves a *process* by which masses of people become increasingly active. This may seem a rather obvious element, but it allows to us to dismiss a number of misconceptions which are sometimes used to deny an Irish revolution. Revolutions are not one-off events which are deliberately and consciously planned. There are no dates set for when they start, there is no leadership or central committee that can decide their course, there is no guaranteed outcome. They erupt when there is a general tumult that arises from deep contradictions in society. Moreover, their starting point is often 'moderate' demands which elites refuse or cannot concede. Thus, the mere fact that the mass of people simply opposed conscription or voted for an independent Parliament cannot be taken as indicators that they had not entered a path of revolution. The Russian Revolution of 1917 had even more moderate ambitions: its main slogan was for land, bread and peace. A revolution is a process which stretches over a significant period of time, where cries of unity are followed by splits and divisions; where seemingly radical phrases are not backed up by action and where allegiances shift and change. It is only if they are successful that there is a final seizure of power by masses of people. Engels summed up this concept for revolution when he pointed out that it is a 'big mistake is to think that the revolution can be made overnight. As a matter of fact it is a process of development of the masses that takes several years even under conditions that favour its acceleration.'[15]

From this vantage point, the events in Ireland between 1918 and 1923 constitute a revolutionary process. They involved a combination of armed struggle, mass boycotts and strikes to defeat the British state. This particular mix did not conform to the patterns by other revolutions but then again revolutions by their very nature diverge from set patterns. In Russia in 1917, the revolution involved mass strikes, the creation of workers' councils and a final successful insurrection. In Ireland, by contrast, the process was in reverse order. There was, first, an unsuccessful insurrection in 1916, which was then followed by a mass revolt which led to a form of dual power. This, however, mimicked the existing state and did not have a distinct class basis. Then, finally, there was a counter-revolution where pro-Treaty forces worked with British allies to crush more radical elements. Nevertheless, for a certain period, control of society was not in the hands of the elites because masses of people intervened to shape their own destinies. It only became an aborted revolution because no political force emerged which could fuse national and social demands.

The revolution involved, first, an intense level of military activity to resist the repressive machinery of the British state. Approximately one hundred thousand people joined the Irish Volunteers in the wake of the conscription crisis in 1918 and a smaller minority engaged directly in military operations. This was because of a restricted supply of weaponry and the varying degrees of commitment amongst those who enlisted. One estimate puts the number of active volunteers at fifteen thousand, but their strength varied in different counties.[16] In Tipperary, for example, there were about a thousand Volunteers,[17] whereas the organisation was much weaker in Mayo primarily because the republicans refused to support the agitation for land redistribution. The strategy of the Volunteers – later renamed the IRA – was to uproot the British administration in local areas and so their primary target was the Royal Irish Constabulary (RIC), an armed police force. In 1919, the IRA killed 18 policemen; in 1920, they killed 182, and in the first four months of 1921, 94 more. The historian Roy Foster claims that overall four hundred policemen and one hundred and sixty soldiers were killed before the Anglo-Irish Truce of 1921.[18] Police stations were burned to the ground and the RIC were eventually driven from many areas. By 1920, the RIC had retreated from five hundred police barracks and huts.[19] The IRA also engaged in extensive road cutting to hamper access to areas by the police and the notorious Black and Tans. In April 1920, scores of tax offices were burnt to facilitate a campaign of withholding taxes and land annuities from the British administration.

However, while the IRA inflicted serious damage on the British forces, it could not do so without an active boycott campaign from the mass of people. Early in the conflict, Sinn Féin called for a ban on all social intercourse with the police, stating that there should be 'No salutations. No social contact. If they attend, you leave.'[20] These injunctions were largely adhered to – and then backed up by military action. RIC barracks were no longer supplied with turf, butter, eggs, or milk and people walked away from church pews if police officers arrived. Stones were thrown and the police were attacked on the streets, until they were eventually isolated. In January 1919, the RIC's inspector general noted that his force was being treated 'with bitter hostility' in disaffected counties.[21] The combination of boycott and military action led to the creation of liberated zones. By 1920, for example, almost half of the 63 police stations in Mayo were closed.[22]

The people also turned their back on the official state institutions.[23] In the general election of 1918, they voted to give Sinn Féin 73 out of the 105 seats and the elected members decided to convene Dáil

Éireann as a constituent assembly of an independent Ireland. When it met on 21 January 1919 they voted for a Declaration of Independence. As if to ensure there was no ambiguity, Cathal Brugha, who was elected acting president, declared 'you understand what is asserted in this Declaration that we have now done with England.'[24] The Dáil then began to formulate laws as if it was the real government of Ireland. One of its first decisions was the establishment of republican courts. Judges – or 'brehons' as they were called after the old Irish term – were to be elected in each chapel by adult suffrage.[25] Clergymen or magistrates who had resigned from the British system were, however, allowed to become judges *ex officio*. A campaign against the British court system quickly ensued. Litigants for the Crown courts were turned away by republican pickets and prospective jurors were told that attendance would be considered an act of treason to the Irish republic. By August 1920, about three hundred magistrates, who were either sympathetic to the republican cause or too frightened to defy them, resigned their positions. Undersecretary for Ireland John Anderson informed the British Cabinet that the British court system 'had virtually come to a standstill and rival courts are functioning openly'.[26] The *Irish Times* noted that 'the King's writ runs no longer in many parts of the country. The Sinn Féin tribunals are jostling British law into oblivion, as fast motor cars jostle foot passengers off the roads.'[27]

Other forms of a boycott of state institutions were less successful. The republicans sought to develop an alternative local government and tax system even while operating under the military power of the British state. Local authorities were asked to pledge allegiance to Dáil Éireann even though the British government had deemed it to be an illegal assembly. The Dáil then instructed these local authorities not to levy rates to meet the costs of malicious damages claims to buildings which the IRA had targeted. They were instead to collect rates to finance an alternative government structure. The republican local government structures were, however, very shaky, because they tried to replicate the institutions of the British state without having the military apparatus to back them up. This became apparent in 1920, when Michael Collins, who functioned as minister for finance as well as IRA leader, decreed that taxes should be sent to Dáil Éireann rather than the British authorities. However, this plan failed because of lack of support from the wealthier elements of society. As David Fitzpatrick put it, 'Farmers and men of substance feared seizure of their land or assets if they refused annuities or taxes [to the British government] and those who did not showed no eagerness to send them to the Dáil instead.'[28]

Labour Mobilises

The other key element in the revolt against the British government was workers' action. On a number of occasions, the sheer strength of the workers' movement forced the British government to retreat.

The first was the attempt to introduce conscription in April 1918. As soon as it was announced, the Irish Trade Union Congress called a rally in Belfast and between eight and ten thousand people attended. A special congress was held on 20 April and delegates voted for a general strike to be held three days later. The resolution declaring the general strike stated that it was hoped it 'will be a signal to the workers of all countries at war to rise against their oppressors and bring the war to an end.'[29] On the day of the strike, the ITUC issued a manifesto, warning that any employer who assisted the authorities by dismissing men to force them into the army, would be met by a sympathetic strike.[30] The strike was a magnificent success: most of the country closed down – the exception being Belfast. Despite deaths of many Protestant workers from the 36th Ulster Division in the Battle of the Somme, loyalty to the Empire was still strong. Another reason was that labour's campaign against conscription had become absorbed into a pan-nationalist alliance endorsed by the Catholic bishops. Nevertheless, the power of the labour movement across the rest of the island forced Lloyd George to withdraw his threat, and Ireland became one of the few countries that was free of conscription during the First World War.

After the victory against conscription, a strike was called by the small but militant Irish Automobile Drivers Union against a requirement that all motor vehicles obtain a permit from the military. At the time, driving was a skilled job and many vehicles required the use of hired drivers. Members of the ADU walked off work and the *Dublin Evening Telegraph* reported that 'throughout the country traffic was greatly reduced.'[31] Unfortunately, the ITGWU leaders did not back the strike because of a sectional rivalry with the ADU and this severely impeded the spread of sympathetic action. Despite this, there was some support from grass-roots members of the ITGWU. Yet the ADU was eventually forced to back down, winning only the deletion of a clause forcing their members to re-apply for permits every time they changed employer.

The next intervention of labour came with the declaration of a soviet in Limerick in April 1919. The immediate cause was the imposition of martial law on the city by the British Army. Even before the declaration of a soviet there were signs that Limerick workers were moving dramatically to the left. The year before, ten thousand had attended a May Day rally where a resolution was passed to pay 'particular tribute to our Russian comrades who have waged such a magnificent struggle for their social and political emancipation.'[32] It can hardly be an accident that a year later the same workers borrowed the Russian term 'soviet' – which means 'workers' council' – as the name for their own protest against British rule.

The events which triggered the soviet started with attempted rescue of Robert Byrne, a republican prisoner and a prominent trade unionist, who had been jailed for possession of a revolver. During an escape attempt, Byrne and a policeman were killed and the British authorities responded by placing the city under martial law. Anyone entering parts of the city were required to hold a permit issued by the British Army. Workers at the Condensed Milk Company struck in protest at this ruling and a meeting of the Trades Council then decided to call a local general strike until martial law was lifted. It had a resounding response as fifteen thousand workers walked off their jobs. The Trades Council – now renamed a Strike Committee – then began to take a number of measures to ensure the functioning of the city. They ordered the rationing of hotel meals and granted permits – enforced by pickets – for shops to sell bread, milk and potatoes. A subcommittee organised food supplies from the rest of Ireland and from unions in Britain. They enforced a ban on cars appearing in the streets without permission of the strike committee. A propaganda subcommittee published a daily 'Workers' Bulletin'. They permitted picture houses to open as long as the profits went to the strike fund. They even printed their own money to ensure a supply of credit.

The Limerick Soviet did not reach the level of similar organs in Russia because it confined itself to the demand for the abolition of martial law. It also had a more limited level of mass participation as it was not based on delegates who could be recalled from workplaces. But it represented an impressive development in class consciousness as workers took a lead in opposing British repression. The tragedy was that the militancy of Limerick workers was not matched by their union leaders. The British TUC instructed unions not to pay out strike pay while Tom Johnson, one of the leaders of ITUC, made the bizarre proposal to evacuate the city. In Johnson's case, it was a case of left rhetoric being used to cover an abject failure to spread the struggle. In the end, the Limerick Soviet ended with a promise that military permits would not be required to the same extent as before.

The confidence of Irish labour was growing throughout these events and its next major action came with a food embargo. On 31 March 1920, the British government announced that the fixed pricing of bacon and butter was to end. Speculators then began to buy up these foodstuffs in the hope of making hefty profits when they were exported for sale. All of this evoked historic memories of the Great Famine and there was a fear of higher food prices. There was a growing clamour to stop the exports and the actual ban began with Catholic dockers in Belfast. It then spread to Dublin where the Irish Council of the National Union of Dock Labourers declared an embargo on food exports. Enthusiasm for this action ensured that not only bacon and butter but all foodstuffs were scrutinised by dockers and only exported with their permission. When bacon-curing employers in Limerick and Cork objected, the ITUC informed them that

> We do not recognise the right of the owners of bacon factories to withhold their premises and machinery from use at their discretion against the common interest. These material structures have been built and adapted by workers for a social purpose i.e. to provide bacon for the people. If those who hold these things in trust fail to fulfil their trust the people must relieve them of their trust.[33]

The labour movement's action, however, became part of a pan-nationalist campaign headed up by an All-Ireland Committee for food supplies which included Dáil representatives, farmers as well as trade unionists. It eventually reached a settlement whereby in return for lifting the embargo on 70 per cent of bacon exports, 30 per cent would be sold in Ireland at controlled prices.

The next major action by workers was hugely significant. On 5 April 1920, 36 prisoners in Mountjoy gaol went on hunger strike because they had been imprisoned without even being charged. The prisoners included republicans, trade unionists and one revolutionary socialist, Jack Hedley. As news of the hunger strike spread, people began to gather outside the jail and by the end of the week, forty thousand people were at a protest confronting British armoured cars. The ITUC called a general strike and the response was electric. The country ground to halt and workers' committees began to take over the running of towns. Food committees organised the distribution of food and seized any vehicle found without permits. In some towns, shops were allowed to open only for an hour and were supervised by pickets. The signs of workers' control were evident to both participants and outside journalists. The *Watchword of Labour* – the newspaper of the union movement – contained the following report from Galway:

> Well, the Workers Council is formed in Galway and it's here to stay. God speed the day when such Councils shall be established all over Erin and the world, control the natural resources of the country, the means of production and distribution, run them as the workers knows how to run them, for the good and welfare of the whole community and not for the profits of a few bloated parasites. Up Galway![34]

A correspondent from the *Manchester Guardian* also drew attention to the manner in which workers councils took control of towns. In Clonmel, for example, he noted how permits and passes bearing the superscription of the Workers' Council of Clonmel were necessary for travel and trade:

> It is particularly interesting to note the rise of the Workers Councils in the country towns. The direction of affairs passed during the strike to these councils, which were formed not on a local but class basis. In most cases the police abdicated and the maintenance of order was taken over by the Workers Councils … In fact it is no exaggeration to trace a flavour of proletarian dictatorship about some aspects of the strike.[35]

The sheer scale of the action broke the resolve of the British government and in an act of panic, Lord Lieutenant of Ireland John French decided to release all the untried hunger strikers. However, even a face-saving exercise, of forcing the prisoners to sign a document to state that they would attend a future trial, failed. They simply refused to sign, but were still released. The *London Morning Post* summed up the predicament of the British government when it described the release of the hunger strikers 'as a situation of unparalleled ignominy and painful humiliation.'[36]

The next intervention of labour was directly influenced by events connected with the Russian Revolution. In May 1920, dockers in London refused to load coal onto a munitions ship, the *Jolly George*, which was taking arms to the White armies which were trying to crush the Russian Revolution. This successful boycott inspired Irish trade unionists to make the connection that if workers can boycott British arms going to Russia, why cannot the same be done for Ireland? Shortly afterwards, Dublin dockers refused to unload two ships, the *Anna Dorette Boog* and the *Polberg*. News of the boycott spread and workers at Harcourt Street station refused to unload rifles for the RIC, while dockers in Cobh boycotted another ship carrying machine guns. Then the railway workers declared that they would refuse to transport any military cargo or armed men. The railway companies responded by sacking train drivers, but the movement kept on growing. By July, Commander-in-Chief of the British Army in Ireland General MacCready was describing the action 'as a serious setback for military activities during the best season of the year.'[37]

British soldiers responded to the train drivers' action with naked intimidation. One union leader described how soldiers would get up on the footplate of trains and say to the driver 'you have to drive this train.' They would then 'put a revolver to his head and say "you will get the contents of this if you don't drive."'[38] Despite this pressure, workers stood firm and from July to October there was stalemate, as neither side conceded; as a result, passenger services virtually ceased all over Ireland. By this stage, however, the resolve of the union leaders was beginning to wilt. Fifteen hundred drivers had been sacked, money had to be raised to support them and there was widespread disruption to the wider economy. The union leaders either had to escalate the action or withdraw. They took the latter course and on 11 December 1920, the ITUC leaders called off the boycott. The fact remained, however, that workers' action had hampered the activity of the British war machine for six months.

The sheer scale of the struggles for national liberation – which we have just briefly sketched here – indicates that a genuine revolutionary process was underway; yet the school history books and academic studies have largely ignored its significance. Just as slave revolts or the contribution of women to science or art have been 'hidden from history', so too have workers' action during the Irish revolution. Among the honourable exceptions are Conor Kostick's marvellous *Revolution in Ireland* and Emmet O'Connor's *Syndicalism in Ireland 1917–23*. The omission of mass action from historical memory is profoundly political. The Southern elite want to pretend that the Irish are a naturally conservative people, so that no future attempt will ever be made to shake their rule. Their attitude is encapsulated in a statement by Kevin O'Higgins, the key figure in the post-Treaty counter-revolution, who boasted that 'we are probably the most conservative minded revolutionaries that ever put through a successful revolution.'[39] If by 'we', O'Higgins meant the upper-class, 'Donnybrook set' who jumped into Sinn Féin, he might be right. But of course this 'we' never 'put through any successful revolution' – they did everything they could to restrain and squash it. The actions of the mass of people in backing an armed struggle and taking action themselves testifies to a very unconservative outlook.

The British Response

The sheer scale of the Irish uprising initially left the British authorities reeling and, to make matters worse, 1919 was a year of revolt across the Empire. There was major unrest throughout England, Scotland and Wales as mutinies broke out in the army, the police went on strike and unions fought for a 44-hour week. In Egypt, a revolution was launched against a British protectorate rule, with women to the fore in organising demonstrations. Over eight hundred people were murdered in an attempt to suppress it. In India, over a thousand people were murdered by British soldiers in the Amritsar massacre as they tried to put down a non-violent protest in the Punjab. The Empire was facing its greatest challenge and its leaders were haunted by a fear of 'bolshevism'. They were disorientated and so failed to embark on a concerted strategy to defeat the Irish revolt until mid-1920.

The main outlines of the British response only began to emerge when General MacCready was appointed as commander-in-chief in Ireland. MacCready already had a reputation for brutality – he had previously threatened to shoot striking Welsh miners. He demanded an immediate increase in the number of his forces and soon the Black and Tans began arriving, followed by Auxiliaries from August onwards. The British government's strategy was to frame the Irish revolt as a criminal conspiracy that was carried out by murdering gangs of fanatics. They, therefore, deemed its suppression to be police work and the 40,000-strong British Army was officially only playing a support role. The Black and Tans were to bolster up police numbers and were stationed at their barracks. The Auxiliaries were originally supposed to be a more elite paramilitary force – a special gendarmerie that operated separately from the police and concentrated on raids. By 1921, there were seven thousand Black and Tans and six thousand Auxiliaries in Ireland.[40] The aim of the British strategy was to restore morale to a battered RIC which was experiencing mass resignations and a lack of recruitment. The situation was so bad that a top civil servant told the British Cabinet in July 1920 that 'within two months the Irish Police force as a Police force would cease to exist.'[41] The principle way of restoring morale was by allowing the police to murder opponents and to engage in collective punishment against towns which showed any sympathy with the IRA.

One of the first operations of a police death squad was the murder of Cork's Mayor Thomas MacCurtain in March 1920. A subsequent coroner's report did not mince its words when it stated that 'the murder was organised and carried out by the Royal Constabulary, officially directed by the British government.'[42] The following week, another republican urban councillor, Michael McCarthy, was assassinated in Thurles and to facilitate the use of death squads, a special Restoration of Order in Ireland Act was passed in August 1920. This abolished coroners' courts and so ended embarrassment caused by the likes of the judgement in the MacCurtain murder. The pattern was now set for immediate and brutal revenge assassinations in return for any IRA killing. After an informer was executed by the IRA in Galway in October 1920, a death squad abducted a republican city councillor, Michael Walshe, and dumped his body in the docks. The following month, after a police officer was killed, a republican priest, Father Griffin, was abducted by a death squad and his body was found in a shallow grave in Barna. In February, another elected republican, John Geoghan, a district councillor from Moycullen, was murdered.[43]

Alongside these targeted assassinations, collective punishment of towns and village became a standard response. The most infamous was Bloody Sunday, which came in response to Collins's execution of 14 members of the Cairo gang, an elite British intelligence unit. A large contingent of RIC officers and British soldiers opened fire on a crowd in Croke Park, killing 13 civilians and wounding 70 others. But this was only one of a series of reprisals or collective punishments that the British government put at the core of their strategy. In Tuam in July 1920, the police destroyed the town after the killing of one of their comrades. An English reporter later noted that 'it recalled nothing so much as some of the ruined Belgium and French towns.'[44] In September, after the killing of an RIC constable, a detachment of Black and Tans smashed up the town of Balbriggan, burning down over thirty buildings and then executing two known republicans. In the same week, Miltown Malbay, Lahinch, Ennistymon, Trim and Mallow were subjected to the same treatment.[45] After an ambush in Cork in December 1920, a combined force of Auxiliaries, Black and Tans and regular soldiers burnt and looted Cork City. Two civilians were murdered without provocation and fire hoses were cut so that fires could not be extinguished. Aside from the burning of towns, other forms of collective punishment included floggings of republicans, mock executions, and the destruction of creameries to destroy local economies.

These actions have sometimes been portrayed as those of the ill-disciplined Black and Tans, but this rather misses the point of how they were a clear part of British strategy. Contrary to later myths, the Black and Tans were not a force made up mainly of ex-convicts, and were often only following the example of RIC officers in carrying out 'reprisals'. There is little doubt that the signal for death squads and collective punishment came from the very top. After a near-mutiny of the police in Listowel, for example, the Munster Commissioner for the police told his officers, 'the more you shoot, I will like you and I assure you that no policeman will get into trouble for shooting any man.'[46] Certainly, the 'reprisals' – as the British authorities called them – were seen to have a marked effect on the IRA and the wider population. MacCready later noted that it curbed their activities and 'on these grounds were justified or at all events winked at by those in control of the police.'[47] The authorities regarded police rampages as a necessary measure to restore morale but sought to direct them in a more targeted direction. After the sack of Balbriggan, for example, Assistant Undersecretary for Ireland Andy Cope reported that 'the RIC were not out of hand but are systematically led to reprise by their officers.'[48] His counterpart at Dublin Castle, Mark Sturgis, replied that indiscriminate burnings were idiotic but 'a little quiet shooting' was effective.[49] He noted that the head of the security apparatus, Hugh Tudor, was reported as saying that 'LG is all against burning but not gunning, and told him as much himself'[50] (LG being, of course, the initials for Lloyd George).

The second element of the British strategy was a rapid move to partition Ireland and establish a separate Northern state by creating facts on the ground. Originally, Unionists were opposed to a separate parliament and wanted only to participate in the imperial Parliament at Westminster. However, faced with the republican uprising, key figures in Unionism moved to make partition a reality. In 1919, a subcommittee of Irish Unionists chaired by Walter Long produced a report favouring the partition of the North-East and the creation of two Irish parliaments. The Long Report recommended that all nine Ulster counties be included, but other Unionists were more attuned to the brutal sectarian realities. They knew that inclusion of three Ulster counties with Catholic majorities would de-stabilise a Protestant parliament for a Protestant people. 'We quite frankly admit that we cannot hold onto nine counties', declared Charles Craig, MP.[51] He also indicated that Unionists wanted their own parliament because of their 'profound distrust' of the Labour Party.[52] With a legislative assembly in Belfast, they could overrule any backsliding from Labour and insist on their role within the empire.

With the Government of Ireland Act of 1920, the Tory majority in the House of Commons gave the Unionists everything they wanted. It proposed the formation of two separate parliaments, so setting the stage for the construction of a Northern state on an entirely sectarian basis. The British elite's endorsement of the Northern state was a tactical shift to weaken the impetus behind the Irish revolution. It allowed them to use a rhetoric of championing minority rights and this, they thought, helped to improve Britain's image in an era when the US President Wilson was promoting a new order based on self-determination. Lord Birkenhead explained the motivation behind the new measure. It afforded 'an ingenious strengthening of our tactical position before the world. I am absolutely satisfied that Sinn Féin will refuse it. Otherwise in the present state of Ireland I could not even be a party to making the offer.'[53] However by constructing a new state on the basis of nothing more than a sectarian headcount, the

British authorities must have been aware that it would unleash inter-communal conflict.

They certainly turned a blind eye to the creation of the illegal Ulster Volunteer Force and in fact actively colluded with it. In April 1920, Edward Carson wrote to his old ally, Bonar Law, urging the government to recruit Ulster Loyalists as an auxiliary force to suppress the IRA. However, even before the answer came back, enlistment into the UVF began. Basil Brooke, a large landowner organised a loyalist vigilante force and requested that they be recognised as a special constabulary. Advertisements were placed in the press looking for new recruits for the UVF and arrangements were made to ship in guns. By August, the British Army were supplying intelligence material on Sinn Féin and the Northern IRA to the still illegal UVF. When sectarian riots broke out after the first ever nationalist election victory for Derry City Council, the full extent of the collusion became evident. Loyalists began firing on Catholic areas and UVF patrols took over the city centre, yet the British Army stood aside. When they finally imposed a curfew on the city, they concentrated their efforts on the Catholic population. Searches for arms were also concentrated in Catholic areas and six Catholics were shot dead.

The Derry riots were a harbinger of what was to come. In July 1920, there was a ferocious speech from Edward Carson when he urged loyalists to take matters into their own hands in dealing with the rebellion. Shortly afterwards, a meeting was held in the Belfast shipyards 'to drive the Sinn Féiners out' and over the next few days, all Catholics and 'rotten Prods' who held radical or labour views were expelled. In August, after a local police officer was killed by the IRA, almost all Catholics were driven out of Lisburn. Despite this, the leader of the UVF, Wilfred Spender, held a meeting with Hamar Greenwood, the chief secretary for Ireland, where he was told that the UVF had Lloyd George's tacit approval 'but that it would be politically unwise to announce this publically [sic]'.[54] By October 1920, the UVF had raised an army of between 20,000 to 30,000 members and by that stage it was only a matter of giving it legal cover. This came with government approval to create an Ulster Special Constabulary which consisted of full-time 'A Specials', part-time 'B Specials' and a reserve force of 'C Specials'. From the very start, it was a sectarian force that effectively integrated the UVF into the state apparatus.

The third element of Britain's strategy now came into view. Even while stepping up its military repression and colluding with sectarian forces in the North, the British government started sending out feelers to the republican leadership. The man charged with doing this was Andy Cope, and under Lloyd George's instructions, he made links with Michael Collins.[55] John Andersen, the joint undersecretary for Ireland, thought that 'firm measures' had to be accompanied by a 'declaration of policy and an appeal to moderate opinion' to create an atmosphere and prepare 'for an ultimate settlement by consent'.[56] In other words, they operated a two-pronged strategy of repression while leaving open a space for a peace settlement. By mid-1921, however, they faced a choice. They could either further intensify military operations by imposing martial law on the whole country, or they could seek to move rapidly to a negotiated settlement. MacCready suggested 'the utmost thoroughness' would be required to carry out the first option and it would have to include measures such as capturing de Valera and putting him on trial for his life.[57] By contrast, Churchill argued that there were good reasons for offering a truce to the IRA:

Where is the disadvantage? There is no military disadvantage … If kept, you'll have tremendous advantage; they'll have a great difficulty in getting men to go back; if they break, you are in a far stronger position with public opinion; your troops are all in position; they can begin at any moment and in the interval you'll have got information. It is a matter of psychology when you should time it.[58]

After a long series of debates, the British Cabinet came around to the negotiation option. On 11 July 1921, a truce commenced between British forces and the IRA and 18 weeks were to elapse before the signing of the Anglo-Irish Treaty. That treaty in turn would pave the way for an eventual counter-revolution. But to understand how it occurred we need to examine the politics of one element of the Irish revolutionary tradition: republicanism.

CHAPTER FOUR

Republicanism and Counter-revolution

In the aftermath of the Easter Rising, British propaganda targeted the so-called 'Sinn Féin' rebels as the insurgents. This was the name of the party founded by Arthur Griffith to promote the idea of a dual monarchy. He believed that an independent Ireland should share a monarchy with Britain rather than abolishing it. The 'Sinn Féin' label stuck because there was no other open political organisation to which responsibility for the rebellion could be attributed. James Connolly had not built a substantial socialist party and Patrick Pearse believed in the primacy of the gun rather than political organisation.

Ironically, Arthur Griffith had not participated in the 1916 Rising and had toured Bray on Easter Sunday urging Volunteers to respect Eoin MacNéill's order not to take part in it.[1] Griffith was a militant advocate of Irish capitalism, arguing that it was 'not capitalism but the abuse of capitalism that oppresses labour' and this abuse, he thought, came primarily from English policy.[2] He wanted a Gaelic Manchester where Irish capitalists could hire cheap labour and make enough profits to compete with their British counterparts. He believed in an Anglo-Irish empire and, like many aspiring imperialists, he had little compunction about whipping up racism. He called, for example, for a boycott of Jewish people, during the Limerick pogrom of 1904.[3] He detested Larkinism, socialism, English-based trade unions and any form of working-class militancy. At the time of the Rising, Griffith's political fortunes had actually sunk to a low point because the Sinn Féin organisation was virtually defunct by 1916, with only one branch in Dublin.

Nevertheless, as a result of British propaganda, Sinn Féin became the focal point for open political organising. It also became the means by which the wealthier, more respectable elements of Irish society could reconnect with the growing resistance to the British Empire. This took place symbolically at a convention in the Mansion House in Dublin when 1,700 delegates attended a reborn Sinn Féin gathering on 25 October 1917. Symbolically, Griffith stepped aside as president to allow Éamon de Valera to assume that role. He knew that many grass-roots activists were antagonistic to him because of his support for dual monarchy and his opposition to the Rising. But de Valera argued that the new republican movement had to unite in the national interest and successfully backed not only Griffith but also Eoin MacNéill for the national executive. A month after this convention, another meeting of the military organisation, the Irish Volunteers, took place where de Valera was also elected president. The republican movement now had both a political and a military wing and this became the classic template for subsequent generations. Key elements of the modern tradition were in place – an emphasis on national unity which cut across social classes, a postponement of debate on what type of free Ireland they were fighting for, and a military wing that officially complemented the political wing but which, in reality became its prime mover.

After the conference which established the new Sinn Féin, the stage was set for a major expansion. Elements of the old Irish Parliamentary Party began to join and even the Catholic hierarchy started to endorse the movement. P.S. O'Hegarty, summed it up:

> ... what had happened was not that Sinn Féin captured Ireland but that the politicians in Ireland and those who make them, all the elements which had sniffed at Sinn Féin and libelled it, which had upheld corruption and jobbery, had realised that Sinn Féin was going to win and had come over to it en masse.[4]

Sinn Féin became a political movement that combined different class interests because, it was suggested, the Irish nation demanded unity. Of course, nobody explicitly defined republicanism as an all-class alliance – it was just that class was deemed to be an irrelevance to the cause. However, this silence was more advantageous to the wealthier elements because they could rely for their protection on existing structures of economic power. As long as these were not challenged by explicit policy for transferring wealth, they were safe.

However, this amalgam of different social interests had an impact on Sinn Féin's political strategy because the inclusion of wealthier elements led to compromises on national freedom itself. The respectable elements were anxious to make their peace with the Empire, as soon as possible, and could easily sacrifice the purer republican principles to win their place in the sun. But as the 1917 conventions illustrated, there was a safety exit for the stauncher elements. They could look to the army – the IRA – as the safeguard of republican principles and view any backsliding as the work of softer politicians. Behind the unity of the 1917 convention, the contradictions which were to beset Irish republicanism were already in evidence. As Father O'Flanagan, vice president of Sinn Féin noted, 'the split was there from the beginning.'[5] But if the split was there from the start, so too was an explanation for how the movement could move on. It had only to vest authority in the Army Council of its military wing to stay strong. The historic dialectic of armed struggle–constitutional compromise–armed struggle was therefore built into the republican DNA from the very beginning.

In the early post-Rising period, none of this seemed to matter because the overwhelming emphasis was on national unity. Griffith put it in blunt clinical terms, stating that 'Sinn Féin is not a party: it is a national composition. If it is a party, it is a composite party. No part of that composition may claim its own individual programme until the national ideal has first been attained.'[6] De Valera spoke for the

stronger republican element in the new Sinn Féin but he expressed
the same view – even while indicating his sympathies with labour:

> There are tendencies to try to make it appear that Sinn Féin is
> opposed to labour. We are not opposed to labour or the just
> aspirations of labour. We say to labour: you have your own work
> to do, organise and make yourself as strong as you like, but for the
> present moment we have the big question of Irish liberty on hand,
> which will take all the energy at the present moment, and we cannot
> in the present moment in our fight deal with labour problems.[7]

Outside the ranks of Sinn Féin, the same pressure for national unity
was exerted. The Labour Party was urged not to stand in the 1918
election but to give way to Sinn Féin – and its leaders agreed. Economic
strikes that were not related to the cause of national independence
were discouraged. In 1919, the illegal Dáil set up a Department of
Labour headed by Constance Markievicz who was, in reality, only a
figurehead. The primary aim of the 'department' was not to promote
labour interests but rather to act as a forum for conciliation between
labour and capital. As Emmet O'Connor explained, it aimed to solve
'grievances, usually on the basis of precedents set by the British
government machinery'.[8] Republican arbitration courts were also
established to quell agitation to redistribute land. In 1920, Griffith
told the Dáil that the arbitration courts 'had prevented the land
question from being used to divert the energies of the people from
the national issue'.[9]

However, the focus on national unity did not preclude occasional
rhetorical lurches to the left. In 1919, for example, the First Dáil
adopted a 'Democratic Programme', which promised a 'general and
lasting improvement in the conditions under which the working
classes live and labour'.[10] The programme had been written by the
trade union leader, Tom Johnson, and even though his original
proposal was diluted down by Sean T. O'Kelly, it nevertheless still

expressed a radical sentiment.[11] However, the programme was not a guide to actual republican strategy, but was written to suit an Irish labour delegation that was seeking recognition of an independent Irish state at a Second International conference in Berne. Left rhetoric was used in an instrumental way to garner support for national unity – it was not to be taken too seriously in practice.

Alongside the IRA military, the Sinn Féin leadership hoped to make gains on two major fronts. First, they wanted official recognition for an independent Irish republic from other heads of state. They sought support from Soviet Russia, but their key objective was to gain backing from the US political establishment. To counter the appeal of the Bolshevik revolution, US President Woodrow Wilson had developed a progressive rhetoric about nations having a right to self-determination. Sinn Féin wanted Wilson to act on this rhetoric by granting Ireland a seat at the Paris peace conference and at the League of Nations. Arthur Griffith placed a particular emphasis on gaining US support because he thought Wilson to be a 'sincere man who was struggling against the forces of tyranny, imperialism and lusty world powers'.[12] But the Irish did not even get a reply to their request. The imperial alliance between the US and Britain was far more important than rhetorical flourishes about self-determination.

Second, Sinn Féin set out to create a counter-state to the official state. The Republic was to be both a pure ideal and an underground reality. This strategy was originally proposed by Arthur Griffith and envisaged as a gradual, peaceful evolution in statehood but, in practice, the development of a counter-state paralleled the armed struggle. Even as the IRA was desperately waging a war against overwhelming British forces, ministers of the republican government were going through the motions of overseeing departments dealing with forestry, fisheries and local government. They were even provided with the trappings of office, such as ministerial salaries and secretaries. Some of their plans never left the drawing board but, despite this, an entirely illegal apparatus of government departments was constructed. The problem was that the counter-state did not have either the financial resources or the full arsenal of repression to behave as a proper state. Its principal source of funding, for example, was to come from the US where bonds were taken out for a Dáil Loan. One effect, however, was that the Dáil became even more determined to avoid any entanglement in social issues lest it upset wealthy contributors.

While the population at large showed an impressive determination to transfer allegiance to the new Republic, there were limitations. People could withdraw from the British justice system and look to the republican courts but they could not prevent the British-controlled state from taking taxes or administering hospital or schools. The strategy of creating a counter-state which mirrored the enemy's was, therefore, inherently unstable. As a result, the armed struggle became the main tactic and the IRA fought the full might of the British forces without any way of linking the fight for national freedom with social advance for the mass of people.

The Social Explosion

This strategy of 'national liberation first and discuss social issues later' did not fit with the experience of workers, small farmers, or agricultural labourers. As a general rule, once the poor enter a political process, they tend not to confine themselves to distinct stages. They would not first 'fight for Ireland' and then forget their own burning grievances which affected their lives. They would not resist oppression of a purely British sort and then forget about the Irish oppressors who sheltered behind the British state. As they mobilised for national independence, the poor saw an opportunity to gain land or better wages or conditions. In brief, there was a tendency for the national revolt to spill over into social questions.

In post-war Europe after 1918, there was also a ready-made language of radicalism which could give expression to demands of the poor. The Russian Revolution had shown that it was possible to re-fashion society in the interests of workers and peasants. On 4 February 1918, ten thousand people attended a rally in Dublin and passed a resolution to 'hail with delight the advent of the Russian Bolshevik revolution.'[13] As a result, the word 'soviet' – a Russian term for 'workers' councils' – came to be used in a number of workers' struggles that coincided with the fight against the British Empire, most notably in the designation 'the Limerick soviet'. In an age when mass communications were far more limited than today, the spread of this term was significant. A Sinn Féin commentator, Aodh de Blacam, wrote that 'never was Ireland more devoutly Catholic than to-day ... yet nowhere was the Bolshevik revolution more sympathetically saluted.'[14] The language of the Russian Revolution was often combined with Connolly's rhetoric about a 'workers republic' to express an aspiration for a different Ireland. One example is James Good, a Cork union official, who was explaining why Irish workers were tired of the conservative British leadership of their union, the National Union of Railwaymen:

> The railwaymen in Ireland should be given complete control of their Organisation. They asked to be left alone and they would leave Englishmen alone. All they wanted was a Workers' republic, like the Republic of Russia, and on the day that they had it, the death knell of Capitalism and profiteering would be sounded.[15]

This aspiration for a 'workers' republic' came from a minority but there were many more who wanted to combine a revolt against the Empire with a social revolt. This came in three main forms.

There was, first, a demand for land redistribution, principally in Connaught. In 1911, there were 328,743 Irish farmers but about a third of them farmed less than ten acres. At the other end of the hierarchy, there were 32,000 farmers who had more than a hundred acres and who had, as a common saying went, 'the fat of the land and the silk of the kine' (the best cattle).[16] Within this group was a smaller elite of 'graziers' who held over two hundred acres and who were also known as 'ranchers' and these became the main target of calls for land redistribution. The cessation of emigration led to an upsurge of land hunger and the Irish countryside became a scene of bitter class conflicts. Although these land conflicts are often ignored in subsequent standard accounts of the War of Independence, contemporary observers were very aware of their relevance. The *Irish Times* told of how its wealthier readers were experiencing sleepless nights as the spectre of 'agrarian bolshevism' swept the land. The Catholic clergy also spoke out against a 'greed' for land that was breaking one of God's laws – respect for private property.[17]

Despite its own strategy, the IRA was drawn into these struggles. This sometimes happened because local units wanted to garner support by lurching leftwards and using the land agitation in an instrumental way. As Michael Brennan, the principal IRA officer in Clare, put it: 'I hadn't the slightest interest in the land agitation, but I had every interest in using it as a means to an end ... to get those fellows into the Volunteers ... and up to that they were just an unorganised mob.'[18]

Others, probably the poorer elements within the IRA, were more sincere and, under the guise of attacking 'anti-national landlords', supported the seizure of land. Eventually, however, the strategic emphasis of republicanism on national unity overrode these instinctive sympathies and the Sinn Féin arbitration courts became the means by which land agitation was quelled. Art O'Connor, minister for agriculture in the republican Dáil, attacked 'land seizures as a grave menace to the Republic', adding that 'the mind of the people was being diverted from the struggle for freedom by the class war.'[19]

Republican police moved against the land agitators to stop any breaches in national unity. This brought them into confrontation with poorer farmers and landless labourers who often used a tactic of cattle driving. In the dead of night, gangs of young men and women drove away cattle from the land of the 'ranchers' to scare their owners and pave the way for land redistribution. Sean Moylan, a senior IRA officer and subsequently a Fianna Fáil minister, later explained how republicans responded:

> I know what the IRA were doing in 1920–21, they were engaged in an unselfish struggle for the freedom of this country ... I remember very well a discussion by the IRA headquarters officers on the question of cleaning up the cattle drivers in County Mayo – and they were cleaned up by the IRA and by the County Mayo IRA.[20]

As the IRA cracked down on seizures, the big landowners began to look to the republican courts for protection rather than the British courts. But this also meant there was a marked decline in enthusiasm for the national struggle in parts of Connaught that had been most severely hit by land hunger. When the IRA took up the policeman's baton to protect the big farmers, there were many who asked if the Republic was really worth fighting for.

The second flashpoint was the extraordinary struggles launched by landless labourers. These were generally organised by the Irish Transport and General Workers Union and mainly focused on a demand for higher wages. Sometimes, however, they also spilled over into demand for land redistribution. The ITGWU won its reputation as a fighting organisation among the landless labourers when it began to organise militant countrywide strikes. These often involved sabotage on big farms, disruption of markets and the deployment of armed pickets with clubs to prevent the movement of goods. An alliance with dockers was often the key to victory. Dublin and Drogheda dockers, for example, boycotted the 'tainted goods' of Meath farmers during a strike in 1919.

After this victory, the ITGWU grew rapidly among farm labourers and the agitation spread around the country. In Fenor, in east Waterford, there were pitched battles between three hundred labourers and the RIC with revolver shots, batons and bayonets freely used. In Kerry, the Listowel RIC reported that 'the labour and small

farmer class was [sic] responsible for the great majority of outrages.'
In Carlow, the Watchword of Labour described the union's campaign:

> The Red commandants had perfected their plan of campaign, and
> the rank and file are ready. This was to have been no mere stay out,
> holiday strike. The time is past when battles are won by men on
> holiday. The experience of last year's land strikes has proved that if
> the proletariat of the land are to win against the organised farmers,
> victory only comes through organised aggression, not organised
> passivity ... Terrorism is the most potent of Labour's weapons, and
> while every other weaponry in our armoury must be used, it is on
> the Red Terror that our greatest reliance must be placed.[21]

The threat of 'Red Terror' in Carlow does not easily fit with a narrative
of the good clean fight against the British. This statement sounds
extraordinary to modern ears, attuned to the more conventional
story of the Irish War of Independence. There is, however, an
important context. Ireland was in the throes of both a national and
social upheaval. At the same time, big farmers were also organising
into a 'farmers freedom force' to put down 'labour, socialism and
bolshevism'.[22] The labourers were fighting an arrogant landowning
class that was used to deference. Unlike factory workers, the ratio of
workers to employers was quite small and the union members were
spread over a wide geographical area. All of these factors combined to
make the struggles of the landless assume a violent form.

The republican movement made little effort to tie the issue of
landlordism to the British Empire because they saw these issues as
separate. Landlordism and the aspirations of the landless were to be
dealt with at a later stage after independence had been won. As the
writer Sean O'Faolain explained, 'The policy of Sinn Féin has always
been, since its foundation, that simple formula: Freedom first, other
things afterwards.'[23] They, therefore, simply referred these disputes
to conciliation councils founded by the Dáil or, in at least one case,

intervened to stop blockades of big farmers. In December 1921, for example, Campile in Wexford witnessed the bizarre scene of both the Black and Tans and the republican police arriving simultaneously to quell a strike in the area.[24]

The third factor was workers' struggles for higher pay and shorter hours and then later, after 1920, resistance to wage cuts. The manner in which national and social aspirations fused together during the Irish revolution was evident in a huge growth in union organisation. In 1916, there were 100,000 unionised workers in Ireland but by 1922, this had grown to 225,000. Inside the union movement there was also a strong militant syndicalist influence – this was the idea that there needed to be one big union that would become strong enough to lock out the employer class and bring about a new society for workers. As the numbers of unionised workers grew, so too did the depth and quality of organisation. Trades Councils – which brought together different workers – were often renamed as 'workers' councils' and they co-ordinated strike action on a city- or town-wide basis. After 1918, there was a big push for higher wages and this was often fought for by local general strikes. The town of Charleville, for example, saw five local general strikes between 1918 and August 1923 while Dungarvan had eleven.

The popularity of the Russian Revolution was indicated by the number of occupations which were called 'soviets'. The first use of the term occurred during a workers' occupation of a tailor's workshop in November 1918; two months later, it was the turn of a Monaghan asylum to declare a soviet. In a more sustained struggle, 13 Limerick creameries were occupied, the red flag hoisted over the central depot in Knocklong and a banner was displayed with the words, 'We Make Butter Not Profits'. At Arigna, in Leitrim, a mine was seized from its owners for two months and operated as a soviet. In Cork, the port was seized by dockers and a new workers' commissioner installed as its director. Emmet O'Connor makes the reasonable point that there was still a long way to go between these Irish occupations and the Russian soviet but nevertheless suggests that

> ... there is no denying the extraordinary class triumphalism that gripped the people. Red banners, Mayday rallies, workers aeraiochtai [festivals], soviets, and the mosquito press are merely the archival remains of a spirit that once electrified vast sections of the labour movement ... This counter politics stood for the rejection of capitalism, and the celebration of solidarity, spontaneity, and direct action.[25]

With the labour movement on the offensive, the most important strike occurred in Belfast, demanding a 44-hour working week. On 14 January 1919, 20,000 shipyard workers downed tools and marched to the City Hall for a mass rally; within days, they were in effective control of the city. Once again the *Manchester Guardian* noted that 'the Strike Committee, have taken upon themselves, with the involuntary acquiescence of the civic authority, some of the attributes of an industrial soviet.'[26] Electricity was only allocated with workers' permission and no traffic could travel down major streets without workers' permits. The authorities were terrified because they were facing similar upheaval in Glasgow and elsewhere. The loyalist labour organisation founded by Edward Carson to co-opt workers became irrelevant, while the Orange Order decided not to take sides. Despite Belfast's sectarian history, the leader of the Strike Committee, Charles McKay, was a Catholic and the majority of strikers were Protestant. The conduct of the strike, however, largely remained in the control of the union leaders. They eventually called it off and the Amalgamated Society of Engineers even suspended its Belfast and Glasgow district committees.

Throughout the whole period of the strike, there was not a word of solidarity from the Dáil. At one level, this silence was all the more extraordinary because British troops were moved up to the North to break it. Nevertheless, at another level, it flowed logically from the republican strategy. Sinn Féin and the IRA were fighting for national independence pure and simple and did not want that mixed up with other struggles. However, their silence had implications for the relationship with Protestant workers. These workers were predisposed to having a unionist outlook and the only way that their loyalty to the Empire could be questioned was through an appeal based on social class. The failure to say anything to Protestant workers when they were engaged in a major fight with their Orange employers meant that the republican struggle was seen as totally irrelevant to their interests.

By 1921, however, a post-war slump took its toll and the balance of power shifted to employers, who engaged in a concerted effort to reverse the gains that the workers had won in the previous two years. However, they encountered stiff resistance because, as O'Connor points out, the Irish labour struggles did not follow a similar pattern to Britain where the defeat of a few 'big battalions' quickly determined the fate of other ranks. The Irish workers' movement was more diverse and organised into different sectors, so defeats did not immediately impact on each other. It therefore took employers two-and-a-half years to complete their wage-cutting offensive and, even then, they needed the support of a counter-revolutionary state. In the meantime, workers put up a militant defensive resistance. In 1922, for example, there were another spate of workplace occupations. Attempts to cut the wages of workers in the dairy sector, for example, led to further declarations of 'soviets' even though these were disowned by the ITGWU.

The fact that the republicans turned their back on these struggles had an important impact on the outcome of the national movement itself. Essentially, it meant that the struggle for national liberation was reduced to a guerrilla war and once it started on this path it was bound to be contained by the superior military power of the British Army. The IRA was successful enough in fighting the Empire to a stalemate – but it could not break through. The left-wing republican, Peadar

O'Donnell, grasped this afterwards, when reflecting on how the anti-Treaty republicans lost. He argued that they had been defeated even before even the Civil War started: 'We lost out in 1921 because there was no day to day struggle making for differentiation so that in those days we were forced to defend ranches, enforce rents and be neutral in strikes ... the Free State was in existence long before the name was adopted.'[27]

However, before considering the counter-revolution that occurred and the subsequent Civil War, let us examine why there was no challenge from the left.

The Missing Link

The remarkable feature of the Irish revolution is that there was no coherent left-wing organisation that could combine a fight for national independence with a strategy of fomenting social struggles. Yet Irish Marxism had been represented in the 1916 Rising by the figure of James Connolly. By contrast, Arthur Griffith went missing in the days of the Rising – yet his ideas played a far more dominant role than Connolly's. How did this occur?

James Connolly was a brilliant Marxist who towered above many others in the socialist movement. He wanted the revolutionary overthrow of capitalism rather than simple piecemeal reform and he embraced a syndicalist strategy as the way of doing this. This put a focus on building up militant unions and, accordingly, Connolly placed less emphasis on political organisation. He thought that the instinct to reform capitalism, rather than seek its overthrow, arose from craft-based trade unionism because it focused on sectional struggles. Militant, industrial unionism by contrast would lead workers naturally to revolutionary socialist politics. This syndicalist outlook, which prioritised the unionisation of unskilled workers above all else, explains why Connolly made little effort to recruit or build a distinctly revolutionary party. When Home Rule appeared to be imminent in 1912, he supported the formation of a broad-based Labour Party to contest elections in the event of Home Rule. But this was only a means to supplement the real struggles that took place in workplaces. As legislation on Home Rule slipped away, his proposal for the unions to form a Labour Party died away and that party only took on an existence after his death. Connolly was also a member of left-wing political groups – such as the Independent Labour Party (Ireland) – but these did not have clear political positions. When the First World War broke out, for example, some of his fellow socialists in Belfast actually supported the war. When he spoke against war, he had to acknowledge that 'like all other parties, his own was divided. For that reason he made it clear that his opinions were personal.'[28] There was, therefore, no coherent revolutionary socialist organisation that could take up Connolly's ideas after his death.

There was one other fault-line in Connolly's politics that was magnified by his later 'followers'. Throughout his life, Connolly had sought to incorporate the republican tradition into socialism. He thought that genuine republicans who wanted the 'reconquest' of Ireland would have to uproot capitalist social relations because these had been imposed by the Empire. He was critical of republicans who advocated 'all-class alliances', or who elevated conspiratorial manoeuvres above mass politics. But despite these criticisms, he still thought there was a left-wing dynamic inherent within the republican tradition. Connolly, it should be noted, did not have the experience of seeing a national liberation movement come to power. If he had, he might have realised that a number of such movements – whether in the shape of the African National Congress or the Palestine Liberation Organisation or the IRA – would not only embrace capitalism but, sometimes, partake in its most corrupt and repressive varieties.

Those who claimed to represent Connolly's ideas after his death were primarily trade union bureaucrats who used left rhetoric to cover their own cowardice. For example, the playwright Sean O'Casey accurately captured the mindset of the ITGWU leader, William O'Brien: he 'had no look of a Labour leader about him, but rather that of a most respectable clerk at home in a sure job ... His clever, sharp mind ... was ever boring in a silent way through all opposition to the regulation and control of the Irish labour movement.'[29]

O'Brien was accompanied by Tom Johnson at the helm of the ITUC, who thought the best way to defy the British government was to win the support of politicians and lawyers while simultaneously allowing the British armed forces to take whichever side they chose![30] A more unlikely pair of revolutionaries could not found.

They owed their prominence solely to the fact that there existed no alternative sizeable left-wing party. The Irish Citizens Army, which Connolly had founded, had been rebuilt but it had almost severed its links with the ITGWU. According to one of its participants, it no longer held the same social and economic views as those who participated in 1916.[31] An apparently more 'revolutionary' organisation, the Socialist Party of Ireland, was founded in February 1917, but was effectively controlled by O'Brien and Johnson. There was a smaller more genuinely revolutionary faction within the Socialist Party, but it was effectively shackled to this pair throughout much of the period.

Initially, O'Brien and Johnson expressed support for the Russian Revolution but despite their rhetoric, they positioned themselves as supporters and advisors to Sinn Féin. They ensured that the Labour Party withdrew from the 1918 election because, as an Irish Labour Party and Trade Union Congress manifesto put it, the workers, 'should willingly sacrifice for a brief period their aspiration towards political power if thereby the future of the nation can be enhanced.'[32] They had no interest in carving out a distinct socialist position in the fight for national freedom or developing a class-based anti-impe-rialist position that could appeal to Protestant workers. In fact, they regarded the whole upheaval as a distraction from their preferred road of peaceful parliamentary reform. The Socialist Party of Ireland even stated that 'the preoccupation of the people with the struggle against

British imperialism has been an obstacle of importance in preventing the spread of revolutionary socialism.'[33]

O'Brien and Johnson's sole aim was to expand union membership but, whereas Connolly saw this as a strategy to foment revolution, they saw the revolution as an opportunity to gather union dues. To do this, they placed the labour movement in a subordinate position in its alliance with republicans. In Peadar O'Donnell's words, they took up a position on the 'prompters' stool'.[34] They joined a Dáil committee to devise a labour policy. They encouraged workers to use the Sinn Féin conciliation machinery to settle strikes. They refused to condemn the Treaty. Their aim was to display enough loyalty to the republican leadership as would guarantee a seat of influence in an independent Ireland. It was only in October 1921, that O'Brien and Johnson were expelled from the Socialist Party of Ireland and a Communist Party was formed under the leadership of Connolly's son, Roddy. This, however, was a tiny organisation with a membership of just twenty or so active members.[35] By that stage, there was a truce between the IRA and the British forces, and negotiations for an Anglo-Irish Treaty were under way.

Independence and Counter-revolution

The truce between the IRA and the British forces was concluded on 11 July 1921 and eighteen weeks later, the Anglo-Irish Treaty was signed on 6 December. This granted a limited degree of independence to the 26 counties but it also entailed partition. Despite private assurances given by Lloyd George to Michael Collins that two counties with a Catholic majority would be allowed to secede, the six-county state became a reality. Dáil deputies were obliged to take an oath of loyalty declaring 'they would be faithful to H.M. King George V, his successors and heirs, in virtue of common citizenship of Ireland with Great Britain.'[36] The British Navy retained three bases in Irish territory. The Irish Free State also agreed to assume liability for the public debt of the United Kingdom and pay war pensions in proportions that would later be agreed.

Support for the Treaty came primarily from Arthur Griffith and Michael Collins, the key figures in the delegation sent to London for the negotiations. In their different ways, they represented the main strands of counter-revolutionary thought that would later prevail in Ireland. Griffith had always advocated 'dual monarchy' and so had little difficulty with the oath. His concern was to build up Irish capitalism and he wanted both a connection with the British Empire and a degree of independence to support its growth. One advantage of independence, he thought, was that there would be no danger of any costly social insurance scheme. He was totally opposed to a pre-war insurance scheme introduced by the Liberals because it led to a situation where virtuous Ireland would have to pay for English 'bastardy'.[37] Dominion status within a wider empire would give him the opportunity to dispense with such legislation and develop a tooth-and-claw version of Irish capitalism. Michael Collins typified the military wing of Irish republicanism. His ideas on the type of post-independence Ireland were very vague, combining a desire for more co-operatives with distaste for state socialism and strikes.[38] He had no time for land agitation or workers' occupations. He saw the Irish revolution as a purely military affair, with himself as its leader, and his support for the treaty was conditioned by that perception. He looked at the balance of military forces after the British had increased the level of repression from 1921 onwards and thought there was no option but to settle. Justifying the Treaty later, he noted that 'we had an average of one round of ammunition for each weapon we had … The fighting area in Cork was becoming daily more circumscribed, and they could not carry on much longer.'[39] Collins's exclusive focus on the military side meant that, ironically, the former gunman became the most enthusiastic advocate for a settlement. It was a path trodden by other IRA leaders afterwards.

The prosperous elements in Irish society and the Catholic hierarchy immediately backed the Treaty. As soon as news of it became public, six Catholic prelates issued a statement supporting it, with one bishop claiming that 'the men who made the treaty would be immortal.'[40] On the left, James Larkin denounced the Treaty, stating that 'we propose carrying on the fight until we make the land of Erin a land fit for men and women – a Workers' Republic or Death.'[41] Unfortunately, this was highly charged rhetoric with little substance, as it was written from an American prison cell and there was no network of revolutionary socialists to which it was addressed. The main opposition to the Treaty came from IRA volunteers led by Liam Lynch. These purists framed the matter in terms of how the oath would dismantle 'the Republic' that had been created during the revolution. The more political wing of the anti-Treaty movement was led by de Valera and supported by Austin Stack and Cathal Brugha. While these moved away from the 'straitjacket' of the republic, they still advocated greater independence through 'an external association' with the Empire.

The most amazing thing about the Treaty debates was just how little was said about Ulster or partition. One of the few who spoke on the issue was Sean McEntee and, ironically in view of his later career as a Fianna Fáil minister, he warned that people in the North 'are going to be driven, in order to maintain their separate identity, to demarcate themselves from us, while we, in order to preserve ourselves against the encroachment of English culture, are going to be driven to demarcate ourselves so far as ever from them.'[42]

Although framed exclusively in cultural terms, this echoed Connolly's warning that partition would produce a carnival of reaction. However, this prophetic point was lost in a debate that was essentially framed in terms of the degree of independence of the South from Britain. A 26-county identity was making its first appearance, but was hidden amidst the acrimony of symbols and oaths.

Yet behind the symbols, there was an important point at issue. The anti-Treatyites sensed their former comrades were accepting a dependency relationship with their imperial foes. Although they articulated their opposition with reference to a mythical, abstract republic, they were not entirely wrong. Griffith and Collins' endorsement of the Treaty did in fact lead into a greater entanglement with their former imperial masters. This became abundantly clear when they agreed to work closely with the British to crush their former republican comrades. They claimed that they were merely restoring law and order, but it was an order where the poor knew their place and where there would be no more talk of land redistribution or better conditions for workers. With the first shot of the Civil War, the Irish counter-revolution had begun.

At 4.15 a.m. on the night of 27 June 1922, the Irish Civil War started. Anti-Treatyite forces had previously occupied the Four Courts but, after the assassination of Sir Henry Wilson in London, the British government demanded that action be taken against them. Ironically, Wilson's assassins were not anti-Treatyites but were working for Michael Collins.[43] Even before the assassination, Churchill had been bombarding Collins with letters demanding a crackdown on social anarchy. 'Rich and poor turned out of their homes at two hours' notice … The cattle are killed, the lonely white peacocks hunted to death … some of the scenes are like those of the French revolution', Churchill declared.[44] Wilson's assassination became an excuse to intensify the pressure and on 24 June 1924, the British government drew up its own plans to attack the republicans in the Four Courts. A proclamation justifying the attacks was written and ships were dispatched to Dublin to take prisoners away but then, suddenly, the operation was halted. Instead, talks began between British military authorities, Griffith and Emmet Dalton, a major general in the Free State Army, about supplying artillery so that the Provisional Government itself could carry out the attacks. It was only after two 18-pounder field guns were supplied by the British Army that the attack began. Afterwards, Churchill wrote back to Collins, 'If I refrain from congratulation, it is only because I do not wish to embarrass you. The archives of the Four Courts may be scattered but the title deeds of Ireland are safe.'[45]

The Provisional Government prosecuted the Civil War with an extraordinary ferocity, because they wanted to finish it as rapidly as possible lest the British be tempted to get involved. They feared that if the British intervened, republicans would unite in opposition and matters would then spill out of control. Kevin O'Higgins, who was set to become the strong man of the Free State regime, put it succinctly 'What lies ahead? A social revolution? Reoccupation by the British with the goodwill of the world … These possibilities, none of which are attractive, are not mutually exclusive.'[46]

To gain advantage, the Free State took two measures which were to prove decisive. First, even before the attack on the Four Courts, they started to take weaponry from the British. Between 31 January and 26 June 1922, the British government supplied them with 11,900 rifles, 79 Lewis machine guns, 4,200 revolvers and 3,504 grenades. In August, another eight 18-pounder artillery pieces arrived and by 2 September, total British weaponry amounted to 27,400 rifles, 246 Lewis guns, 6,600 revolvers and 5 Vickers guns.[47] Second, the Provisional Government began a huge recruitment campaign to their army and money appeared to be no problem, as they were effectively bankrolled by the British state. At the start of the Civil War, the National Army had 8,000 troops, by November this number had grown to 30,000 and by the end of the ten-month war, to 50,000 solders. This gave the Provisional Government overwhelming superiority over their republican opponents who had an estimated 13,000 soldiers. The new recruits to the National Army were not particularly motivated by any political ideals but were often attracted by the prospect of pay and excitement.

The anti-Treatyites were further weakened by internal divisions and a cautious military strategy. Co-ordination between units was poor and there appeared to be no definite plan of campaign with local units deciding on their own strategies. In the first two months of the war, the National Army made a number of bold offensive moves while the anti-Treatyite forces withdrew from Dublin to concentrate on a defence of their Munster republic. However, beyond these military difficulties, there were much deeper problems.

After fighting for independence, the population was tired of war and dreaded a return to armed conflict, yet the leaders of the republican forces offered nothing but a purely military strategy. When the Provisional Government announced repressive measures, the anti-Treatyites hit back with assassinations and gun attacks. They ignored the continuing social discontent and conducted the fight as if it were simply about the niceties of constitutional arrangements. They presented themselves as living for a higher moral ideal and saw no link between rejecting the Treaty and improving the lives of the poor. Liam Mellows summed up this attitude: 'We do not seek to make this country a materially great country at the expense of its honour. We would rather have the country poor and indigent, we would rather have the people of Ireland eking out a poor existence on the soil, so long as they possessed their souls, their minds and their honour.'[48]

Mellows would later move away from this absurd attitude but between the signing of the Treaty and the start of the Civil War, the republicans continued with the old policy of suppressing or regulating social conflict through republican courts. When ITGWU members in Clonmel, for example, picketed a shop that would not sell butter from a soviet creamery, they were attacked by anti-Treatyite volunteers firing shots over their heads.[49] When the Civil War broke out, the republicans became less concerned to impose order, but they still made no effort to relate to a wave of workers' strikes and land occupations. When Roddy Connolly met with the anti-Treatyite leader, Liam Lynch, and urged him to adopt a social programme, he was brushed aside. Lynch's attitude was that 'it is a waste of time to be thinking too much about policy.'[50] This disastrous approach meant that the republicans fought on a purely military basis against far superior forces.

During the course of the civil war, the Provisional Government transformed itself into a brutal, authoritarian regime which brushed aside all considerations of human rights, to inflict terror on their opponents. It introduced emergency legislation to set up military courts. These were given powers to impose a death penalty on anyone who took up arms against the state. It decreed that for every republican outrage, three republicans would be executed. Seventy-seven republicans were eventually executed – more than three times the number of IRA volunteers executed by the British before truce. After Sean Hales, a pro-Treaty TD, was killed by the anti-Treaty forces, four leading republicans were executed. Liam Mellows, Rory O'Connor, Joe McKelvey and Dick Barret had been imprisoned at the time Hales was murdered and the emergency legislation passed. It made little difference because the Free State was determined to demoralise its enemies with sheer terror. The Provisional Government also used death squads to eliminate their opponents. A Criminal Investigation Unit, headed by Joseph McGrath, abducted and killed over twenty anti-Treatyite volunteers in Dublin while in other areas, most notably in Sligo, prisoners were murdered after capture. Kerry saw the worst of the brutality and in a horrific incident in Ballyseedy, nine republicans were tied to a landmine that was then detonated. This act was a reprisal for the killing of five Free State soldiers in a nearby village, but more revenge was to follow. Of the 32 anti-Treatyities killed in Kerry in March 1923, only five died in combat. The Civil War was an extremely brutal and bloody affair and both sides engaged in horrific killings. The republicans thought they could win by fighting hardest, but in the terror stakes they were no match for the state forces.

The victory of the Free State forces heralded a counter-revolution where the ideals of the Irish revolution were destroyed. By the end of the Civil War, its two key leaders, Arthur Griffith and Michael Collins, had died, the first from natural causes and the second killed in an ambush. The formal leader of the new regime was William Cosgrave, an old associate of Griffith and a member of the dual-monarchist Sinn

Féin from its early inception. The key figure, however, who embodied the counter-revolution was Kevin O'Higgins. He belonged to the Catholic upper professional class and detested the 'anarchy' of the revolutionary period. O'Higgins had attended the elite private school in Clongowes Wood College and had been a 'wag' in the UCD Literary and Historical Society before joining the legal profession. The speaker of the Free State Dáil, Michael Hayes, who was certainly no radical, had the measure of him when he said, 'he didn't understand ... what the whole struggle had been about. He reduced it to the notion of the Irish people getting a parliament.'[51] O'Higgins saw the period of revolution as one where the moral fabric of society was torn apart and was determined to mend it. He despised the 'attitude of protest, the attitude of negation, the attitude sometimes of sheer wantonness and waywardness and destructiveness which ... has been to a large extent a traditional attitude on behalf of the Irish people'.[52] He was determined to cure the patient and establish respect for 'the rule of law'. To do so, he surrounded himself in the Cabinet with ex-Clongowes boys and members of the Catholic upper professional class, who barely concealed their contempt for a lawless but land-hungry peasantry. By 1926, there were more ex-Clongowes boys in the Cabinet than veterans of the 1916 Rising.

All of the prejudices of the Catholic upper professional class came into view. These had enjoyed the privileges of working within the structures of the Empire but now wanted to replicate these same institutions in their own state. Many were sympathetic to the ideas of Arthur Griffith and had no difficulty with the concept of empire – they only wanted their own share of it. O'Higgins summed this attitude up during the Treaty debate when he openly acknowledged that it left Ireland bound to the Empire: 'Yes, if we go into the Empire, we go in, not sliding in, attempting to throw dust in your people's eyes, but we go in with our heads up.'[53] Not surprisingly, therefore, this social class sought to restore the same type of order they had learnt to admire under the Empire – only this time with an Irish flag.

This involved a restructuring of the state apparatus so that the vestiges of the revolutionary period were removed. All the elements of the counter-state that had been created during the War of Independence were to be replaced with more straightforward versions of the British model. In 1922, O'Higgins moved against the republican courts after they had granted a habeas corpus for republican internees. Two years later, after the republican courts were abolished, he introduced a Courts of Justice Bill to adopt the British model. Judges were no longer elected but were instead appointed from the same class that O'Higgins hailed from. They even adopted the wigs and pomp of the British system. The civil service machinery of the Empire was also refurbished and its existing structures were simply taken over, with the addition of just over a hundred Dáil servants and others who had been dismissed by the British government. To ward off the danger of dissidents using the local government system – as the republicans had previously done during the War of Independence – a highly centralised government structure was created. Local government Acts were passed to allow ministers to dissolve local authorities and replace them with commissioners. Inside the apparatus of the central state, the Department of Finance was given a crucial role and all legislation being submitted to the Dáil had to be scrutinised by the department in advance. As the Department of Finance's central mission was to maintain 'balanced budgets', a conservative bias was built into the Free State from the very start.

The first sign of fiscal rectitude came with Ernest Blythe's decision to cut the old-age pension by eight shillings and to slash the wages of teachers. Even the mildest proposal to develop an active state that might promote social justice was scoffed at. When William O'Brien, now a Labour Party deputy took up Pearse's suggestion and proposed that Ireland's natural resources be vested in the state, O'Higgins claimed that it would be unwise 'to embody in the constitution what certainly looks like a communist doctrine'.[54] A proposal to guarantee citizens free education up to an age prescribed by law was rejected by O'Higgins because it might open the door to free secondary education.[55] Although it was faced with a major crisis of unemployment, the new Cumann na nGaedheal government believed that the state should not create jobs. Instead Minister of Industry and Commerce Patrick McGilligan put its philosophy bluntly, when he stated that 'It is not the function of the Dáil to provide work and the sooner this is realised the better ... people may have to die in this country of starvation.'[56] He was only expressing the core attitude that lay at the heart of the counter-revolutionary state – it backed business and big farmers, but not social rights.

The victorious post-Treaty state was also deeply hostile to any form of militant trade unionism – particularly if it came from its own state employees. O'Higgins boldly declared, 'No State, with any regard for its own safety, can admit the right of the servants of the Executive to withdraw their labour at pleasure. They have the right to resign; they have no right to strike.'[57] He made this statement when postal workers struck in 1922 over a pay cut, and he included them in the category of civil servants who had no right to strike. The workers were particularly incensed that the same government that ordered their pay cut had increased their own ministerial salaries from £700 to £1,700 a year. Soon after the strike began, strikers were shot at by the National Army, pickets were beaten up and preparations were made to employ ex-postal workers to break the strike. The Free State government was determined to defeat them because as Postmaster General J.J. Walshe later recalled, 'at this critical juncture to smash such a well organised strike was a salutary lesson to ... general indiscipline.'[58]

There was also plenty of 'indiscipline' on the land that the Free State was determined to crush. Small farmers continued not only to demand land redistribution but sometimes had ceased paying rent or annuities to landlords. The Free State's answer was the Enforcement of Law (Occasional Powers) Act of 1924 to give greater powers to bailiffs. These could immediately seize property from recalcitrant farmers, sell them off within 24 hours and charge the cost of their seizure to the victims. A special mobile unit of the Irish Army was also established to capture cattle that had been 'driven' from big estates. 'The bailiff, as a factor in our civilisation, has not been particularly active or effective in recent years', O'Higgins declared and he intended to fix that.[59]

The Free State, however, offered its population one compensation for the dashed hopes of the revolutionary years – strict Catholic morality. Despite their own self-image as cosmopolitans who disdained the crudities of the Gaelic revival, the Free State elite were the first to forge a tight bond with the bishops. They saw them as agents for control and rewarded their loyalty to the state with measures to enforce a Catholic fundamentalist ethos. The Free State completely banned divorce by closing off all loopholes and imposed strict censorship on films, including even the posters used for advertising those films. It targeted unmarried mothers and created a framework for punishing those who were 'recidivists'. It established a Committee on Evil Literature in 1926 to identify publications that were deemed offensive on sexual matters. It adopted a particularly vindictive attitude to women who sought to be politically active outside the home or simply more engaged in the wider society. Some women had played a prominent role in the anti-Treaty side and these were denounced as 'Furies', who had been turned into 'unlovely, destructive minded begetters of violence'.[60] The solution, according to the Free State propagandist, P.S. O'Hegarty, was to keep them out of politics. In 1927, O'Higgins introduced his Juries Bill that excluded women from jury service and brought about a return to the pre-revolutionary practice.

Contemporary Irish politicians of all hues claim an allegiance to the 1916 Rising and, with a certain nervousness, suggest that the Irish state owes a gratitude to those 'who gave their life in 1916'. However, the current Irish state is not a product of the Rising – it owes its existence to the counter-revolution of 1923. That state established clear structures that survived for decades – even after it was modified by subsequent Fianna Fáil governments. It was an authoritarian state that kept a battery of repressive legislation at the ready for dealing with dissidents. It was a highly centralised state which left little room for local democracy. Free market conservatism was built into its apparatus from the very start and 'fiscal rectitude' and 'balanced budgets' became its catch cries to ward off claims for social rights. The top civil servants, who controlled the Department of Finance, had an inordinate influence and restricted any legislation that could help develop a welfare state. The demands of labour were regarded with suspicion – unless its union leaders could be co-opted into the national project of building up Irish business.

The central project of this state was the promotion of Griffith's notion of a Gaelic Manchester and, as a result, corruption was inscribed into it from the very start. Irish capitalism was puny and weak and needed a helping hand from state funds. Consequently, the borderline between private business and the state's interests was never tightly drawn. Covering it all up was a sanctimonious Catholic morality that repressed sexuality and denied women an active role in the wider society. This morality was, in fact, the spiritual anti-depressant offered to the population to encourage them to accept their lot. The elite never took it seriously and believed they had a right to a different lifestyle. While Kevin O'Higgins was lecturing the population about the evils of divorce, he was conducting an affair with Hazel Lavery, wife of the painter, Sir John Lavery, for whom he sought a state position. Decades later, it was Charles Haughey, who legislated for contraceptives for 'bona fide' family planning purposes only. And at the same time, he conducted his own extramarital affair and again sought a state position for the jilted husband. Venial acts, maybe, but symbolic of the type of state that emerged from Ireland's victorious counter-revolution.

CHAPTER FIVE

A Most Conservative Country

Just off the Dublin Road coming out of Tuam, if you turn into a small working-class estate, you will come across a monument set in a peaceful collection of houses. It commemorates six republicans – Seamus O'Maille, Martin Moylan, Francis Cunnane, Michael Monaghan, Sean Newell and Sean Maguire – who were executed at a military barracks in the old workhouse in the town. They had been captured by Free State soldiers during the final month of the Civil War and shot dead in cold blood.

If you look behind the monument, you will see a gate with a white cross and behind it a small patch of grass leading to a statue of the Virgin Mary in a glass case. Buried beneath the grass are an unknown number of children, who were housed in the same workhouse which had been turned into a Mother and Baby home after 1925. This was run by the Bon Secours sisters until 1961 and was part of a system whereby unmarried mothers were hidden away until their babies were either fostered out or adopted. However, a high proportion of the babies did not make it out: a staggering 23 per cent of children born in the Tuam home died there. In absolute figures, 796 children died during the 36 years that the Bon Secours nuns were in charge – which is about one child death every two or three weeks.[1] In 1939, Alice Lister, an inspector with the Department of Local Government and Public Health noted that 'The chance of survival of an illegitimate infant born in the slums and placed with a foster-mother in the slums a few days after birth is greater than that of an infant born in one of our special homes for unmarried mothers.'[2]

The children were malnourished and often died of normal illnesses that were treatable even then. After their deaths, they were buried in church grounds with no coffins or headstones because, prior to 1994, the religious were exempt from laws about notifying the authorities about a death or the conduct of burials. So without any markers, the dead babies of Tuam were forgotten until an assiduous local historian, Catherine Corless, unearthed the story in 2012. Meanwhile, the Bon Secours sisters moved on to manage the largest private hospital group in Ireland. They no longer specialised in the care of the 'poor and destitute' and could only issue a bland statement through their PR agency when news of the burial site at Tuam became known.

The juxtaposition of a monument for republicans, murdered during the Civil War, and a nearby unmarked burial ground is a testimony to a dark, hidden Ireland that, after the counter-revolution of 1923, had become an unusually conservative country. School history books did not discuss the Civil War and, until the 1990s, there was little talk of the abuse that occurred behind the walls of Church-run institutions. The sheer scale of the conservative hegemony was astounding as each element re-enforced the other. Southern Ireland had an overwhelming Catholic majority – with 93 per cent affiliated to this Church up to 1981. Religious practice was extremely high, with 90 per cent of Catholics attending weekly mass until the early 1970s.[3] Compare this with Austria in the same period where attendance was only one-third, in urban Italy 28 per cent, and in France just 20 per cent.[4] Ireland was also a country, which unusually in a European context, had virtually no left–right divide. The population voted overwhelmingly for two right-wing parties, Fianna Fáil and Fine Gael, which traced their origins to the Civil War. The Labour Party was small and weak, and could barely be described as a social democratic party. Its main function was to act as a prop to Fine Gael when they occasionally got a chance to form a government. The conservative hegemony that overtook Southern Ireland after the counter-revolution rested on the twin pillars of the Catholic Church and Fianna Fáil.

The Catholic Church

There were a number of features to the Catholic Church in pre-independence Ireland which helped to secure its future. It was neither a large landowner nor was it linked to a landed aristocracy and so it did not encounter opposition from a peasant movement. During the great period of land agitation in the late nineteenth century, most of the junior clergy sided with the Land League – even if the bishops remained hostile or suspicious. By contrast, in Spain, the Catholic Church was identified with big landowners and gravitated to the fascist side in the Spanish Civil War. The Irish Catholic Church also had the aura of an oppressed Church, even if it enjoyed certain privileges from the British Empire. Up to the 1780s, it was officially subject to the penal laws which allowed for the deportation of Catholic bishops or members of religious orders. The same legislation also prohibited Catholics owning property. The oppression of the Church, therefore, coincided with the experience of the wider population. The Irish identity which emerged through a conflict with the Empire became intertwined with Catholicism. However, by the start of the nineteenth century the penal laws fell into abeyance and the British state came to look on the Catholic Church as an ally in their fight against the French Revolution. It supported the formation of Maynooth College to train priests and this allowed the Church hierarchy to build up a centralised and disciplined organisation. It also conceded to the Catholic demand for control of their own schools – and funded a primary school system organised on confessional lines. All of this enabled the Catholic Church to establish a dense institutional structure even before independence.

After independence, the Catholic Church acquired a special role in enforcing moral control over the population. This had begun with the Cumann na nGaedheal government which used the bishops' threat to excommunicate republicans during the Civil War to demoralise their enemies. Once the counter-revolution was successful, they cemented the alliance with the bishops by passing sectarian legislation that brought the state into conformity with a Catholic ethos. Even while in opposition, Fianna Fáil presented themselves as more Irish and, therefore more Catholic, than their rivals. In a celebrated case, de Valera supported the decision of the Mayo County Council not to appoint a Protestant librarian. The post, he pompously declared had 'a propagandist education character' and 'as over 98 per cent of the population is Catholic [they] are justified in insisting on a Catholic librarian.'[5] It was a signal that Fianna Fáil intended to construct a Catholic state for a Catholic people to mirror the Protestant state for a Protestant people north of the border.

Once in power after 1932, Fianna Fáil was as good as its word. In 1935, they passed the Criminal Law Amendment Act to prohibit the sale and importation of contraceptives. They introduced a clause into the Conditions of Employment Act giving the Minister for Industry and Commerce power to exclude women from certain industries. In a further move to shore up the male breadwinner model of the family, they banned married women from the post of primary school teacher – this measure lasted from 1934 to 1958.[6] They even passed a Public Dance Hall Act which made it a requirement to obtain a licence from a district justice for all public dances. Dancing was viewed by priests as 'occasions of sin' and had to be regulated. However, even beyond this legislation, Fianna Fáil established a shadow theocracy whereby proposed legislation were first filtered through the partnership of Éamon de Valera and John Charles McQuaid, the Archbishop of Dublin.

McQuaid was fanatically anti-Protestant, anti-Semitic and anti-socialist. He saw the *Declaration of the Rights of Man*, a product of the French Revolution, as the foundation document for a dangerous political creed which influenced most modern democracies. This creed, which had emphasised the separation of church and state, McQuaid perceived as the work of the Freemasons and Satan. He, in contrast, believed that the bishops had a 'divine right to guide the faithful ... whenever political or social or economic doctrines are at variance with the Divine Law'.[7] In line with this, McQuaid bombarded de Valera with letters, almost daily and, sometimes, twice daily.[8] His letters ranged from instructions about promoting Catholic medical interests, to calls for more censorship, to offering advice on how to handle strikes. He regarded the latter as the source for 'the venom of communism'[9] and volunteered himself as a mediator to prevent them. He had a network of spies which monitored books, magazines, university students, plays and, above all, 'communists'. He built a Catholic social action movement that dominated the professions and the judiciary. In the Tilson case in 1950, for example, the President of the High Court Gavan Duffy ruled that a Protestant father had to fulfil his *ne temere* agreement which promised that his children would be brought up as Catholics. The judge, who was a member of an elite Catholic action body, An Rioghnacht (The League for the Kingdom of Christ) had taken covert guidance from McQuaid.[10] The fruits of the partnership between de Valera and McQuaid was the Constitution of 1937, dedicated to the Holy Trinity which recognised the 'special position' of the Catholic Church.

But what was the central purpose of this hegemonic project? Was it just about controlling sex as is sometimes thought? It is often assumed that Catholicism has an unhealthy obsession with the regulation of sexual activity and there is some evidence for this in its official teachings, but Catholic populations do not always conform to such dogmas. The sexual mores of Brazilian workers, for example, were by no means the same as Irish workers at this time – yet both were equally Catholic. The reality is that people interpret official religions according to their social circumstances and the degree of control exerted over them. In post-independence Ireland, Catholicism became a spiritual compensation for the failure to achieve the real improvements many had hoped for during the revolution. The more Catholic and respectful you were of the priests, the more you asserted your victory over the Brits. This was linked to a romanticisation of rural life because, as Curtis put it, there was a conviction that 'life on a small Irish farm represented a purity and decency of life that set Ireland apart from more commercial societies that surrounded them.'[11] Even if there were few jobs and thousands had to emigrate, Ireland could keep clear of the moral 'filth' of British urban life. It could be both self-sufficient and avoid the 'materialism' and immorality of modern life. These ideological attitudes – which ultimately grew out of the counter-revolution of 1923 – gave the Catholic Church a ready-made audience.

The core of the Catholic priesthood was drawn from the countryside. Out of the 429 students, for example, who entered Maynooth Seminary between 1956 and 1960, a massive 72.5 per cent came from the 'open countryside' or small towns and villages.[12] This strata had imbibed the strict repression of sexuality from the farming class and transmitted it to the cities. The Catholic Church also had the means to push its message of 'purity' and 'modesty', as it controlled the schools and hospitals, and had constructed so many churches – by 1997, there was one church for every 1,092 Catholics.[13] It also had a huge army of priests who could also visit – and morally inspect – family homes. A national survey in 1973–74, found that nearly half of all Irish homes had been visited by a priest in the previous six months.[14] With these institutional means, a rural-based Church was largely successful in imposing its sexual morality on cities, because here too there was an identification of Irish nationalism with Catholicism. For the minority of women who were disobedient, there were always the Church-run Mother and Baby homes and the Magdalene laundries.

However, controlling sex was only one aspect of the Church's project. A deeper purpose was to inculcate obedience to authority into the population. In his first pastoral letter in 1941, McQuaid stated that parents must regard their children as souls to be prepared for the carrying of the cross of Christ: 'It will be impossible to train youth to the maturity of Christian virtue unless from infancy the habit of obedience has become, so to speak, an instinct.'[15] Control of the schools was the main mechanism for achieving this and so corporal punishment and rote learning became the norm. The last thing that either the clergy or the politicians wanted was critical thinking. There was an implicit understanding with the state that the clergy would instil obedience in school children and in return get to indoctrinate them in Catholic teaching. It was certainly understood by de Valera that the church and the state were working together to coerce the population into obeying both their temporal and spiritual leaders. After a minor dispute with one of the bishops, de Valera wrote to the Papal Nuncio urging him to remind the clergy to 'secure their active co-operation in inculcating in the people that respect for lawful authority without which the continuance in their country of a Christian church and a Christian state would soon become impossible.'[16]

This was the essence of the Fianna Fáil-Catholic Church project. It was a case of rendering unto Caesar and unto the clergy a respect and a subservience which were mutually beneficial to both.

The Catholic Church periodically attacked the very idea that the state could give citizens extensive social rights; the primary argument used for this was the principle of subsidiarity. This suggested that the state should only delegate to itself functions which could not otherwise be performed by groups in civil society. This wider society ought to be permeated by Catholic principles of social justice and as, the Papal encyclical *Quadragesimo Anno* put it, 'social charity ... ought to be as the soul of this order, an order which public authority ought to be ever ready effectively to protect and defend.'[17] This principle was rigorously applied in Ireland and an unholy alliance was formed between the mandarins of the Department of Finance and the Catholic hierarchy to discourage social spending. Under McQuaid's leadership, an extensive charity and voluntary social care network was established. Instead of developing a welfare state, the state encouraged voluntary Catholic organisations to develop a safety net. J.J. McElligot, the secretary of the Department of Finance, spelled out the practical implications of the principle of subsidiarity:

> The principle has not been generally accepted that the state
> has responsibility for the relief of poverty in all its degrees – the
> principle underlying any social measures undertaken by the state
> in this country up to the present is that the state's responsibil-
> ity is limited to the relief of destitution i.e. extreme cases where
> employment and the minimum necessities of existence is lacking.[18]

This ideological principle was not always upheld because the political
elite were subject to pressure to provide some social protection,
especially after the Beveridge Report was published in Britain in
1942. Nevertheless, the principle of subsidiarity created a framework
by which social rights could be limited.

The proposal by Noel Browne to introduce a Mother and Child
scheme to provide free health care for children up to the age of 16
illustrates succinctly how this occurred. As soon as Browne's plans
became public, he was ordered to a meeting at Archbishop McQuaid's
palace. A statement was read to him which claimed that 'the right to
provide for the health of children belongs to parents, not to the state.'
He was told that the bishops would oppose him because his free
health measures would 'constitute a ready-made instrument for future
totalitarian aggression'.[19] Browne had considerable popular support,
but such was the hegemony of the Church that few formal organisations came out in his favour. Inside the government, one of Browne's
most vigorous opponents was the leader of the Labour Party, William
Norton.[20] The ITUC, which had originally backed the scheme before
the bishops' condemnation, went silent. The tragedy was that no
element of the Irish labour movement came to Browne's defence
when he tried to establish a rudimentary national health service. The
hysteria about state control and dictatorship was only a cover to allow
the bishops to work with the Irish Medical Organisation to create a
two-tier medical system which protects privilege and the doctors'
lucrative private practice. It is a system that works against the poor to
this very day.

The debacle over the Mother and Child scheme illustrates the dominance that the Catholic Church exerted over workers at this time. Behind it lay a highly conscious strategy to prevent the growth of left-wing ideas. The wedge was driven into the labour movement through a sustained campaign against communism but, like the McCarthy campaign in the US, 'communism' was a catch-all term used to target union militants who were deemed to be un-Irish or un-Catholic. The *Catholic Standard* worked closely with leaders of the ITGWU to help split both the ITUC and the Labour Party in 1944 on the grounds of alleged communist infiltration. After the more anti-communist group, the Congress of Irish Unions, was established, McQuaid led a delegation of its union leaders to meet Pope Pius XII. The following year, the CIU sent a telegram to the pontiff to state that they were 'humbly prostrate at the feet of his Holiness'.[21] A Catholic Education Programme for Trade Unionists was also established to inculcate Catholic social teaching into its leadership cadre and to ward off dangerous left-wing ideas. Unions were also encouraged to have a spiritual director and to dedicate their headquarters to the Blessed Virgin Mary. When the Bakers' Union did so, their spiritual director explained that Mary provided the best safeguard for the legitimate interests for workers![22] The hegemony of the Church reached right down to the grass roots of the union movement, as workers collected money to build religious shrines and statues in their workplaces. Through such methods, a bulwark was created against almost all left-wing ideas and the revolutionary tradition was squashed.

Fianna Fáil

The Catholic Church was, however, only one pillar of Irish conservatism – it needed its alliance with Fianna Fáil to preserve its domination. Fianna Fáil was a remarkable party in many ways. Up to the 1970s, it occupied government office for a longer period than any other party in Western Europe – with the significant exception of the Unionist Party in Northern Ireland. At its heyday, it had 100,000 members and defined itself not as a 'mere political party' but as a 'national movement'.[23] Its tentacles reached into every area of Irish society. If you served on a local GAA committee, you were likely to encounter Fianna Fáil members. The primary school teachers' union, the INTO, contained many active Fianna Fáilers. If you wanted to get a local council house or even a state job for a son or daughter, you went to a Fianna Fáil clinic. But the most remarkable thing of all was that Fianna Fáil had a voting base that was class neutral – it received approximately 40 per cent of the votes from all the social classes, and this meant it took the natural working-class constituency of Labour and the left. These achievements were all the more astounding, as Fianna Fáil singularly failed to make any progress on its key aims. It promised to restore the Irish language as the main medium of conversation, yet less than 3 per cent of the population spoke it regularly. It promised to remove partition and win a united Ireland. Yet as former Fianna Fáil Cabinet Minister Kevin Boland suggested, the party founded to remove partition, had become its greatest bulwark.[24]

In reality, Fianna Fáil's electoral domination arose from the economic agenda it advocated for the 26-county state. It translated the language of republicanism into the plain speak of economic advance and turned that state into its central point of reference. Talk of a 32-county Ireland was confined to rhetorical flourishes at its conference – the practical focus was exclusively the 26 counties. It first developed this project in the late 1920s by using a radical language that appealed to workers – while at the same promoting the building of native capitalism. The space for making this cross-class appeal arose from the fact that the Irish Free State was a neo-colony of the British Empire. Cumann na nGaedheal's primary strategy had been to secure the position of the big farmers who were exporting livestock to Britain. They turned their back on Griffith's advocacy of protectionism to foster Irish industry and adopted a rigid policy of fiscal rectitude to reduce taxation. When de Valera described the country as 'an outgarden for the British',[25] he was only giving an accurate description: 97 per cent of all Ireland's exports went to Britain and at least two-thirds of these were agricultural products. Fianna Fáil challenged this model of capitalism and was able to offer improvements to workers through a different mode of development. They set out to construct an industrial block that was allied to the rural poor in order to overturn the agro-export model of Cumann na nGaedheal.

It is often forgotten, but in its early stages Fianna Fáil used a more radical left republican rhetoric than the present-day Sinn Féin uses to win a base among workers. Its newspaper, *The Nation*, denounced the 'imperialist Labour party'[26] and supported strikes against wage cuts. It called for public control of the transport industry. At its first Ard Fheis in 1926, de Valera proclaimed his allegiance to James Connolly, and the party declared that 'the resources and wealth of Ireland are subservient to the needs and welfare of all the people.'[27] It joined with left republicans like Peadar O'Donnell in launching a campaign against the payment of land annuities to Britain – though significantly, like the current Sinn Féin approach to water charges, it did not favour a boycott.[28] It attacked the banks as 'satellites of the Bank of England'[29] and the prominent Fianna Fáil politician Frank Aiken demanded that 'banks should not amass profit … [but] should [have] managed credit and issued money for the benefit of ordinary people.'[30] It even favoured the abolition of the standing army as an imperialistic relic and Sean Lemass proposed that it be replaced with a volunteer force.[31] Nevertheless, even while engaging in this radical rhetoric, Fianna Fáil discouraged militant action that would break the law, and kept a primary focus on promoting 'native industries that minister to the needs of the people.'[32] This was to be done by tariff protection and a break from the neocolonial model of Cumann na nGaedheal.

Just as the Peronist movement in Argentina needed to construct a populist bloc of social forces to move beyond their neocolonial status, so too did Fianna Fáil. They used more left-wing-sounding economic policies to promote industrial expansion and a more progressive distribution of income. Through these policies, the party was able to mobilise voters after the Wall Street crash of 1929 and take control of the state. It had no need to change the structures of that state, as it was merely advocating a different capitalist road. So it continued with the patterns that had been laid down by the counter-revolution. It merely re-directed the state away from its ties to the big farmers and used it to create a space for native industrialists.

The key feature of both these social classes was their relative weakness. The big farmers vigorously objected to Fianna Fáil's policies of raising tariffs because it led to an economic war with Britain that endangered their livestock trade. They, therefore, backed a 'Blueshirt' movement led by the former police chief Eoin O'Duffy in the hope of driving Fianna Fáil from office. But the fascist attempt to seize power via a march on Dublin in 1933 was easily defeated and Fianna Fáil did not need the same degree of labour mobilisation that Peron had needed in Argentina. The native capitalists were also very weak and needed state support as well as tariffs in order to foster their growth. Fianna Fáil, therefore, had to develop a more active state to create more favourable conditions for capital accumulation. In quick succession, they established an Industrial Credit Company and an Irish Sugar Company in 1933, Bord na Móna in 1934, Aer Lingus in 1936 and an Irish Life Assurance company in 1939. Far from being intrusions on capitalism, these were designed to bolster it.

Once it took full control of the state machine, the radical elements of Fianna Fáil's rhetoric disappeared and it relied on two mechanisms to maintain its hegemonic bloc. First, it cemented its alliance with the Catholic Church and used anti-communist rhetoric to break up any left-wing challenge. 'Communism' was defined as a foreign and, more specifically, a British import and Fianna Fáil forged a tripartite alliance with the leaders of the ITGWU and the Catholic Church to combat this mythical enemy. After an upsurge of working-class militancy in 1941 over a wages standstill order, this alliance targeted British-based unions as well as the Larkin's Workers Union of Ireland to foment a major split. This in turn weakened the labour movement and made it more amenable to the Fianna Fáil's project of constructing native capitalism. However, this ideological offensive was not sufficient to guarantee Fianna Fáil hegemony. Its second mechanism was to use the space it gained from challenging Ireland's neocolonial status to give some substance to its promise of social advance for the population.

The loosening of Ireland's economic dependency on Britain created a space which allowed Fianna Fáil to grant limited reforms to workers and the rural poor. The Land Act of 1933 gave the Land Commission more powers of compulsory purchase than had been granted under the previous 1923 Land Act. The latter had included many exemptions which protected the big farmers, but within four years of the passage of the new Act, nearly 353,000 acres were divided among 25,802 allottees.[33] Although Cumann na nGaedheal denounced the moves as 'the purest of communism',[34] the redistribution was limited and did not satisfy the demands of the rural poor. However, even these limited measures gave Fianna Fáil a more popular image and allowed them to develop a patronage system whereby those looking for land could approach a Fianna Fáil cumann to improve their chances. In the cities, Fianna Fáil were also able to show some benefits as they sought to expand the economy rather than simply maintain its neocolonial status. Between 1932 and 1942, for example, 13 new county hospitals and 17 district hospitals were established.[35] A free milk scheme for poorer children was introduced and a major house-building programme was undertaken. More crucially, the number of jobs in industrial employment increased from 110,000 to 166,000.[36] The jobs were often low paid and a high proportion of juveniles were employed but, nevertheless, Fianna Fáil's hegemony grew as they seemed able to bring limited gains.

After 15 years, the limits of the protectionist strategy were reached and when Fianna Fáil was no longer able to provide gains, the party's support base began to erode. The period after 'the emergency' – as the Second World War was known in Ireland – is a case in point. In its annual report for 1947, for example, the ITGWU noted that not since 1923 had there been so many strikes.[37] Teachers, bus workers and Electricity Supply Board (ESB) workers joined in battles to win wage increases or a reduction in working hours, while the newly formed Federation of Rural Workers led a major fight for farm labourers and turf workers. But while the militancy was intense, its political expression remained entrapped within the framework of Fianna Fáil republicanism. Discontent flowed into Clann na Poblachta which was effectively a recycled version of the radical Fianna Fáil of earlier years and led by another ex-IRA leader, Sean McBride. Fianna Fáil was thrown out of office in 1948 and this, combined with the long depression of the 1950s, signalled that another strategy was necessary to shore up their project of developing native capitalism.

After 1958, Fianna Fáil did an about-turn and removed clauses in the Control of Manufactures Act which restricted foreign investment coming into Ireland. Instead of relying on tariffs to foster native Irish capital, there was a shift to an export economy which was to be driven by foreign capital. Some on the left – such as Noel Browne – regarded the shift as a sell-out of Fianna Fáil's original ideal of self-sufficiency. However, this was to mistake the wrapping for the content, as the party's central aim was to build up native capitalism by whatever means possible. The foreign firms that located in Ireland used the country as a platform for exporting elsewhere. Their economic dynamism created new opportunities for Irish businesses and – and after some initial concerns – these slotted in, becoming junior partners of the multinationals. Henceforth, the Southern state looked after the joint interests of foreign and native capital. Irish companies benefited from the same tax breaks and grants that were used to attract the multi-nationals and even received a higher level of grant per job created.[38] The new alliance also helped to shore up Fianna Fáil's base amongst workers because economic success appeared to lend truth to the claim that 'a rising tide lifts all boats.'

Fianna Fáil's partnership with the Catholic Church allowed them to discipline the population and inculcate 'anti-communist' values. This, however, had to be supplemented with improvements in material conditions, so that the strategy of building native capitalism won support.

The Carnival of Reaction

Conservatism in Ireland's 26 counties found their mirror image in the North's six counties where the key mechanism was the domination of the Orange Order and its association with the Unionist Party. The nature of the Orange Order has been somewhat obscured by the Good Friday Agreement, which placed an emphasis on understandings between two cultures. In 2012, for example, it was announced that the Orange Order was to receive €4 million in grants from the European Union's Peace 11 programme to build two interpretive centres. The chief executive of the funding body hoped that 'open and honest dialogue will lead to a positive understanding of Orangeism and its place within our society.'[39] The implication was that the Northern conflict was the result of a conflict between two 'cultural traditions' and that dialogue and understanding between them would ensure long-term peace. This, unfortunately, is a rather bland fairy story that misunderstands how Orangeism was a political movement designed to discipline the Protestant population so that they accepted leadership from the landlord and business class. It was at the core of the sectarian oppression that characterised the Northern state until it erupted in 1969.

The Northern state was born amidst violence and repression. By the end of 1922, the Ulster Special Constabulary, which drew its original membership from loyalist paramilitaries, had 48,000 members.[40] Although the A Specials were disbanded after 1926 when the borders of the six counties were secured, the B Specials continued to function until 1970. They maintained an order of constant petty intimidation against the Catholic population. A Special Powers Act which allowed for internment and suspension of all civil liberties was passed in 1922 and remained on the statute book until 1973. This arsenal of repression was designed to keep Catholics in their place as second-class citizens.

The Unionist Party, which controlled the state, was led by an elite which had little concern for the Protestant working class. At its core was a landowning class whose members, in the words of Peter Gibbon, were a 'branch of the traditional English ruling class' and gathered around them assorted business elements.[41] The big landowners provided three of Northern Ireland's premiers – Craigavon, Brooke-borough and O'Neil – but industrialists did not lack representation. Of the seven ministers in James Craig's Cabinet from 1921 to 1937, three were former presidents of the Belfast Chamber of Commerce, one was a partner in a large firm of solicitors, another an industrialist and company director, and another the titled owner of one of the large landed estates.[42] Their primary aim was to defend the interests of Northern capitalism by keeping open access to British imperial markets. The industrial base of the North was concentrated in textiles and ship building, and was mainly dominated by family firms which required both export markets and a quiescent labour force to survive and compete. Northern businessmen saw Home Rule and Irish independence as a threat, because it would lead to protectionist tariffs designed to foster the weaker Southern industry. Unionism was the political means to secure their links to the Empire, while the Orange Order was their means to integrate and discipline Protestant workers.

This disciplinary mechanism worked at a number of levels. First, the Orange Order was mobilised at any time Protestant workers showed the slightest sign of drifting leftwards. In 1932, for example, Protestant and Catholic workers struck together to demand higher pay on the Outdoor Relief schemes. After a ban on marches, rioting took place on the Falls and Shankill roads in solidarity with each other. The Orange Order, however, pointed to the real enemy, declaring 'We desire to impress on all loyal subjects of the King, the vital necessity of standing guard against communism.'[43] They followed this up with a demand that Protestants should employ Protestants and, in response, Basil Brooke, later Lord Brookeborough, made his infamous statement:

> Many in the audience employ Catholics but I have not one about the house … In Northern Ireland, the Catholic population is increasing to a great extent. Ninety seven per cent of Roman Catholics in Ireland are disloyal and disruptive … If we in Ulster allow Roman Catholics to work on our farms we are traitors to Ulster.[44]

The strategy of displacing working-class anger into a sectarian conflict was successful. Within a short period after the joint struggle of the Catholic and Protestant unemployed, Belfast was to see another orgy of sectarian rioting when three hundred Catholics were driven from their homes and nine people died.

The other mechanism for cementing Unionist unity was to turn the ballot box into an Orange and Green headcount. This was achieved by abolishing proportional representation, because PR allowed for expressions of different shades of unionism and nationalism. In 1925, for example, the Unionist Party lost eight seats when votes went to Labour, independent unionists and a tenants' group. In response, the Unionist Party abolished PR and James Craig explained why: 'What I want to get in this house and what I believe we will get very much better in this House under the old fashioned plain and simple system, are men who are for the Union on one hand, or who are against it and want to go into a Dublin parliament, on the other.'[45]

Democracy under capitalism functions by allowing for limited debate on alternative economic strategies. Democracy in Northern Ireland functioned solely as a device to reinforce and cement sectarian loyalties. However, the main mechanism which ensured Unionist hegemony was a guarantee of marginal privileges to Protestant workers. The central government in Stormont was, in the words of

Belinda Probert, 'more of an administrative or co-ordinating body than a controlling power' because there was a deliberate strategy of reducing state spending.[46] Between its foundation and 1945, for example, only 8,000 new council houses were built in the whole of Northern Ireland.[47] In Craig's words, the main function of government was 'to distribute the bones'.[48] In a situation of mass unemployment and limited public spending, local councils became a key source for jobs and housing. They were also best able to institute discrimination as they had a highly accurate knowledge of who was orange and who was green. Discrimination in housing was widespread and linked to the maintenance of Unionist control over electoral wards. In 1958, for example, although there were seventy vacant houses in Dungannon, not one went to a Catholic. Later, the Cameron Commission noted that in the same council, there was not one Catholic employed in the administrative, clerical and technical grades.[49] Overall in the civil service, the number of Catholics holding positions remained at a constant 6 per cent between 1927 and 1959.[50] Discrimination in the public sector was paralleled by a favouritism·shown to Protestant workers by family-owned firms run by members of the Orange Order. Typically, Catholics tended to be pushed into unskilled labouring jobs while Protestants secured more skilled and secure employment.

The main mechanism for discrimination were the Orange lodges. These had originally been formed in the countryside to protect Protestant tenants from Catholic competition and were later used to break the United Irishmen. When the lodges moved into the cities, they became centres of cultural and political life. Officially, they claimed to defend the civil and religious liberties of the Protestant tradition, but the contemporary assertion of Orangeism was mainly about superiority. Protestants were seen as more thrifty, industrious and upstanding, and that was why they supported the Empire. Catholics were feckless, lazy and undisciplined, and that was why they were rebels. In the local lodge, the Protestant worker mixed with his betters and saw himself as a member of a superior grouping. When his lodge paraded on 'the queen's highway', he displayed that superiority by his right to march with lambeg drums through Catholic areas. More prosaically, it was the lodge that gave the worker contacts that got him jobs and houses. At its height, the Orange Order had nearly 100,000 members and was the principal mechanism for integrating Protestant workers into the Unionist machine.

However, while Protestant workers gained marginal privileges over Catholics, both sets of workers lost out overall. Even though the North had a comparatively high trade union membership – 200,000 in 1960 – sectarian divisions meant that the unions were weaker at a workplace level. Even on the most recent estimate, Northern Irish workers are still earning just 80 per cent of the equivalent rate for the same position in the rest of Britain.[51] Workers certainly benefited from the expansion of the welfare state after 1945, but this had to be pushed on a reluctant Unionist administration. Permanent right-wing control in Stormont meant that services were often limited to the bare statutory minimum. Childcare and facilities for elderly care, for example, were the worst in the United Kingdom.[52] Up to 1971, 37 per cent of Catholic and 28 per cent of Protestant homes did not have hot water or an inside toilet. The segregated nature of Northern Irish society meant that hospitals and schools had to be duplicated – leading to a waste of resources. The sectarian nature of the state also bolstered the most backward ideas on the status of women and gays. Despite claiming to adhere to the civil and religious liberties of British culture, there was no extension of the 1967 Act which permitted women to obtain abortions. Moreover, while the Sexual Offences Act decriminalised homosexuality in Britain in 1967, it took another 15 years before the Act was extended to Northern Ireland. And this was only after a successful human rights case was taken to the European Court of Justice and in the teeth of opposition from a 'Save Ulster from Sodomy' campaign. Overall, the sectarian divisions created an atmosphere which ensured the hold of the most right-wing and backward views.

The tragedy was that this held true for both 'communities'. There is sometimes a myth that oppression drives people to the left and to radical politics. However, it also unites populations around traditional leaders who promote reactionary ideas. Sectarianism led Catholics to identify even more closely with their priests and bishops, and these in turn promoted the most virulent forms of anti-communism. Eamonn McCann tells of growing up in Derry where the Nationalist Party held sway and was so closely associated with the Catholic Church that its 'candidates were not selected; they were anointed.'[53] When even the most mild-mannered Labour candidate appeared at election time, the Nationalist Party sent out loudspeaker cars to say the Protestants were voting for him. In this situation, according to McCann, 'the fear that it was possibly sinful to vote against the Nationalist Party was quite real.'[54]

All these elements of reaction tended to reinforce each other and obliterate the space available for any left or revolutionary tradition. The more the Catholic population identified with its Church, the more it confirmed the message of the most bigoted elements of the Protestant population. The more that Protestants behaved in a bigoted sectarian fashion, the greater the hold of the Catholic Church over its flock. The overarching framework for all of this had been produced by the counter-revolution of 1923. British imperialism had intervened in Ireland to partition the country and help construct two opposing identities. It then came to an accommodation with a section of republicans around Collins and Griffith who turned their guns on their former comrades. To bolster their position, they had forged an alliance with the Catholic bishops to offer the population a spiritual anti-depressant. And, not to be outdone, the 'more Irish' republicans around de Valera outbid their rivals in Catholicism. What emerged were two conservative sectarian states that reinforced each other. The more the 'special position' of the Catholic Church was enshrined in the law and practice in the South, the more Protestant workers were wedded to their Unionist leaders.

And while de Valera had not the slightest intention of re-taking the 'fourth green field', he was happy to use the national issue as a totem to unite the Southern population around a Fianna Fáil-Catholic alliance. James Connolly's prediction about a carnival of reaction has been more than fully borne out.

Sparks or Embers?

The period from 1923 to 1968 was a very barren period for the Irish revolutionary tradition. The republican movement dwindled dramatically, as it was hit by both heavy repression and co-option by Fianna Fáil. In 1933, the IRA had 12,000 members but by 1938, membership had declined to just 2,000. Those who survived were drawn to a futile militarist strategy which, at its lowest points, led them to make links with Nazi Germany. During the Second World War, the IRA even declared that 'if the German forces should land in Ireland, they will come as friends and liberators of the Irish people.'[55] After the Second World War, the IRA took up right-wing stances and called for 'a reign of social justice based in Christian principles'.[56] When it launched the 1956 border campaign, it was operating according to pure nationalist principles. Brendan Behan described the more typical member as 'your wrap-the-green-flag-round-me junior Civil Servants that came into the IRA from the Gaelic League, and well ready to die for their country any day of the week, purity in their hearts, truth on their lips, for the glory of God and the honour of Ireland'.[57] One of the heroes of the 1956 border campaign made famous in the song 'Sean South of Garryowen' was a member of the extreme right-wing Maria Duce organisation who thought that Hollywood was a 'Judeo-Masonic controlled conspiracy' to 'warp and corrupt the minds of our youth.'[58]

The left fared little better. At the end of the Civil War, Jim Larkin founded the Irish Worker League with five hundred attending its first rally and six thousand marching with the League when Lenin died the following January. In Belfast, the Revolutionary Workers' Groups played a leadership role in bringing Catholic and Protestant workers together during the Outdoor Relief struggles. But the connections between the left and Moscow did the left a great disservice. The Catholic right repeatedly pointed to links with Stalin's dictatorship – even when they themselves gave full support to dictators such as Franco in Spain and Salazar in Portugal. The notion of a left-wing party controlled from Moscow did not fit well with a political culture that was steeped in anti-imperialism. Worse, after 1940, a tiny left shifted to fully supporting Britain's war effort because it was an ally of Moscow. The Communist Party in Northern Ireland benefited by growing to a thousand members as a result of its support for the 'patriotic war'. Loyalism and Stalinism blended into an uneasy mix, with the Communist Party meetings even being advertised in the Unionist press. In the South, however, the left's opposition to Irish neutrality created a weak spot which was aptly exploited by its opponents. They were portrayed as mouthpieces for Churchill, while right-wing labour leaders presented themselves as anti-imperialist.

However, during this whole period, there was one event that stood out: the formation of the Republican Congress in 1934. This was a rupture within the republican tradition and occurred because of a number of factors. The depression of the 1930s and the mass unemployment that followed led to a powerful questioning of capitalism. The weakness of mainstream republicanism was also exposed as IRA members drifted towards Fianna Fáil. There was a need for a left-wing critique of Fianna Fáil as the party of Irish capitalism, but the IRA leadership refused to do just that. Finally, the impressive unity displayed between Catholic and Protestant workers during the Outdoor Relief struggle meant class struggle was seen to offer a new way forward for those who genuinely aspired to a unity of 'Catholic, Protestant and Dissenter'.

The Republican Congress came together on a manifesto that declared that 'a Republic of a united Ireland will never be achieved except through a struggle which uproots Capitalism on its way.'[59] From the very start, it operated in a way that was different to all previous – and future – republican organisations. It declared itself to be for an alliance with labour organisations rather than assuming its leadership was the real, legitimate government of Ireland. Instead of simply supporting the Irish nation in an economic war with Britain, it argued that there first had to be a critique of native capitalism. It placed a strategic focus on winning Protestant workers to its ranks, declaring that its Belfast organisation 'must place their main emphasis on the anti-imperialist forces developing among the working-class organisations'.[60] Against a background of clerical reaction, it made a special appeal to women to join its ranks. Most crucially, the Republican Congress saw itself as an agency that promoted mass working class struggle. It stated:

> If there is a workers' strike every ounce of our power must be exercised to see that the strike is carried to victory. There must be no more of the lonely picketing by a few workers while the great stream of workers passes by unheeding. The whole power of the Ireland assembled into the Congress must back the workers in their industrial struggles; must champion the rural youth in their demand for the land; must rally round housing fights.[61]

This was by no means empty rhetoric. The Republican Congress joined in mass pickets at workplaces which were on strike and as a result its members were arrested. One of those jailed, Charles Donnelly, declared, 'a picket becomes too large for legality as soon as it becomes large enough to be effective.'[62] It formed a Tenants' League and organised a demonstration where thousands participated with slogans such as 'No work: No evictions' and 'No rent for Rat Pits!' Through this mass agitation, it managed to win a small but significant minority of Northern Protestant workers to its ranks. In June, these attended the annual Wolfe Tone commemoration at

Bodenstown behind a banner inscribed 'Shankill Rd Belfast Branch. Break the Connection with Capitalism'. However, they were attacked by right-wing IRA leaders, who ordered the 'communist' banners to be taken down. The next day the Belfast contingent marched to Connolly's grave, where a Shankill man, Robert McVicar, gave a memorable oration:

> We do not pretend to speak on behalf of the majority of Belfast workers. We are a body of Protestant workers, the vanguard of the working class ... [come from Belfast] to pledge our determination at the graveside of Connolly to do all we can to carry out [his] message ... to break all connection with England and to smash Irish capitalism.[63]

The intervention of the Shankill workers was highly significant. It showed that a body of Protestant workers could break from loyalism and adopt an anti-imperialist stance, but they would only do so by also opposing Irish capitalism. The editorial in the following week's issue of *Republican Congress* spelled this out eloquently:

> Sectarianism dies out slowly when the fight against it is one of words. Sectarianism burns out quickly where there is team work in common struggle. Those who see in Partition just a reflection of sectarian strife see no way forward except in foolish talk about toleration, charity, real religion etc. Those who see in partition the link between Irish capitalism and Imperialist finance, see in the common struggle for the Workers Republic the solution of partition, and in the destruction of exploitation, the withering away of sectarian strife.[64]

This statement brought a new clarity on the linkage between the national and class question. But there remained one problem which torpedoed an extremely promising project – the umbilical cord to the republican tradition was not cut. At a Congress held in September 1934, attended by 186 working-class delegates, that ambiguity exploded wide open. A section of the Congress led by the former IRA leader Mick Price and two of James Connolly's children, Roddy Connolly and Nora Connolly O'Brien, called for the creation of a new political party that would lead the fight for a Workers' Republic. If they had been successful, Ireland would have seen its first revolutionary socialist party, with substantial roots in working-class communities and with a claimed membership of between 6,000 and 10,000. However, another faction led by Peadar O'Donnell and the tiny Communist Party did not want to make this fundamental break with the republican tradition. They wanted to hold open the possibility of attracting 'sincere' republicans back into a fight for 'The Republic'. Or to put it differently, they did not want to jump a stage in the struggle but wished to confine it to a framework that could attract fellow republicans. O'Donnell put this succinctly when he said, 'We dare not jump through a stage in the fight, now raising the slogan of a Workers Republic and leaving Fianna Fáil to say they were standing for one kind of republic and we stand for a different one.'[65]

Peadar O'Donnell's position won out narrowly and the Congress broke up in disarray. A major advance in winning a small but significant section of Protestant workers to the left was lost. So too was the clarity about the links between partition, capitalism and socialism. It would take another 35 years before these issues were re-examined.

CHAPTER SIX

The Rise and Fall of Radical Republicanism

In January 1960, after the abject failure of the IRA's border campaign, republican internees were released from prison but there were few people to welcome them at the gates. Jimmy Drumm felt himself to be part of 'a forgotten race of people' and noted that 'some of the people in the street [where] we lived didn't even know we were in prison.'[1] Republicanism had reached its lowest point since the pre-1916 period. Throughout much of the decade, the IRA remained a virtually defunct organisation. On the fiftieth-anniversary commemoration for the 1916 rising, a large crowd marched to Casement Park in Belfast, but one of the young participants, Danny Morrison, noted that 'As far as we were concerned, there was absolutely no chance of the IRA appearing again. They were something in the history books.'[2] In the same year, the Belfast contingent could only send a minibus to the annual commemoration at Wolfe Tone's grave and even when the North erupted in 1969, there were less than sixty people in the Belfast IRA.

The following two years, however, transformed the republican movement into the most important fighting force since the War of Independence. This transformation began in January 1970, with a split between the leftist Official IRA and the more traditionalist Provisional IRA over dropping the tactic of abstentionism from the Dublin and London parliaments. After civil rights protestors were attacked by the police and B Specials, the Provos – as they were called – grew rapidly and gained huge popular support in Catholic working-class areas. Doors were opened for IRA activists involved in an armed struggle, thousands stored guns and hid weaponry, while tens of thousands attended republican ceremonies. The young Danny Morrison's claim that the IRA belonged to the history book was not only disproved – he himself eventually became one of its leaders.

The shift from failure to success for the republican movement represented a turning point in Ireland's revolutionary tradition. Many of its members endured enormous hardships but the transformation was not simply the result of individual effort. It grew out of deep contradictions in Northern Ireland and the impasse of alternative politics. The most traditional forms of republicanism were grafted on to a mass rebellion but eventually the tradition itself was jettisoned. The great irony was that the initial 'success' turned into the death of radical republicanism and with it, one strand of the Irish revolutionary tradition.

All Change

The Unionist monolith, which bound together Protestant workers with their Orange employers, cracked apart in the 1960s, under pressure not from any communist or republican bogeyman but from capitalism itself. 'All that is solid melts into air', the Communist Manifesto proclaimed, referring to the constant change inherent in the system.[3] Northern Ireland was a dramatic illustration.

Partition was originally supported by British imperialism to keep hold of the industrial triangle that linked Manchester and Glasgow to Belfast. Maintaining this arrangement also had the effect of weakening the industrial development of the South. This, in turn helped to secure the South as a neo-colony of Britain, supplying agricultural produce but a minimal amount of manufactured goods to the metropolis. The North, it was also hoped, would become a net contributor to the British exchequer. In return for these benefits – and the political advantage of minimising the impact of the Irish revolution on its other colonies – Westminster turned a blind eye to how the Unionist

Party ran its state. Under a 'convention' in place in the late 1940s, the North's internal affairs were scarcely ever discussed in the House of Commons. The Unionist Party was allowed to run a sectarian state in whatever way it chose. In the five years preceding the riots of 1969, the House of Commons devoted less than 0.16 per cent of its time to discussion of Northern Ireland.[4]

By the 1960s, however, the economic basis of partition had eroded. The big bastions of Unionist industry – the family-owned firms in shipbuilding, linen and textile – were in terminal decline. Between 1949 and 1967, employment in the linen industry fell by 50 per cent, while numbers in shipbuilding declined from 25,000 to 10,000. The Northern economy became more reliant on foreign multinationals. For example, synthetic fibre manufacturers such as Dupont, Chemstrand, British Enkalon, and so on, replaced the linen mills. These did not have the same interest in discriminating against Catholics. Dupont managers sent over from New Jersey didn't join local Orange lodges to rub shoulders with workers. Higher capital investment meant extra productivity and they preferred to simply negotiate with moderate union officials.

The growth of the welfare state in the 1950s and 1960s was also a significant factor. The North's status as part of the UK meant that it enjoyed this extension of state provision, but its declining industrial base meant that, on its own, Stormont couldn't fund it. One result was that far from the North contributing to the British exchequer, it became a drain on the exchequer. However, a more positive result of the welfare state was that Catholic youth gained access to higher education. In the past, it was joked that the only way that a Catholic could get into Queen's University's medical school was by leaving their body for research. By 1967, the number of Catholics studying science and technology had doubled as a percentage of the student intake, compared to the previous decade.[5]

These developments meant that it was necessary to modernise Unionist rule. But on top of that, Britain's own interests in Ireland were changing. By the early 1960s, the Southern economy had opened up to foreign multinationals and British firms were the first to arrive. The South also established a free trade area with Britain, which facilitated its reintegration into the global economy. All of this encouraged the British and Irish ruling classes to forge a new political relationship. Britain's interest was no longer just confined to the North – it had developed a strong all-Ireland focus. The British now had an incentive to clean up some of the sectarian mess in their own backyard. Hence the pressure on Unionist leader Terence O'Neill to modernise. O'Neill was an upper class squire who talked the language of reform but could not disguise his patronising tone. After he left his office he made known his views:

> It is frightfully hard to explain to Protestants that if you give Roman Catholics a good job and a good house they will live like Protestants, because they see neighbours with cars and television sets. They will refuse to have eighteen children, but if a Roman Catholic is jobless and lives in a ghastly hovel, he will rear eighteen children on National Assistance.[6]

Although it infuriated his own backbenchers, O'Neill shook hands with nuns, he met the Southern leader Sean Lemass, and talked a new language of inclusion. But the rhetoric only raised the expectations of many Catholics. This was expressed in more determined opposition to discrimination and support for civil rights marches calling for an end to gerrymandering, fair allocation of housing and 'one man, one vote'. However, the Orange machine that had been constructed over decades was not so easily dismantled. It had been maintained by constant propaganda about Protestants being under siege from a hostile Southern state and the need for vigilance against disloyal Catholics. While the British elite might demand a more modernised capitalism, the Orange machine had developed interests of its own. It had bestowed marginal privileges on Protestants and these would not be given up so easily. And, as Eamonn McCann, pointed out 'the Orange machine, in a real sense, was Northern Ireland.'[7]

These dynamics played themselves out in the crucial years between 1968 and 1971. Civil rights marchers were attacked by Orange mobs, the RUC and the B Specials. When Catholics responded by attacking an Orange march in Derry, it escalated into the Battle of the Bogside. A few days later, a virtual pogrom occurred in Belfast, as Protestant mobs laid siege to Catholic housing estates in the Falls and Crumlin-Ardoyne area. Afterwards, eight people lay dead, 750 people were injured and 1,800 had to flee their homes. Westminster responded by deploying the British Army and announcing a reform programme to disband the B Specials and disarm the RUC. This in turn led to rioting in loyalist areas and the growth of a harder right around Ian Paisley and William Craig. Then as support for 'moderate' Unionists was draining away, the British Army moved to crack down on Catholic areas, ostensibly to display 'even-handedness'. Orange marches were forced through an area adjoining the largely Catholic Ballymurphy district and a brutal curfew was imposed on the Lower Falls Road. Houses were ransacked, three people died from gunfire and one was crushed by an army vehicle. Many drew a sharp lesson from these events: The Northern state could not concede equality to its Catholic citizens and the British Army would simply prop it up. What had started with a modest demand for civil rights had led to the raising of the 'national question'. The very existence of two states was now at issue.

The strategy of building up a civil rights movement had come from the left. Desmond Greaves of the Connolly Association – an organisation of Irish emigrant workers that had close links to the British Communist Party – had championed the idea for some time.[8] It was promoted actively by Roy Johnson and Anthony Coughlin, two left-wing intellectuals who had joined Sinn Féin and who were sympathetic to CP politics. When the Northern Ireland Civil Rights Movement was formed in 1967, future members of Official Sinn Féin and the CP had considerable influence within it. They based their strategy on two key considerations. First, the movement should focus exclusively on civil rights within the Northern state. At a later stage, the achievement of these demands would create the space for pursuing the idea of a united Ireland by purely political means. Talk of socialism would have to be postponed until after a united Ireland had been won. This was the 'stages theory'. Second, in line with the thinking on 'popular fronts' which was common in communist politics, unity inside NICRA was to be enforced by a studied moderation that would not frighten off any 'progressive' elements. When the struggle for civil rights escalated into a confrontation with the state itself, these beliefs became straitjackets. Instead of recognising the unreformable nature of the Orange state, the leadership of the Official Sinn Féin began to blame the 'ultra-left' and the 'sectarian Provos' for provoking a backlash from loyalism. They opposed demands for the abolition of Stormont even as the movement itself was putting its existence under question. Starting from the correct premise that the interest of British capitalism was changing to embrace an all-Ireland focus, the Officials argued that the abolition of Stormont would only increase imperialist control over the whole of Ireland. 'Less Westminster is required, not more', they proclaimed. A 'democratic Irish structure' in Stormont could be utilised to bring about a better all-Ireland settlement.[9] In brief, the more Catholic working-class youth moved into confrontation with the Northern state, the less they adhered to the role ascribed to them by the stages theory. And the left dogmatists were sticking with their theories.

One organisation that grasped some of these dynamics was People's Democracy. It started as a student 'ginger group' in Queen's University, holding marches for civil rights but, unlike NICRA, it placed no faith in the ability of Stormont to reform itself. When O'Neill called for a truce on demonstrations in late 1968, PD refused to abide by it. The PD's Burntollet march, which set off on a four-day trek from Belfast to Derry on New Year's Day in 1969 (modelled on Martin Luther King's Selma–Montgomery march), was repeatedly attacked by off-duty B

Specials. This dramatically exposed the sectarian nature of the state. PD grew into an explicitly revolutionary organisation that developed a different understanding of the national question to both the civil rights moderates and the Provos. Here is Michael Farrell spelling it out:

> Firstly the border must go because it is a relic of imperialism, and in order to root out imperialism we have to root out the neo-imperialist set-up in the South and the neo-colonial one in the North.
>
> Secondly, Northern Ireland is completely unviable economically and only exists as a capitalist entity at the moment because of massive subventions from Britain. Similarly the South on its own is an area of small farms with very little industry. It too is completely unviable on its own and as a result is also dependent on Britain.
>
> The unification of Ireland into a socialist republic is not only necessary for the creation of a viable economy, it must also be an immediate demand, because only the concept of a socialist republic can ever reconcile Protestant workers, who rightly have a very deep-seated fear of a Roman Catholic republic, to the ending of the border.[10]

PD tried to implement some of these policies by staging a series of dramatic events. Later in 1969, for example, it organised a march to Dublin to 'arouse the anger of working people against the exploitation of Green Tories'.[11] However, the organisation did not develop into a coherent revolutionary party and it was unable to develop tactical positions or more specific socialist policies in a rapidly evolving situation. It was also unable to recruit to a clearly defined organisation. It loomed large when it staged its own imaginative events, but was largely absent when numbers of organised activists were required in local areas. As a result, it eventually fragmented and, later, the remainder of the organisation developed a mistaken perspective where they thought a civil war and loyalist-fascist takeover was distinctly possible.[12]

So although the left had initiated the civil rights strategy, it had neither the politics nor the coherence to deal with its escalation. The Provos, by contrast, had a simple but traditional message – the battle was under way for Irish unity and the way to achieve it was by armed struggle. It was a message that fitted with Catholics who found themselves besieged in ghettos for daring to ask for more equality.

The Provos

In republican mythology, there is an unbroken line of succession to the past. The IRA training manual, the Green Book, states 'the Army is the direct representatives of the 1918 Dáil Éireann, and as such are the legal and lawful government of the Irish Republic.'[13] This is not just rhetoric – it was a literal claim. The IRA sees itself as the custodian of the First Dáil and so its army council is the real, legal government of all Ireland. This direct continuity provided the moral justification of the IRA's right to conduct a war. Yet despite the emphasis on tradition, the IRA's progress over the past thirty years comes from a series of dramatic ruptures. There were four main phases in the history of Provisional IRA/Sinn Féin.

In the first phase, from 1970 to 1972, the IRA's campaign grew out of a *mass resistance to the Northern state*. Recruitment was driven by the role they claimed as military defenders of Catholic ghettoes. Joe Cahill, one of the IRA leaders at the time, explained, 'There was no grand plan about an immediate offensive. Most volunteers were involved in defence work in certain areas – I believe that was the thought that was uppermost in people's minds.'[14] The Catholic ghettoes were very fearful of loyalist attacks and, so for a brief period, they looked to the British Army for protection. However, after the Falls Road curfew when 3,000 soldiers ransacked houses in this compact Catholic area, this changed. Defence came to mean warding off both loyalist attacks and repression from the British Army. Support for the Provos escalated after the introduction of internment in 1971, which was directed exclusively against the Catholic population. A nationalist response became inevitable when organisations which claimed to be 'non-sectarian' refused to take a stance. The Northern Ireland Committee of the ICTU, for example, neither openly condemned internment nor organised any protest action against it.[15]

During this period, the IRA came closest to justifying its claim to be a 'people's army'. One IRA member, Gerry Bradley put it like this:

In 1971, it wasn't republicans in the third battalion: it was the people. The areas of the third batt [sic] were constantly under attack from loyalists, from British army raids. The IRA were defenders of the area. You had a hundred houses to stay in. Every door was open. Popular support was enormous. Everybody was behind us. We genuinely believed that we could beat the Brits this time.[16]

By August 1971, the Provisional IRA had grown to 1,200 members and was organised under brigade staff and companies, or active service units. There was also a dramatic change in the social base of Irish republicanism. During the previous upsurge from 1918 to 1922, the IRA mainly drew its recruits from the countryside and most of the military activities took place in the Munster area. Now, the IRA won a mass base among working-class Catholics in Belfast and Derry. It was an urban guerrilla army with mass popular support. Brendan Hughes, described its class composition: 'There was no rich people in the IRA then ... We were all working class, we were all pretty poor. There may have been one or two who would be seen as well off, like Hugh Feeney whose father owned a pub ... but that was as far as the wealth gap meant.'[17]

Yet despite this overwhelmingly working-class character, the ideology of the Provos was that of a highly traditional organisation. Their leaders rejected 'extreme' socialism and wanted a return to the Comhar na gComharsan (Neighbourhood Co-operation) policy that had originally been developed by IRA leaders in rural Ireland in

1939.[18] This was described as a midway position between the twin evils of capitalism and communism, which conformed to Catholic social teaching. The IRA leaders were anti-communist, but did not support a society based on wealth and privilege. Rather, they combined a radical anti-imperialism with deep-seated traditional Catholicism. Here is, for example, Séan Mac Stíofáin: 'I am very radically left wing in everything except religion. And I am opposed to abortion. I reluctantly accept there is a case for divorce. But divorce should be controlled. I don't like the idea of people just being able to get divorce on demand.'[19]

The Provisional IRA leadership, however, identified left-wing politics with running down the armed struggle and were determined that it should not happen again. They claimed that 'Red agents' had infiltrated the IRA and 'brainwashed young men and girls' into departing from the traditional republican emphasis on armed struggle.[20] The traditional way of warding off compromise in the republican tradition was to put the military wing in control. So the political wing, Sinn Féin, was made subservient and no one would gain any standing in the movement unless they served their time in the army. Sinn Féin was put under the command of the Army Council.

One result was that the Provos adopted a purely military strategy that played down mass mobilisation. After internment, tens of thousands took part in a rent and rates strike and 8,000 people in Derry took part in a one-day strike.[21] But the main republican response was to engage in a bombing campaign that focused on economic targets. Pubs, offices and shops in town centres were deemed to be legitimate targets and bombed. This, it was believed, would make the North ungovernable and force the British to leave. When nationalist sentiment was rising, the loss of civilian lives from the bombing campaign and sectarian responses from the IRA to atrocities against Catholics did not significantly detract from their support – albeit that many continued their support through gritted teeth.

This period culminated in January 1972, when the British forces murdered 13 people in Derry – Bloody Sunday – both to crush the IRA and, more importantly, as far as senior British officers were concerned, to smash the Bogside area – 'Free Derry' – where the people had taken control of their day-to-day affairs. The result was a spontaneous eruption of mass action throughout the 26 counties, as well as in the Catholic areas in the North. On the Monday after the shootings, workers in the South walked out of work in protest. Airport workers refused to service British aircraft or unload their cargo and dockers boycotted British shipping. Tens of thousands marched in Southern cities and occupied British-owned business. In Dublin, the British embassy was burnt to the ground. The Southern government were terrified that the 'troubles' might spill over to the Southern state and lead to an uprising. Yet throughout this period, the Provos' only response was to urge people to join the IRA and engage in a bombing campaign. They had no political strategy for dealing with the Lynch government in the South and this gave the Southern state the space to set about defusing anger. In reality, the IRA's unrelenting focus on a bombing campaign only assisted Lynch in winning back the Southern population.

The second phase of the IRA campaign lasted from 1972 to 1975 was one of *misplaced military optimism and near defeat*. It began when the British government responded to the mass upsurge of protest by abolishing the Stormont regime and promoting the Sunningdale agreement. This agreement established a power-sharing regime within the North and a Council of Ireland to develop all-Ireland co-operation. The agreement split the nationalist movement, as more middle-class Catholics saw their opportunity to gain status within Northern Ireland. But reform from above also provoked a massive response within Unionism, which was still capable of uniting in opposition to British directives. A loyalist strike, backed up by considerable intimidation, tore down the Sunningdale agreement. In its aftermath, loyalist paramilitaries such as the 'Shankill butchers' – a cover name for the UVF – embarked on a campaign of terror. This campaign was also directed toward the Southern state when – most probably with the help of British intelligence – 33 people were killed in the Dublin and Monaghan bombings in 1974. The Southern government used the bombings to undercut republican support and to introduce special emergency powers. They calculated, correctly as it transpired, that Southern support for the struggle in the North was relatively 'soft' and that most people feared any possibility of the violence spilling over the border.

The IRA strategy of bombing their way to the negotiating table therefore, played directly into the hands of the British and Irish governments. A few months after the fall of Stormont, the IRA set off twenty car bombs in Belfast in just over an hour, killing nine people in what became known as 'Bloody Friday'. The scale of the killings revolted many and led to a considerable loss of support. The Southern population had no direct experience of loyalist attacks or the brutality of the British Army and were even more outraged. The result was a growing alienation and an isolation of the struggle to the Catholic ghettoes. Moreover even within these areas, support for the IRA was draining away. When the IRA called for a boycott on voting for a reformed Stormont regime, the majority of Catholics ignored them and supported the SDLP. Ten days after Bloody Friday, the British Army used the public's revulsion at the IRA's actions to launch Operation Motorman. Five thousand soldiers bulldozed their way through the barricades of the no-go area of Free Derry and re-took it.

To compound these difficulties, the IRA leadership made no attempt to assess the changing political environment. They simply stuck to their purely military strategy and believed that if only this was conducted in a more ruthless and determined fashion, the British would be driven out. Dáithí Ó Connaill explained the strategy:

> The Brits can be beaten. Collins, for example, demonstrated the effectiveness of ruthless, well directed actions in smashing the

British secret service in Dublin. It was this sort of attitude that was lacking in the '56 campaign. That was fought with kid gloves. That attitude has now been eliminated.[22]

This approach bordered on the illusionary. In January 2004, *An Pobhlacht*, the Sinn Féin newspaper, ran with the headline '1974 – Bliain an Bua – Victory Year'. Four months later, the headline was 'Brits Get Ready to Pull Out'.[23] In September, Sinn Féin President Ruairi Ó Brádaigh told their Ard Fheis that he was concerned about the possibility of 'a secret or sudden withdrawal' by the British and did not want them to leave 'without proper plans and precautions' being made.[24] Based on this gross overestimate of their own impact and a misreading of British intentions, the IRA entered a truce with the British government.

The republican leadership thought that 'Her Majesty's government wished to devise a structure for disengagement from Ireland', and so they embarked on lengthy talks with senior civil servants.[25] In reality, the British were attempting to divide them and win away more moderate elements. The IRA was allowed to establish seven incident centres with a 'hotline' to the British authorities, and these effectively gave them power to police their own areas. However, the British were also using the truce to increase their surveillance of the IRA as their volunteers broke cover. This was a relatively successful tactic because in the first five months of 1976 after the truce broke down, 400 people were charged with violent offences.[26] The British also used the space provided by the truce to prepare a new strategy for dealing with the IRA known as 'Normalisation, Criminalisation and Ulsterisation'. Northern Ireland was to be presented as a normal society that was confronting a criminal conspiracy. Instead of the British Army being to the forefront, there was a new counter-insurgency strategy based on locally recruited forces who would extract confessions against IRA 'criminals' by using supergrasses to gain evidence.

From Left Rhetoric to Pan-nationalism

The third phase of the IRA campaign, which lasted from 1976 to 1987, might be termed the period of *the long war and leftist rhetoric*. It began when a group of prisoners led by Gerry Adams criticised the republican leadership for the truce. They presented themselves as more hard-line and suggested that the Southern-based leadership of the IRA lacked a strategic sense. Writing under the pseudonym 'Brownie', Adams argued that 'there is only one time to talk peace and that is when the war has been won not while it is raging. The time to talk peace is when the British have left Ireland, otherwise they will find some excuse to remain.'[27]

In recognition of the demoralised state of the IRA, all talk of imminent victory was dropped and instead a new 'long war' strategy was adopted. The guerrilla movement was reorganised into a cell structure. This was thought to have two main advantages: it was more difficult for informers to penetrate, and a smaller IRA would become less dependent on public support.

The criticism of the old leadership was also broadened out into an attack on the federalist proposals of the Eire Nua (New Ireland) policy position. This had envisaged a united Ireland being based on four provinces and in one of these Ulster Parliaments, Dáil Uladh, the 'unionist orientated people would have a working majority' and so could guarantee their own civil rights.[28] This was attacked by the younger Northern leadership as a 'sop to loyalism' and, using language borrowed from the remnants of PD, it was argued that the Protestant workers were a 'labour aristocracy', who would only play a progressive role after a united Ireland had been achieved. On the basis of posing as more hard-line and closer to the realities of Catholic working-class ghettoes, the Adams leadership set out to modernise republicanism.

There was a strategic thinking that started from a recognition that the movement was based on a minority of a minority within the Northern state. Breaking out of this required winning Catholic workers away from a middle-class SDLP leadership and gaining a base among Southern workers. The key to this was the embrace of a left rhetoric. The South was characterised as a neo-colony where the ruling class was 'not based primarily on native capitalism but is an agent class, acting as agents for foreign capital'.[29] The economic ills that Southern workers were suffering from were, therefore, directly linked to British interference. The IRA struggle was presented as a vanguard movement that was fighting against a direct colony in the North and a neo-colony in the South.

In terms of militant rhetoric, the tone could not be stronger. In a landmark speech given in 1977, Jimmy Drumm enunciated the new leadership line. There was a 'need to take a stand on economic issues and the everyday struggles of the people' and for 'the forging of strong links between the Republican Movement and the workers of Ireland and radical trade unionists'. He added:

We are not prepared even to discuss any watering down of our demands. We can see no future in participating in a re-structured Stormont, even with power-sharing and a Bill of Rights. Nor certainly will we never accept the legitimacy of the Free State, a fascist state, designed to cater for the privileged capitalist sycophants. No. Even to contemplate acceptance of either of these partitionist state would be a betrayal of all that Tone preached and died for.[30]

The IRA was declared to be a socialist organisation and, in a document written for the IRA known as the 'gray document', Adams argued:

Furthermore with James Connolly, we believe that the present system of society is based on the robbery of the working class and that capitalist property cannot exist without the plundering of labour. We desire to see capitalism abolished and a democratic system of common or public ownership. This democratic system, which is called socialism, will, we believe, come as a result of the continuous increase of power of the working class.[31]

The militancy of the language may, at first sight, come as a surprise. But nationalist movements have always been Janus-faced – they can look in two directions at once, because loyalty to the nation trumps any class interests. This allows them to shift easily between different registers as a means to garnering support. Even in the heyday of this rhetoric, there were clear signs that the republican use of socialist language was entirely instrumental. It was a means to an end – one of broadening out support for the IRA.

An early sign came when Gerry Adams told a journalist. 'There is no Marxist influence in Sinn Féin … I know of no one in Sinn Féin who is a Marxist or who would be influenced by Marxism.'[32] The claim that there was not a single person who was influenced by Marxism in an organisation whose aim was, apparently, the overthrow of capitalism, is quite extraordinary. But the real purpose of Adams's contradictory message was to signal that republicans were not straying too far from their traditions. He went on to add, 'To be a Republican in the true sense you have to base it on the 1916 Declaration which in itself is a radical document … Also as radical was the Democratic Programme of the First Dáil.'[33] In other words, there were no foreign influences and whatever about the rhetoric, this generation of republicans would be going no further than their predecessors. Significantly, even while engaged in left rhetoric, the republican leadership began its long-term relationship with a very right-wing US Republican party member, Peter King.[34]

The rhetoric about socialism also lacked an important element: any recognition that it was the working class, as a class, that could free itself. The IRA volunteer remained the key agent of change. Adams argued that the armed struggle provided the 'vital cutting edge' and that other forms of struggle would 'complement' it.[35] Workers' action was not deemed to be essential for change but was merely supportive of IRA volunteers. There was no acknowledgement that armed struggle was a tactic that might be judged by how much it furthered working-class action. And as for Protestant workers, these were simply dismissed as a reactionary bloc who could be ignored until after Ireland was united.

There was one other shift in this period that appeared to be borrowed from the left. During the fight for a restoration of political status for prisoners and the subsequent H-Block hunger strike, left wingers such as Bernadette McAliskey had argued for a 'broad front' strategy and participation in elections. They suggested that support for the prisoners should not be confined to those who backed the armed struggle, and that an attempt should be made to reach out to non-republican forces in order to build up mass support. One way to do this was to participate in elections and McAliskey therefore ran for the European election in 1979. She won considerable support for backing prisoners who were then on a no-wash protest. This was despite the fact that the Adams leadership denounced her for not giving 'unequivocal support' to the armed struggle and Martin McGuiness urged people to boycott the election on the slogan 'Back the prisoners, back the war'.[36]

However, the republican leadership soon did an about-turn and embraced both the broad front approach and participation in parliament. But the tactics employed by McAliskey and other left wingers, which were geared to generating mass support amongst workers, took on a different hue. Instead of focusing on workers' action to win support for the H-Block prisoners' hunger strike, the republican leadership placed an emphasis on winning Fianna Fáil, the SDLP and the Catholic Church hierarchy. These were seen as having more clout in the corridors of power and, therefore, more important allies. Lobbying the nationalist wing of the political establishment rather than encouraging the small but significant strike action that followed the death of the hunger striker, Bobby Sands, became the key to advance.

In 1986, Sinn Féin finally dropped its abstentionist position on the Dáil and Stormont because continuing refusal to participate led to a very low vote. Traditionally, socialists have normally participated in parliaments or considered it a mere tactical issue. But for republicans, participation brought into question their claim to be the real government of Ireland based on an unbroken legacy that stretched back to the First Dáil. The Adams leadership dealt with this conundrum with a triangulation strategy. In order to move forward, they upped their more traditional rhetoric. The grass roots were promised an 'armalite and ballot box' strategy but were informed the first was primary. According to Martin McGuinness:

> We know that elections, while important ... will not achieve a British withdrawal. If Sinn Féin were to win every election it contested, it would still not get an agreement on British withdrawal ... We recognise the value and the limitations of electoral success. We recognise that only disciplined, revolutionary armed struggle by the IRA will end British rule.[37]

The fourth phase of the IRA campaign, which lasted from 1987 to 2005, was based on *pan-nationalism and de-commissioning.*

At the end of the H-Block hunger strike, the IRA prisoners issued their own judgement on the Catholic Church, the SDLP and Fianna Fáil. They denounced Fianna Fáil as 'accessories to murder' and thought that the SDLP were 'middle-class Redmondites', who were 'devoid of principles'.[38] More widely, republicans regarded these groups as 'servants of the queen' and 'imperialist lickspittles'.[39] Yet remarkably, within a decade, the republican leadership declared them to be allies in a pan-nationalist front that would solve Ireland's national question. The shift was accomplished by two main techniques.

There was a move away from a principles-based framework to one of tactical agility. Instead of sticking to pure principles, the aim was to bring about a continual movement forward. This was articulated most clearly by Danny Morrison when he pointed to one of the main strengths of the republican leadership. This was a talent for 'finding vulnerabilities in the armour of our enemies, seizing the high moral ground and using the ingenuity for which we are renowned'.[40] The emphasis on tactical ingenuity was both a break with republican traditions and a logical consequence of it. The IRA campaign had lasted longer than any previous struggle and had outlasted many other urban guerrilla movements. But by the 1990s, it was clear that it could not break through and that the risks of defeat had risen. The political psychology behind 'bombing to the negotiating table' rested on an ability to carry off repeated 'spectaculars' that shook the establishment. When these became less likely, the element of surprise had to be internally generated and dramatic political stripteases rather than bombings became the way to trip up the enemy.

The shift away from armed struggle was also accompanied by further forms of triangulation. After landing a number of shiploads of weaponry from Libya, IRA members were energised by the possibility of launching a 'Tet offensive' in 1987–88. The aim was to hold, even for a brief period, liberated territories. However, the comparison with Vietnam was totally misplaced. The Vietcong were a large army that had a base amongst the peasantry – the IRA was a smaller, compact force of a few hundred guerrillas based mainly in cities. But even as talk of a 'Tet offensive' spread throughout the ranks, the first tentative steps of a 'peace process' were under way. In May 1987, the Redemptorist priest, Father Alex Reid, delivered a message from Gerry Adams to Charles Haughey. It suggested the possibility of a ceasefire that 'could mean taking the gun out of nationalist politics forever'.[41] The failure of any Tet offensive cleared the way for a peace process.

The first major change was that nationalist rivals, who had previously been denounced as agents of imperialism, came to be seen as allies. The strategic aim of Sinn Féin was now to 'construct an Irish nationalist consensus with international support' and thus create a pan-nationalist alliance.[42] There was an open acknowledgement that the armed struggle could not bring progress and so it was necessary to gain support from the political establishment. A 'Tactical Use of Armed Struggle' (TUAS) document distributed to the IRA stated:

> Republicans at this time and on their own do not have the strength to achieve the end goal. The struggle needs strengthening most obviously from other nationalist constituencies led by SDLP, Dublin government and the emerging Irish-American lobby, with additional support from other parties in the E.U. rowing in behind and accelerating the momentum created.[43]

Far from aiming at the overthrow of the Southern state, the political establishment were now to play a positive role. Moreover, after the fall of the Berlin Wall, it was suggested that the US and Britain were no longer trapped into an imperial dynamic and could also play a progressive role. The US could pressure Britain to change direction, and Britain in turn could become 'persuaders' for a united Ireland among Protestant workers. Instead of the earlier republican vision – that a united Ireland would come through a revolt against both states – there was a belief that it could be forged from above.

However, the engagement with new allies entailed even more dramatic consequences. The peace process documents that were exchanged between Sinn Féin and the British and Irish governments were premised on the concept of 'self-determination'. The British government acknowledged that it had no selfish or strategic interest in directing Irish affairs and would accept a united Ireland if that was the will of the majority. But the republicans were also boxed in to accepting that 'Northern Ireland in its entirety remains part of the United Kingdom and shall not cease to be so without the consent of a majority of the people of Northern Ireland.'[44] In other words, that a declaration in favour of a united Ireland would have to come from two jurisdictions – and not arise solely from an all-Ireland vote. To put it mildly, this was quite a change.

Once that principle was accepted, there was little point in maintaining an armed wing. Even during previous defeats, such as at the end of the Civil War or the 1956 campaign, republicans had never handed in their weapons to the state authorities. To do so would be tantamount to giving up on armed struggle forever. This is why Danny Morrison once wrote that 'There will not be de-commissioning. There will not be a surrender ... even by the year 3000.'[45] But as pressure from their new-found allies was intensified, the republicans were forced into de-commissioning their weapons. On Monday, 26 September 2005 it was announced by the Independent International Commission on Decommissioning (IICD) that the IRA had completed the decommissioning of all of its arms. Henceforth, the Provisional IRA was to become a commemoration club.

The armed struggle was abandoned, and the republicans had little conception of 'people power'-style politics. Their tradition had played down the possibility of mass action and so the only vehicle for advance became the state institutions themselves. Sinn Féin claimed that the Good Friday Agreement was 'the most significant political development since Partition',[46] because the North-South Ministerial council could create a dynamic that led to a united Ireland. If there were more Sinn Féin government ministers in both states, there could be greater 'harmonisation' across Ireland. As Eoin O'Broin put it, 'Sinn Féin in government in the North, and at a future date in the South, would place the party in key positions of institutional power from which to drive the agenda for reunification.'[47] This 'institutional power' would be supplemented by the creation of an all-Ireland economy and the combined pressures would then eventually erode partition. The creation of a power-sharing Executive within Northern Ireland was also supposed to help change the perceptions of Protestants. Sinn Féin ideologues presented the Protestant population as fundamentally insecure because 'they don't have a rooted mentality, having one foot on the island and the other on the other island.'[48] By opening a dialogue and promoting shared understanding of different cultures, the republicans hoped to bolster the all-Ireland economy and North-South institutions and so win a united Ireland. The key in all of this was the use of official state structures.

The ending of the armed struggle was overwhelming popular. But welcome as the peace was, it represented a fundamental break with republicanism. It ceased to be a revolutionary force and became a conventional political party. In the early 1970s, republican ideas seized hold of working-class Catholics because they were under sustained attack. But, ironically, areas like West Belfast had never traditionally been republican. They had tended to vote for the more conservative and communal Nationalist Party rather than Sinn Féin. Republicanism was grafted onto this community because it was resisting oppression and became the key to its principal mode of defence. But there was no natural fit. There was certainly no natural embrace of republican dogmas about the IRA being the real, legal government of Ireland, or even the absolute necessity to engage in armed struggle to win a united Ireland. Eamonn McCann has pointed to this paradox underlying the peace process:

> The Republican leaders realized at a fairly early stage, certainly by the mid-eighties, that actually the mass of their supporters, although they were extremely loyal to the Republican leadership … but there hadn't actually been support for the key ideas of Republicanism.
>
> Another way of looking at it is that they were realigning their own movement to meet the actual thinking of the people … [with which they were] out of alignment.[49]

Put differently, the IRA leadership jettisoned the core ideas of republicanisms to align their movement with communal advance for the Catholic population of Northern Ireland.

The Death of Radical Republicanism

In 2000, Gerry Adams predicted that a united Ireland could be achieved by 2016, the anniversary of the 1916 Rising because of the peace process.[50] Martin McGuiness expressed a similar optimism: 'With devolved government up and running we are able to bring together ministers and political leaders from north and south to commemorate the men and women of 1916 who could only dream of the new Ireland we now live in.'[51]

These predictions were, to put it mildly, somewhat optimistic but it indicated how far the republican leadership had come. They genuinely believe that the age-old goal of a united, free Ireland can be achieved by using the structures of two partitioned states.

Yet the harsh reality is that the radical republicans of yesteryear have become government ministers responsible for running a failed Northern state. The economic viability of Northern Ireland is now in question: its manufacturing base has shrunk and what remains of it is highly dependent on grants and subsidies. One study suggested that without these subsidies, there would have been no pre-tax profits in this sector between 1970 and 1992.[52] It has become an economy dependent on low-paid services and a large public sector, where one in three workers are employed, compared to less than one in five in Britain.[53] In the right-wing political discourse, this reliance on the public sector is presented as a major problem. Yet the real issue is the extreme weakness of local capitalists and the opportunist approach of multinationals who use the province as a base for subsidised profit. Lack of private investment means a lower level of productivity and so Northern Ireland competes mainly through low wages. Relative livings standards are, therefore, only 75 per cent of the UK average, even though workers work longer hours.[54] The result is great pools of poverty and deprivation, particularly in areas from which the IRA and other paramilitaries rose. A large proportion of the population is registered as economically inactive and a significant number of households have experienced intergenerational poverty.

The architects of the Good Friday Agreement originally thought that a 'peace dividend' would accrue and that the North could piggy-back on the success of the Southern 'Celtic Tiger' but these illusions have fallen apart. In the immediate aftermath of the peace, the main spurt to growth came from a retail and construction bubble, but only one of the seven new inward investments to West Belfast remained by 2007 and that employed just 27 people. The collapse of the Celtic Tiger and the global economic crash had a further devastating effect. When a comparison is made between the value of Northern Ireland's economy and the rest of the UK, Northern Ireland's is at its lowest level since the current series of records began in 1997. In the dry words of one consultancy group, 'the overall outlook for NI is particularly downbeat.'[55] The key problem is that Northern Ireland is being run on a huge fiscal deficit of an estimated £9.6 billion[56] – at a very time when Britain as a whole is engaged in a major downsizing of its public sector.

The solution that the republican leadership have accepted, as government ministers, is neoliberalism. The North, it is suggested, must be 'rebalanced' to create a stronger private sector and the way to do that is to cut taxes on business. Sinn Féin and the Democratic Unionist Party engage in a hostile rhetoric against each other, but both agree that the main way forward is cutting the rate of corporation tax to 12.5 per cent. This, it is claimed, would lead to 'an unprecedented investment in our private sector', because 'local companies would retain more profits which could then be re-invested into business expansion.' The North could also follow the South in attracting more foreign direct investment.[57] The republicans claim that a cut in corporation tax would help 'harmonise' the two Irish economies, while the DUP suggest it would allow better competition between them. But the reality is that both parties back the same neoliberal programme.

In order to persuade devolved powers to cut corporation tax in 2017, the DUP and Sinn Féin became the principle architects of the Stormont Agreement. This involved an agreement for a 'balanced budget', attained principally by welfare reform and by cutting 20,000 public sector jobs. The Northern Ireland Executive agreed to borrow €700 million to promote these 'voluntary exits' and, on top of that, the cuts in corporation taxes will also have to be funded from other internal sources. According to Richard Murphy, the reduced rates will lead to an immediate loss of between £200 million and £300 million in Westminster subsidies.[58] For the DUP, who have traditionally embraced right-wing economic policies, this is not an ideological problem, even though it does affect their working-class base. But for the former leaders of the IRA, who once claimed to fight for a socialist Ireland, it presents a major contradiction. They will have to explain to the people of West Belfast – where 45 per cent of workers are employed in the public sector[59] – why it is necessary to subsidise big business by cuts to public services.

The way out for both parties lies in an intensification of communal politics. Contrary to some media hype, the Good Friday Agreement was not about eliminating sectarianism, but rather about the management of enmity. Sectarian competition was inscribed into the very structures of the reformed state and a premium was put on 'ethnic outbidding'.[60] The agreement set up a political system whereby the most hard-line representatives of the rival communities were sent to the Northern Executive to fight for their side. Thus the DUP emerged as the largest unionist party by heightening a rhetoric about the Catholics getting everything, while Sinn Féin dominated the nationalist bloc by presenting itself as the strongest at promoting an 'equality agenda' – meaning equality between Protestants and Catholics within Northern Ireland. The result was that each economic 'reform' is filtered through the prism of which 'community' gains most or loses most. Even though both the DUP and Sinn Féin agree on the fundamentals of the neoliberal solution, they shore up their working-class base by constant talk of communal competition. Both parties promote cuts to public services and then claim that it was the 'other side', which pushed the cuts of their community. As Murtagh and Shirlow suggest, 'the DUP and SF have entered a "game-keeper by day" and "poacher by night" scenario in which they promote unity by day and ethno sectarian gatekeeping by night.'[61]

All of this casts a dark light on the optimistic republican perspective of working through the institutions of the state to bring about a united Ireland. The growing economic integration of Ireland under two neoliberal governments will hardly bring the working classes together and may even have the opposite effect. As the two states compete for foreign investment by becoming tax havens, working-class living standards will be squeezed to pay for subsidies on capital. In the absence of a genuine socialist challenge, communal politicians could divert anger onto the other side. Moreover, within Northern Ireland, as sectarian competition is being intensified by the two communal gatekeepers, there is little prospect that Protestant workers will be weaned away from 'insecurity' to embrace a united Ireland.

The plain reality is that modern-day republicanism has settled into becoming the communal representatives of a Catholic minority within the Northern state. Their main hope is that they can use an anti-austerity rhetoric in the South to gain access to state positions and then 'move forward the peace process'. Yet the contrast between the rhetoric against austerity in the South and the practice of implementing neoliberalism in the North is becoming ever more visible. Whatever the outcome, radical republicanism as a revolutionary tradition has died because its original principle of uniting Catholic, Protestant and Dissenter is submerged under the flag of communal competition. The principle of armed struggle has been replaced by a strategy of working through both states, and respectability has become the order of the day.

There are, of course, no inevitabilities and others will try to resurrect the radical elements within the tradition. Dissident republicanism can grow from the failure of the Good Friday Agreement to deliver any real change to impoverished Catholic areas in the North. Moreover, republicanism can still be attractive for many who draw a contrast between the ideals of the 1916 Rising and the realities of Southern capitalism today. However, as an ideology that provides a strategy for revolt, it has died. The most successful republican movement since the War of Independence has followed the same trajectory of its forefathers – it has switched from armed struggle to constitutional nationalism and the management of Irish capitalism. Dissidents who attempt a repeat of the pure tradition must face the prospect that it is highly unlikely that there will ever again be mass support for an IRA struggle. Those seeking revolutionary change must therefore look a different way.

CHAPTER SEVEN

From the Ashes
a Phoenix is Born

'The date of Tuesday, September 30, 2008 will go down in history as the blackest day in Ireland since the Civil War broke out', declared the Fine Gael politician Michael Noonan.[1] It was the date the Southern state was exposed as a servant of big corporations.

At about 1.40 a.m. on 30 September 2008, the Irish government decided to issue a blanket guarantee for the €440 billion worth of debt of Irish banks. The drama had all the appearance of a high farce. The idea of a bank guarantee had originally come from David McWilliams, a popular newspaper columnist, who transmitted it to a distraught Minister for Finance Brian Lenihan, as he chewed raw garlic at McWilliams' kitchen table.[2] However, it was the top bankers of Allied Irish Bank and Bank of Ireland who made it a reality by calling the Taoiseach's office to request an urgent meeting. They wanted a state guarantee to stave off a run on the Irish banks because news of a crisis in the Anglo Irish Bank was about to break. And they got it – just like that. The Cabinet did not even meet in person – but instead its members were later telephoned to ratify the decision at an 'incorporeal meeting'. One minister, Eamonn Ryan, stated that it 'was a chaotic, difficult, crisis period … It was 6 or 7 in the morning [when I took the incorporeal call]. Ridiculous, the whole thing was mad.'[3] There was no proper documentation or costings – ministers and top civil servants simply wrote a blank cheque.

Later, of course, there was confusion about how it all happened. The top bankers could not recall whether it was four or six banks which had been guaranteed.[4] There was also, apparently, a handwritten note from the Secretary General of the Department of Finance suggesting that a bailout of Anglo Irish would cost €8.5 billion and Irish Nationwide €2 billion – but later it was suggested that this was 'just a scribbled note which might not even have been transcribed properly'.[5] The government had commissioned expensive reports from financial experts, but these were entirely misleading. Merrill Lynch was paid €7 million for a report which claimed that 'all of the Irish banks are profitable and well capitalised' and even suggested that 97 per cent of Anglo Irish loans were 'neither impaired nor past due'.[6] Goldman Sachs stated that the loan book of Irish Nationwide 'had real value' but that 'help from the authorities' will be required for their 'liquidity' problem.[7] The real cost of the eventual bailout of Anglo Irish ran to a staggering €29.3 billion while Irish Nationwide came in at €5.4 billion. To put these figures in context , these two banks got more than the G8 leaders allocated for feeding 70 million people who were starving because of the same global economic crash that brought the banks down. Meanwhile, Goldman Sachs walked off into the sunset, Merrill Lynch became the wealth management division of Bank of America, and the top civil servants and politicians went away with fat pensions. The people of Ireland were left to carry the bill.

Sometimes one dramatic event can illuminate a whole political and social pattern. On that fateful night, the state elite displayed their total subservience to big money by taking a reckless decision to impose a debt on their population that will eventually cost an estimated total of €64 billion. They raided the National Pension Reserve Fund of €20 billion and then borrowed the equivalent of €9,000 per person to pay off the private gambling debts of bankers. The consequences of that decision are enormous. Future pensioners will be condemned to poverty because the funds set aside for them have been squandered. The state will also have to pay about €8 billion a year just to cover the interest to bondholders. That is the equivalent of the entire education budget and, with some variation in payments, it will continue until

2053. It means that the population will be deprived of decent public services for decades.

Why did they do it? It was not simply a case of confusion or panic, because a few days later, the main political parties – including Sinn Féin, but not the Labour Party – endorsed the policy. In reality, the bank guarantee was the logical outcome of a wider policy of being 'the best small country in the world in which to do business'.[8] This is coded language for a policy that effectively means cutting taxes on profit, and light regulation. After the mid-1990s, a major focus of state policy became the attraction of financial companies to the Irish Financial Services Centre and, as this was one of the most rapacious sectors of global capitalism, it demanded even more subservience from the Irish state. An IFSC Clearing House group was established, composed of representatives of Bank of America, Citibank, BNY Mellon, State Street and the Irish Bankers' Federation, and it became an embedded lobby group inside the Department of the Taoiseach itself. It effectively was permitted to write policies that allowed for the greater liberalisation of finance. Thus, for example, in 2001, legislation was drafted by the Irish Bankers' Federation and McCann Fitzgerald, a big legal firm, to open up a market in 'covered bonds'.[9] This gave creditors first call on mortgage-backed securities and allowed both IFSC finance houses and Irish banks to borrow €40 billion from money markets.[10] It provided the fuel for a raging property market, and super fees and bonuses for bank directors. The severity of the Irish crash was a reflection of the state's subservience to finance capital – and its response was simply to continue that subservience.

One effect of these policies was to put Ireland under the tutelage of the EU bureaucracy. After the crash of 2008, the EU intensified its neoliberal policies by introducing scorecards to deal with deficits and imbalances. The irony is that the Irish government was advised by the European Central Bank to save its banks in order to ensure that they paid back their debts to the bigger French, German and British banks. Lenihan later stated that 'We consulted the European Central

Bank and I was contacted by Mr. Trichet that weekend. The strong advice we received from the European Central Bank was that we should save our banks at all costs.'[11] But once the government did this – by turning private debt into state debt – it became entrapped in the new EU scorecard regime and it will remain imprisoned in a regime of surveillance for decades to come. This will allow the EU bureaucracy to order spending cuts and issue 'country-specific recommendations' which dictate its budgetary framework. These recommendations are framed in a benign way for public consumption but, by using coded language, they press for measures that undermine social rights. Thus, under the guise of 'labour activation' measures, for example, private companies have been employed as bounty hunters who are rewarded when they place the long-term unemployed in jobs. Behind the maze of bureaucratic speak contained in these recommendations stands a threat of economic sanctions if an elected government does not obey.

In the aftermath of the Celtic Tiger crash, the main aim of state policy was to salvage private capital. One way to do this was to revive the property market by stimulating another artificial boom. The state used a number of measures to do this, such as cutting back severely on social housing, refusing to impose rent regulation on an overheated rental market, and renting a vast amount of accommodation from the private sector. In one extraordinary move, it gave tax breaks to Real Estate Investment Trusts to lure in US vulture funds to buy up Irish property. By 2014, Dublin house prices were recovering faster than those of London or New York and according to the research company, MCSI, the city offered investors the highest rate of return in the world.[12]

Another way that the state helped private investors was by writing off debts. One of the lucky figures, for example, was Denis O'Brien, who has become somewhat of a symbol for Irish capitalism. He purchased two companies after the crash: Siteserv, whose subsidiary installed water meters, and Topaz, a petrol retailer. The Siteserv deal saw the state-owned Irish Bank Resolution Corporation (the new

name for Anglo Irish Bank) write off €110 million of the €150 million
it was owed while, in the Topaz case, the IBRC wrote off slightly
more than half of the €304 million it was owed.[13] These policies were
accompanied by growing pressure to extract more taxes from PAYE
workers even while the proportion of revenue raised from corporations
and the wealthy declined. Table 7.1 illustrates how this has occurred.
Even more remarkably, the tax hikes on workers occurred when the
labour force was in decline and experiencing pay cuts.

Table 7.1   Percentage of tax revenue from capital and labour in Ireland,
2007–13

	2007	2013
PAYE	26.3	33.3
Corporation plus capital gains and capital acquisition tax	16.4	8.8

Source: M. Collins, 'Taxes and income related taxes since 2007', Nevin Institute,
March 2015, NERI WP 2015/No. 25, Table 1b.

Protest

For a period, the Irish population appeared to accept their fate
passively. In Greece, there were several general strikes; in Spain, there
was a rise of an *indignado* movement that occupied town squares; in
Portugal, there were enormous demonstrations against austerity. But
in Ireland, there was quiet. The appearance was, however, somewhat
deceptive – there had been a host of brief, sectional protests over
issues such as the withdrawal of medical cards to the elderly or
hospital closures. Nevertheless, the lack of general anti-austerity
protests was enough to send commentators rushing for explanations.
Some saw it as a 'post-colonial' reflex where people lacked faith in
their own collective ability to bring about change. Others thought
that passivity arose from a deadly combination of Catholicism, which

had led to a 'deference to authority', and consumerism, which made protesting 'not cool' for a younger generation.[14] However, these wildly over-generalising cultural explanations eventually proved to be totally mistaken. The delay in the development of mass anti-austerity protests was the result of much more mundane and specific factors.

First, the decades of reaction after the Civil War meant that the Irish left was very weak and there was no historic memory or readily available language to critique capitalism. This weakness was further exacerbated by the legendary Celtic Tiger which had all the appearance of a free market success story. Rising living standards allowed workers to seek individual solutions to the failure of the Irish state to provide proper public services. At the height of the Celtic Tiger boom in 2007, for example, 51 per cent of the population held private health insurance. This type of individualised solution helped to underpin the decades of electoral dominance by Fianna Fáil. Its promise of real gains for workers through the expansion of Irish and multinational capital appeared to be working. At a wider intellectual level, the mass media pushed a strong commitment to capitalist values. A cult of the entrepreneur was assiduously promoted and key businesspeople were treated as economic rock stars. They were, apparently 'risk takers', who rose to the top without any state support, relying only on their 'innovative' ideas. The Celtic Tiger experience thus created a naïve belief in capitalism whereby the global economic order was seen as a morality play. As long as you played by the rules of the market, rewards would be granted. All of this meant that when the crash happened, Irish workers were singularly unprepared. They had no language or networks of struggle to start resistance and so were subject to what Naomi Klein termed the 'shock doctrine' effect,[15] as the elite moved rapidly to change Irish society.

Second, three decades of social partnership had weakened Irish unions and made them more amenable to co-operating with the state. The Irish Congress of Trade Unions embraced a philosophy of business unionism, believing that what was good for Irish capitalism was good for workers. They supported tax cuts as a way of subsidising low wage rises and, even at the height of the boom, made few demands on employers that would increase their costs. Thus, there were no claims for mandatory pension payments and few claims for enhanced holidays, even though Irish workers had comparatively few paid holidays. These policies led to a significant decline of the unions in the private sector and a broad decrease in membership involvement everywhere. When the crash occurred, the union leaders faced a strategic choice – they could either fight or capitulate to demands of the employers and the political elite. They were entirely predisposed to the latter course and so accepted pay cuts that averaged 15 per cent for public sector workers. These, in turn, became a signal for private employers to launch a similar offensive. In the immediate post-crash period, therefore, there was no national organisation that became a focal point for anti-austerity resistance. In an interview with the *Financial Times*, the Services, Industrial, Professional and Technical Union (SIPTU) leader, Jack O'Connor, acknowledged that the Croke Park agreement he signed with the state, 'took the best organised section of the workforce out of the equation of social protest.'[16]

These two factors help to explain the lateness of the Irish revolt against austerity. By the time Irish workers began to move, the Greeks and the Spanish were looking at governmental solutions for ending austerity. The mass protests in Greece gave rise to Syriza which grew from 3 per cent in the polls to becoming the government of Greece, while in Spain the new Podemos party became very popular. The anti-austerity movement in Ireland also took on a distinctive character: it was based on working-class communities coming together on a very simple issue – the right to water. As the main unions were no longer a focal point for protests, activists in local areas stepped into the vacuum to direct the anger against austerity. This meant that the protests had both an extremely radical character, as there were no 'official leaders' who could dampen its spirit, but they were also unstructured and inchoate. It was a genuine grass-roots movement where there was not one dominant narrative but a host of different perspectives melded into one great radical surge forward.

The first moves to form a broad based anti-water charges movement came on 5 April 2014, when Marcella Oliviera was invited to speak at a conference in Dublin, sponsored by People Before Profit and the UNITE union. Marcella was one of the leaders of the Cochabamba water wars in Bolivia that had defeated price hikes and had eventually led to a movement that overthrew a neoliberal government. The conference came at an opportune time, as many activists were demoralised by a defeat they had suffered in resisting a tax on family homes. They had called for a boycott of the tax but the government defeated them by using the Revenue Commissioners to take it directly from people's incomes. The conference agreed to focus on mass street protests and to create a broad united front of all parties and unions to mobilise for this. After further discussions, a number of trade unions became involved and the Right to Water Campaign was officially launched in August 2014 and it agreed to set 11 October as the first date for mass mobilisation.

Even before this date, smaller protests had begun in working-class areas when Irish Water attempted to install meters. In Togher in Cork, small numbers of people began to block the installation of meters but were soon joined by many local residents. Within a few weeks, other working-class estates in Cork joined the battle and Irish Water was prevented from imposing meters. Opposition to the meter installations soon spread to Dublin. In Clondalkin, a series of street meetings were held in housing estates and residents agreed to block the installation of meters physically. Delegates came together to form Clondalkin Meter Watch council which closed the whole district off to Irish Water. Protests against the installation of water meters also broke out on the north side of Dublin, when residents of Edenmore, Raheny and Kilbarrack joined in direct action to prevent installation. The state's response was to deploy extra police to force the meters into the areas and when that did not work they sent the Public Order Unit, aka the riot squad. The meter companies also went to the courts and took out injunctions threatening to jail protestors.

Meanwhile, preparations for the mass mobilisation continued against a backdrop of television scenes of local confrontations over meters. The organisers were expecting possibly tens of thousands to attend, but on 11 October, there were over 100,000, one of the biggest mobilisations ever seen. From then onwards, the movement simply mushroomed, as working-class communities got involved in street meetings and in building their own networks through Facebook groups. Every time there was confrontation with the police over meters, a mobile phone was at hand to record the events and tens of thousands later watched it on their Facebook pages. Several videos were produced to give instructions on how to decommission meters that had been installed. Almost everywhere was an explosion of working-class creativity as many made their own placards or banners. When the second mobilisation occurred on 1 November, 200,000 attended in over a hundred local demonstrations in towns and villages throughout the country. It was one of the biggest protests movements since the anti-conscription mobilisation of 1918.

The government was forced to retreat and embarked on a dual strategy to counter the movement. It apologised for its mistakes and offered some concessions – water charges were to be capped at €260 until 2019; a pledge was offered that there would be no privatisation, and the threat to turn down the water of non-payers to a trickle was withdrawn. But even while offering concessions, the state set out to criminalise the more militant sections of the movements and split off a moderate centre ground. It was assisted in this by a media campaign spearheaded by the Independent group of newspapers – owned by none other than Denis O'Brien, who coincidentally owned a company installing the water meters. The strategy, however, got off to a poor start when Right to Water called a major demonstration at the Parliament during working hours. About 50,000 turned up to a largely peaceful protest, showing that a significant number did not accept the concessions.

The Right to Water campaign then stumbled somewhat when the union leaders called off a planned mobilisation at the end of January 2015 and the next official mobilisation did not take place until April of that year. This was attended by over 80,000 which was extremely impressive, but the state had used the intervening period to step up a campaign of criminalisation. Paul Murphy, elected a member of Parliament in a recent by-election, and several protestors from Tallaght were arrested and threatened with a charge of kidnapping for blocking a government minister's car. Others on Dublin's north side were jailed for defying a court order. Nevertheless, despite these attacks, the movement remained strong and clearly posed a threat to the government. The next decisive phase occurred when Irish Water sent out its bills. One section of the movement, most notably Sinn Féin, refused to call for an organised boycott campaign. They argued that the only way to defeat Irish Water was to change the government at the next election. The radical left, however, argued for a boycott and in many areas began a new round of street meetings to promote both the boycott and 'burn the bill events'. Over half the population responded to the call for a boycott and refused to pay their first water bill.

Even this cursory account of the movement indicates just how significant it is. However, a more detailed academic study based on a sample of 2,500 participants who took part in demonstrations produced even more extraordinary results. It showed that just over half (54.4 per cent) had never protested before and that a sizeable number had previously voted for the two government parties – Labour and Fine Gael. Despite this, they showed signs of rapidly moving leftwards. Seventy-eight per cent thought that the effective way to bring change was through protesting, while 52 per cent thought voting another way to be effective. When it came to voting, 83 per cent said they would vote left and that included 32 per cent who said they would vote for the two radical left organisations, People Before Profit and Anti-Austerity Alliance; 28 per cent for left independents and 24 per cent for Sinn Féin. The vast majority of the movement (92 per cent) said they would not pay the charge and 80 per cent said that Right to Water should organise more protests. Overall, the survey showed a deep suspicion of the mainstream media which, it was felt, portrayed the movement in a negative light. The vast majority relied on the social media for their source of information about the campaign.[17]

Politicisation

On 1 November 2014, Damian Dempsey sung a magnificent rendition of 'The Ballad of James Connolly' to the assembled crowd of anti-water protestors. There are at least two different ballads about Connolly. In one, he is portrayed as a 'brave son of Ireland', and in the other, he is described as a gallant man 'who has gone on to organise the union so that working men might yet be free'. Dempsey sung the left-wing version and then adapted the last verse by shouting that Connolly's spirit was here at the protest and singing: 'He has joined the great rebellion so that Irish people might be free.' It was a moment that captured the link between the ideals of a socialist who joined the 1916 Rising and the rebellion that the water movement had triggered off.

The water movement became the focal point for major political change. That change had started before the movement began, but it accelerated and helped to crystallise it. In the seventy years from 1932 until 2002, three-quarters of the population voted for right-wing parties and only 11 per cent voted for the very mild Labour Party. In purely electoral terms, Ireland was the most right-wing country in Europe. Even more remarkably, in the 24 years between 1987 and 2011, Fianna Fáil was only out of office for a mere three years. Irish politics, therefore, was based on a two-and-a-half party system – with one large right-wing party, a second 'spare wheel' right-wing party and a Labour Party that acted as a prop for the other two. Even more bizarrely, in recent years, the Labour Party drew its votes predominantly from upper-class professionals rather than the manual working class.

Contrary to impressions, the long right-wing dominance at the ballot box did not reflect an inherent conservatism amongst the Irish. Fundamentalist Catholicism was strong until the 1970s and it used an anti-communist rhetoric to attack all left-wing ideas. But even during this period, there were comparatively high levels of union density and strong aspirations for social rights. The colonial history of Ireland meant that many workers linked hopes for social and economic advance to the progress of the Irish nation. As long as Fianna Fáil could translate national development into economic advance for workers, they sustained their base. But even then, there were short explosions of workers' struggles and, at various times, a rise in left-wing ideas. Ireland was not immune, for example, to the upsurge of revolutionary ideas in the late 1960s when thousands wore Connolly badges on their lapels and joined protests over housing, private ownership of fisheries, the Vietnam War and apartheid in South Africa.

With the crash of 2008 and the subsequent bank guarantee, Fianna Fáil's hegemony fell apart. They were exposed as a party that was entirely in the service of the wealthy and who had little concern about the state paying for bank debt. In the general election in 2011, there was a massive swing to Fine Gael because they promised a 'democratic revolution' and denounced the bankers' debt. Some viewed this 'revolution at the ballot box' as simply a shift in allegiance from one right-wing party to another and further confirmation of the conservatism of the Irish. In reality, however, there was such shock and hatred of Fianna Fáil that the mass of people just wanted the fastest and quickest way of getting rid of them. However, soon after Fine Gael took office, the hollowness of their own rhetoric was exposed when they dropped all talk of writing down the banker's debt. Their own class base also predisposed them to continue the attacks on the poorest sections of society. Even in their moment of triumph in 2011, when they won over the 'floating voter', Fine Gael's voting base was skewed to the upper professional groups, winning 41 per cent of the AB advertising category and 30 per cent of the C, D and E categories – that is, skilled, unskilled and semi-skilled workers. Not surprisingly, therefore, they simply continued the attacks on lone parents, the young, social welfare recipients and public sector workers – only this time ably assisted by the Labour Party.

The emptiness of the rhetoric about a democratic revolution and the continuation of austerity policies has shaken the legitimacy of the whole political establishment. Many people see that all the main parties make false promises to win elections and do the reverse afterwards. Democracy, it appears, just functions for a brief few moments before an election and then stops once the ballot box closes. This pattern occurs in many Western democracies and leads to such cynicism among the electorate that, Peter Mair argues, political elites are now 'ruling the void'.[18] In Ireland, however, this process has gone further and the legitimacy of the political regime itself is under question for a significant minority of people. The old mantras that are spun about 'living beyond our means' or 'sharing the pain during difficult times' have lost their potency. Even before the crash, Irish voters stood at the bottom of an international league table for strong levels of identification with particular parties.[19] But after the crash, low-level endorsement swung to outright hostility. Opinion polls in 2014–15 indicated a consistent pattern whereby the political establishment commanded the support of just over one half of the electorate. Over the various months, the results varied from 50 per cent to 55 per cent for the combined support for Fianna Fáil, Fine Gael and Labour. Nearly half of the electorate looked to Sinn Féin, the radical left, or independents. The latter grouping combined right- and left-wing independents, but left-leaning independents tended to be more dominant. The change has been, quite simply, extraordinary.

How, it may be asked, do these changes affect a revival of Ireland's revolutionary tradition?

For Sinn Féin, the answer is relatively simple. They define themselves as an anti-austerity party in the South and hope to be the dominant partners in government at either the next or the following election. Their presence in government on both sides of the Irish border, they think, will provide ample opportunity to use the institutions of the Good Friday Agreement to advance the cause of Irish unity. And as that unity will be constructed on an 'equality agenda', this will represent the culmination of Ireland's revolutionary tradition. However, there are good grounds for questioning this optimism. Even while the party promotes itself as a progressive anti-austerity force in the South, it agreed to severe public sector cuts in the North. Moreover, it increasingly defines itself as a pro-EU party and therefore is loath to talk of a unilateral writedown of Irish debt. Given its already inconsistent record on fighting austerity and a lack of strategy for dealing with the bankers' debts, the prospect of serious, long-term change from a Sinn Féin-led government is minimal.

Nor will much compensation be found in advances towards Irish unity. Far from the Good Friday Agreement leading to a new understanding among Unionists about an Irish identity, low-level sectarianism has intensified in the North, and Sinn Féin's own activities appear to confirm that. In the 2015 Westminster election, one of its leading members, Gerry Kelly, issued a leaflet calling on voters to 'Make the Change, Make History'. His point being that as the demographics in his North Belfast constituency had finally moved to 46.9 per cent Catholic and 45.6 per cent Protestant, Catholics should vote for him. It was a direct appeal to communal loyalty and, as Eamonn McCann put it, 'The "Vote Catholic" leaflets made a mockery of Sinn Féin claims to have risen above the hibernianism of wee Joe Devlin to connect with the noble traditions of the founders of Irish Republicanism.'[20] It indicated that even if a united Ireland were possible through the avenues Sinn Féin envisaged, it would not remove the poison of sectarianism.

Despite these inconsistencies, Sinn Féin will probably win the support of many who want rid of the political establishment in the immediate future. But a space has also opened up for a more radical left that can reconnect with a revolutionary tradition that stretches back to James Connolly. The basis for this revival will be found among the many working-class activists who have come to the fore in the anti-water charges movement. But the manner in which the connections will be made depends on the outcomes of a number of key debates inside the movement. Ireland's position as a late riser in rebellion means that the anti-water charges movement is engaged in debates about what is happening in Greece and Spain. Sinn Féin, for example, has consciously rebranded itself as the Irish Syriza and has effectively been endorsed in this by Alexis Tsipras.[21] Others look to Podemos in Spain for a model on how a new political organisation can be built to challenge the political establishment. This international dimension has given rise to two key debates.

Neither Left Nor Right?

On 1 May 2015, Eduardo Maura from Podemos spoke at a conference organised by trade unions supporting the Right to Water campaign. He told participants that Podemos in Spain grew because it realised that 'there was a new political space that was neither on the left side of the board or the right side of the board but at the centre.'[22] His remark drew strong applause from one section of the hall but deadly silence from another. It was a glaring indicator of the different strands that compose the anti-water charges movement.

The section which applauded came from the 'Says No' groups who normally take a town or county name such as Clonmel Says No or Dublin Says No. These sprung into life in response to the cost of bailing out banks and typically organised weekly marches on Sundays. From the outset, they adopted what has been described as an 'anti-politics' position. They opposed the presence of political banners on their demonstrations and claimed to speak 'for the people' and not political parties. Although there are only a relatively small number of activists in the Says No groups, the anti-politics mood is far more widespread, both in Ireland and internationally. It reflects a crisis of representation in Western democracies and a deep cynicism about political machines which share a mainstream consensus but use lies to build a voting base. But anti-politics also arises from an experience of defeats where there is no strong labour movement that provides a focal point for the anger in society. In the Irish case, there is also a hostility to the radical left, as its Marxist ideas are seen as foreign to the Irish culture. For the 'anti-politics' wing of the anti-water charges movement, the call for a new force that is 'neither left nor right' sounds attractive.

The theoretical argumentation that underlay Maura's call was originally developed by a group of academics at the Complutense University of Madrid. These were influenced by two former Marxists, Ernesto Laclau and Chantal Mouffe, who reworked Antonio Gramsci's theories about 'hegemony'. Gramsci had used this concept to explain how the viewpoints of the ruling class dominated the whole of society. (The unquestioned use of the term 'competitiveness' serves as an example because it shows how the mindset of corporate executives permeates our very thinking. Why, we might ask, is there no equivalent term which values 'co-operation'?). However, while Laclau and Mouffe used the concept of hegemony, they dismissed talk about social class, arguing that populist leaders could construct an alternative hegemony.[23] The intellectuals who founded Podemos adopted this approach and defined their movement as 'neither left nor right'. They wanted to create an alternative common sense that pitted 'the people' against a 'political caste'.[24] However, this also implied their politics had to be kept vague, because otherwise one would have to enter the murky world about which social class might benefit or lose from specific policy proposals. The project of creating a political force that goes 'beyond left and right', therefore, depends on a slippery use of political meaning where what is unsaid becomes as important as what was articulated. Here, for example, is one of the Complutense intellectuals, Inigo Errejon, explaining the strategy. We need, he argued

> ... an understanding of politics as a battle for meaning, in which discourse is not that which is said – true or false, revealing or obfuscatory – about positions that already exist and have been constituted in other spheres (the social, the economic, etc.) but rather a practice of articulation that constructs one or another position, one or another meaning, on the basis of 'facts' that can take on very different significance according to how they are selected, grouped together, and, above all, counter posed. That meaning is not given but rather is dependent on clashes and balances.[25]

One may need to read this academic-speak a second time for its meaning to become clear. Essentially, it is suggested that politics is not about definite positions but how meanings shift and change according to the balance of forces.

There may appear to be a long road between the academy in Madrid and working-class communities in Ireland but ideas and strategies from one movement can pass over to another. But in a country that has never had a proper, strong left, the call to go beyond the left seems, at best, to be premature.

Let us, however, define what is meant by the term 'left'. In the Catholic rhetoric that pervaded Ireland for many decades, the term referred to political movements that, in varying degrees, aspired to a version of the old USSR. 'Left wing' meant to be in favour of state ownership and lack of democracy. Even in that era, this was a distortion of what genuine socialists stood for and it is certainly not what the modern radical left in Ireland advocates. By left wing we, therefore, mean a politics that starts from the reality of class division and articulates the interests of the working class. That class is not simply confined to factory workers but embraces all who must sell their labour and whose labour is controlled by others. At a minimal level, 'left' means a redistribution of wealth to favour workers. Most left wingers, however, go further and argue that the problems of inequality and economic insecurity arise from the capitalist system itself. Left politics, therefore, envisage a different way of organising society rather than simply managing capitalism. This new society must put the control of enterprises in the hands of the mass of people. This can only occur through an extended form of democracy – one that goes beyond the limited political democracy to include also economic democracy as well. In simple terms, left wing equals more democracy and workers' control.

There are also three problems with the suggestion that Ireland needs a new force that goes beyond 'left and right'.

First, it assumes that Ireland's austerity regime was simply caused by a few corrupt politicians and greedy bankers. The remedy, according to this view, lies in the political sphere. One can either elect honest representatives who are not beholden to any vested interest. Or one can change the constitution to bring about regular referenda to make politicians accountable. There is some truth in this analysis because the political elite in Ireland *are* corrupt and the greed of bankers *is* insatiable. Regular referendums would also be a democratic improvement. The problem, however, is that even if the political establishment was honest and even if there were regular referendums, there are underlying structures that led to Ireland's period of austerity. The demands for greater profits in Irish banks, for example, were not driven solely by the greed of a few executives but were hardwired into the system itself. Even if corporations were run by angelic figures that lived a life of frugal abstinence, they would still try to gain more profit because, otherwise they would be destroyed by their competitors. The logic of capitalism is one of frenetic accumulation and therein lies its extraordinary drive for efficiencies – and its utter madness and irrationality.

When economic crises occur, the state elite *always* tries to restore rates of profit, because this is the very motor that drives the system forward. Where there is no profit, there is no investment and so the chaos of society increases. This inherent logic means, that despite its own rhetoric, the function of the state is not to serve the 'common good' but to serve the needs of capital. It also means that there cannot be purely political solutions.

Second, contrary to the 'beyond left and right' rhetoric, there is not one 'people' or 'one nation', but different social classes with opposing interests. As soon as one moves beyond blaming German Chancellor Angela Merkel, for all Europe's recent economic ills – and she is responsible for some – and enters the world of specific proposals, this becomes clear. Take, for example, the problem of Ireland's national debt and how it is to be solved. Are the multinationals, who enjoy an effective tax rate of just 6 per cent, to pay up – or should there be extra taxes on PAYE workers? Should public sector workers get a restoration of their pay and conditions – or should they be regarded as a privileged layer? Should the national debt be repudiated – or must we respect the rights of Irish and foreign bondholders? Beyond the issue of revenue and public spending, there is an even deeper left–right divide. Everyone agrees that Ireland's calamitous economic collapse was triggered by a few top bankers, but there are disagreements regarding its implications. If so few people can cause such chaos, should there not be permanent public ownership of banks? Or must they revert again to private ownership? And if it is necessary to have public ownership of banks, why not pharmaceuticals or insurance? The answers given to these questions show the fallacy of talk of moving beyond left and right.

Finally, a politics that is neither left nor right is almost always linked to a desire for charismatic leaders. The term 'charisma' was originally coined by the sociologist Max Weber who took it out of its original religious context. In Christian theology, charisma meant having a divine gift of grace, but Weber used the term for leaders who had extra-special qualities. They were like the famous Pied Piper of Hamlyn who could whip up followers into such a frenzy that they forgot all about their material concerns. Populist movements need such spellbinding leaders because their political positions invariably contain ambiguities and omissions. Unless there is a leader who stands above the movement and is almost venerated, questions about these ambiguities inevitably arise. In the case of Podemos, the need for a charismatic leader was built into its theoretical foundations from the very start. Errejon claimed that they were innovative by challenging the 'leadership taboo' that charismatic leaders were incompatible with democracy. He added, 'For Podemos, the use of the media leadership of Pablo Iglesias was a condition sine qua non of the crystallisation of political hope that allowed the aggregation of dispersed forces, in a context of disarticulation of the popular camp.'[26] In more simple language, the charisma of Pablo Iglesias was needed to pull together a movement that was neither left nor right.

Once charismatic leaders are in place, they must develop an extremely hierarchical and centralised organisation. As the leaders are seen as the font of wisdom, they must be allowed to pick their key staff members. The grass roots of a movement must be directly and constantly linked to the leader, rather than having this relationship mediated by local branch structures. In an age of information technology, the simplest way to do this is through Internet plebiscites. Instead of intense local discussions and choosing delegates to represent views, the grass roots simply votes on proposals framed by the leadership. In the case of Podemos, this has produced a strange irony. It grew of the 15-M *indignados* movement that was inspired by the idea of participatory democracy and autonomous spaces. When the party was first established, it was, therefore, built around local 'circles' that chose their own candidates and made their own decisions. But when Pablo Inglesias emerged as its charismatic leader, the influences of the circles decreased. Instead, a structure emerged whereby Inglesias directly chose a 15-person executive, ratified by a citizen council who were chosen directly by Internet voting. Local activists in circles gave way to a direct link between the leader and a more atomised mass membership. The logic of populism undermined grass-roots control.

Ireland's First Progressive Government?

As attacks mounted on the water charges movement, a strong desire emerged amongst activists for a left government. The polls all pointed to a distaste with the political establishment and so a desire grew to create Ireland's first government that was not led by either Fine Gael, Fianna Fáil or Labour. Moreover, in Greece, there was already an example to hand. Syriza had emerged from the margins of Greek political life to articulate the demands of the anti-austerity movement. It broke open the two-party system of New Democracy and Pasok to form the first radical left government in Europe since the Popular Front governments in France and Spain in 1936. Directly influenced by this success, the five unions associated with the Right to Water movement initiated a set of policy principles for a progressive Irish government. These principles began with a preamble from the Democratic Programme of the First Dáil in 1919 and the 1916 proclamation and so the link between historic memory and future aspiration were clear to see.

A left government in Ireland would indeed be a marvellous sight. It would break apart the two-and-a-half party system and the corrupt networks that stand behind them. It would raise the aspiration of workers and allow them to feel, that for once, there was an understanding of their needs. It could also establish some key social rights. Irish workers have no legal right to collective bargaining for their unions. Irish women are still forced to travel to Britain for an abortion. There is no legal obligation on Irish governments to house their citizens or even provide access to state-run primary schools. A left government could change all this – and more. It could also turn the axis of fear in society. Ever since the 2008 crash, the poor are afraid about cuts in their living standards, but a left government could switch fear onto the other side of the social class divide. In the leafy enclaves of Shrewsbury Rd or Ailesbury Rd, it would cause real worry about taxes on wealth or an end to lucrative contracts granted by crony politicians. Imagine, for a moment, the conversations in the boardrooms of a firm like Arthur Cox, for example, which has enjoyed such enormous legal fees.

A similar sort of dynamic went into play immediately the Syriza government was elected. Workers in Greece and in many parts of the rest of Europe rejoiced that there was finally a government to speak up for them. But precisely for the same reason, the EU elite was determined that Syriza must be seen to fail – lest the power of its example spread. Within weeks of Syriza taking office, the ECB terminated a mechanism that allowed Greek banks to fund themselves. This move led to a flight of billions of euros and made Greece more dependent on injections of EU 'emergency liquidity assistance'. In the words of Prime Minister Alexis Tsipras, the ECB was 'holding onto the rope that is around our necks'.[27] They used that rope to demand that Syriza honour deals that the previous right-wing government had agreed. They demanded that any 'reforms' that Syriza wanted to introduce had first to be approved by a 'troika' of lenders. The EU elite wanted to display to the people of Greece, and Europe more generally, that their economic 'realities' could trump democratic wishes. Through this silent form of economic terrorism, the Syriza government was forced to implement an austerity programme, even though its own population rejected it decisively in a referendum.

The advantage of Ireland's status as a late riser in rebellion means that it can foresee the consequences that arise from any strategic choice. In the case of Syriza, they promised both to end austerity and to reach an accommodation with their EU 'partners'. Some even assumed that their anti-austerity programme, which was based on Keynesian economics, offered a better way forward for European capitalism and that its 'partners' could be brought around to seeing this. The reality, however, proved to be very different. Their election intensified the conflict over who should pay for the Greek economic crisis. The EU institutions intervened in this conflict and acted as a key leverage point of pressure forcing them to retreat. This experience must be fed into any strategy that focuses on achieving a left government in Ireland. Instead of simply just hoping for such a government, it is necessary to clarify in advance how it could deal with similar and inevitable blackmail. A number of key principles need to be taken into account.

First, a left government would have to be willing to act unilaterally to write down the national debt. Bankers' debt was imposed on Ireland because the EU elite wanted to ensure that borrowed money would be repaid to their banking system. Yet even after the 'contagion' caused by an Irish bank crash passed, all pleas for a write-down of this debt has been ignored. The outstanding monies are so huge that a left government could not possibly implement a serious programme of reform and continue to pay off this debt. It could certainly ask – as Syriza did – for a European Debt Conference to discuss a general write-down of debt, but such pleas would probably come to nought. A left government would, therefore, have to be willing to act in defiance of the EU and the fiscal straitjacket it imposes.

Second, an Irish left government would have to end Ireland's status as a tax haven for global corporations. Irish society effectively offering these corporations a hidden subsidy by tolerating poor public services because of this shortfall in tax revenues. It is not possible to offer any substantial concessions to middle- and low-income earners and develop proper public services without forcing these corporations to pay up. As a basic minimum, a left government would need to abolish water charges, property taxes and the Universal Social Charge on incomes of €70,000 a year or under.

The ending of these post-crash tax hikes would have to be paid for by taxes on corporations.

Third, a left government would not be able to confront both the EU elite and the wealthy in Ireland without the active mobilisation of the working population. In any conflict between these forces and a small number of left-wing politicians, the former would undoubtedly win. The only way to reverse this is by breaking out from the constraints of conventional politics. 'People power' through mass demonstrations, strikes, boycotts is the most effective way of standing up to the insidious power of money. The willingness of people in Ireland to take such action is also the best way of generating international solidarity action.

All of which raises a question: who or which parties would be willing to take such actions?

Clearly, none of the establishment parties have any interest in such an agenda. One cannot imagine Fianna Fáil, Fine Gael or Labour, for example, agreeing to write down debt or increasing taxes on the large corporations. This is of some relevance because Sinn Féin stresses that its objective is a *left-led* government. Although this may at first sight appear as a quibble, there is a difference between a left government and a *left-led* government. The latter concept implies that Sinn Féin and other left-wing forces would be in a majority in a Cabinet but that a minority component could come from a party like Fianna Fáil. Yet even if a right-wing party was a minority partner, it would still exercise a veto over decision making. It would insist on adherence to EU fiscal rules and would continually threaten to destabilise a government that took serious left-wing measures. There are also major problems with the claim that Sinn Féin is part of a radical left axis that stretches from Athens to Dublin. The hollowness of its left-wing credentials were exposed when it argued for a *reduction* in the tax on corporation profits in the North rather than an *increase* in the rate in the South.

However, a government led by Sinn Féin would still represent a major shock for the Irish political system. The hysterical reaction of the Independent media group to the advance of Sinn Féin is testimony to this. But the anti-austerity movement should not demobilise or simply wait for a progressive government. A continuing active boycott of water bills is important because it empowers people. Workers' action is also better than thinking that unions can do very little until a new government creates a more favourable legislative climate. Huge popular movements can, in fact, force even right-wing governments to buckle under pressure. They also create the historic conditions for a shift in political allegiances and without mass mobilisations, there is a danger of older voting patterns reasserting themselves.

The Connolly Way

The outcome of these debates cannot be foretold in advance but a major social movement against austerity has come into being in Ireland. It began with a demand for a right to water but many have already generalised their experience into a wider critique of the political system. A significant minority are looking at the possibility of revolutionary change. And, by coincidence, they are doing so at precisely the time when the centenary commemorations of the 1916 rebellion are getting under way. The Irish state is using its full resources to project its image of the rebellion through programmes in universities, schools, museums and art galleries. It does so somewhat reluctantly and with some trepidation, fearful that if does not act, other forces will step into the breach. Nevertheless, the coincidence can be highly productive.

Social movements by their very nature are fluid and indeterminate. They rise rapidly in the most surprising ways, but they do not last forever. They establish networks of solidarity between activists who then often move on to other struggles. Nevertheless, the common experience of struggle helps to generate shared understandings about how society works and how to bring about change. At the centre of the diffuse social movements, there is often a distinct organisational and intellectual framework that provides a reference point for its development. The coincidence of the rise of rebellion in modern Ireland with the commemoration of the 1916 Rising, creates favourable conditions for ensuring that this framework has a distinct anti-capitalist hue. The key is all of this is the link between the rebellion of today and the socialist ideas of James Connolly.

Let us elaborate. Throughout the world, there is a new questioning of the links between corporations, democracy and the functioning of the capitalist system. These questions have been forced on masses of people by the way in which the wider economic system appears to be uprooting reforms won by previous generations. Everything from pensions to a proper public health service and the right to a job with basic rights is being challenged. Social movements have arisen in response to these changes and new radical parties have also been created. Tragically, in some countries such as France or Hungary, the far right have hegemonised this space by combining a fake anti-corporate rhetoric with the scapegoating of migrants and minorities. However, the trajectory in Ireland is very much to the left. There is a broad diverse sentiment that the political establishment serves the wealthy elements of Irish society and that 'people power' is a necessary vehicle for bringing change. This sentiment represents a huge leap forward in political understanding, but it needs to be firmed up with the growth of more coherent anti-capitalist ideas. The political programme of the great Irish Marxist, James Connolly, provides the best opportunity for doing this in the current period. He stood for something far more clear than those who talk about creating a 'new republic' or even returning to the well-meaning but vague Democratic Programme of the First Dáil.

Connolly named the source of the problems facing working people: capitalism. He never pretended that that the betterment of the working class would in any way be helpful to the business elite. Far from promising new ways of 'attracting foreign investment', Connolly started out from the blunt assessment that

When our investing classes purchase a share in any capitalist concern, in any country whatsoever, they do so, not in order to build up a useful industry, but because the act of purchase endows them with a prospective share of the spoils it is proposed to wring from labour. Therefore, every member of the investing classes is interested to the extent of his investments, present or prospective, in the subjection of Labour all over the world. That is the internationality of Capital and Capitalism.[28]

In simple terms, business leaders were not 'the partners' of labour but rather its exploiters.

Connolly openly advocated socialism and was very straightforward about what that meant: 'Socialism will confiscate the property of the capitalist and in return will secure the individual against poverty and oppression; it, in return for so confiscating, will assure to all men and women a free, happy and unanxious human life. And that is more than capitalism can assure anyone today.'[29]

He scoffed at the idea that socialism was somehow 'un-Irish' and proudly displayed his internationalism. The tactic of associating socialists with foreign figures and exotic ideas is still a familiar one to this day. Labour politicians, for example, habitually label the radical left as 'Trotskyites' to help shore up their positions with a little nationalist prejudice. Connolly disputed this by stating that 'in Ireland socialism is an English importation, in England they are convinced it was made in Germany … '.[30] He repeatedly emphasised the 'oneness of our interests all over the world' and stressed the international nature of the fight in which the workers were involved.[31] This internationalism did not spring from any mawkish sentimentality about humanity but was a necessary response to the system itself. 'The internationality of Socialism is at most but a lame and halting attempt to create a counterpoise to the internationality of capitalism', he wrote.[32]

Connolly wrote in an era when the main focus on opposition to the system came from workers' organisations. There is no discussion of the role of social movements in his writings – the agent for change was simply the workers. This gives his writings a distinct syndicalist tone because he saw the workplace as the germ for a new type of society. While there were some limitations in this, there were also some positive pointers. Connolly's notion of socialism was fundamentally linked to an extension of democracy to the economic sphere. He wrote that, under socialism,

> ... administration of affairs will be in the hands of representatives of the various industries of the nation; that the workers in the shops and factories will organize themselves into unions, each union comprising all the workers at a given industry; that said union will democratically control the workshop life of its own industry, electing all foremen etc., and regulating the routine of labour in that industry in subordination to the needs of society in general ... that representatives elected from these various departments of industry will meet and form the industrial administration or national government of the country.[33]

The emphasis on workers' action may seem quaint to some, but Connolly's argument about the potential power of workers to effect change is extremely relevant. After the crash of 2008, a series of movements, such as the Occupy movement, sprang up to challenge the rule of the 1 per cent. They typically occupied squares or city centres and pointed to the bankers and corporate leaders who held society hostage. But they were positioned *outside* the banks – sometimes literally sitting in squares outside their headquarters. They had no mechanism for challenging the banks' sheer economic power, bar the use of moral outrage. This weakness often leads social movements to look for other strategies once they reach a cul-de-sac. They sometimes move away from creating 'autonomous spaces' where participatory democracy prevails to the more conventional march through the institutions. The case of Podemos is the sharpest illustration of this.

Connolly's point about the crucial role of workers' action offers a way out of the polarity between 'spontaneous apolitical revolt' and a conventional strategy of electioneering. It suggests that the anger and creativity that arises from social movements should be taken beyond the town squares and into the workplaces where the profits of capitalism are generated. This linkage is vital for the progress of the anti-austerity movement in Ireland because, despite the huge street mobilisations, workers' action has been comparatively modest. The main reason is that the Labour Party still holds a death-grip over SIPTU and the Irish Congress of Trade Unions. Despite their use of Connolly's image, the leadership of these organisations has about as much relationship to his ideas as an embalmer has to the body he is mummifying. Yet if the anti-water charges movement could link up with the many disgruntled workers who reject the Labour Party's control of their unions, the scene could be set for major changes in Ireland.

The way to bring about these changes, Connolly suggested, was through revolution. He never thought that change would come from 'practical' politicians who set out to reform the system. He argued that 'Although it may seem a paradox to say so, there is no party so incapable of achieving practical results as an orthodox political party; and there is no party so certain of placing moderate reforms to its credit as an extreme – a revolutionary party.'[34]

Being practical, in this sense, meant thinking 'in the grooves those who rob you would desire you to think'.[35] It meant sticking to the rules they had drawn up for the game of politics. To be 'impractical' meant thinking in a different frame and seeing mobilisation from below as the key to change. Ironically, this was also the best way to wrest even minor reforms from the elites.

It is precisely at this point that the ideas of James Connolly and those of many in the anti-water charges movement converge. The betrayals and lies by conventional politicians have convinced many that 'people power' is the only sure guarantee of change. It is only when they get on the streets in huge numbers, block the water-meter installers, disrupt the economic life of a country, that a ruling elite is forced to listen. For Connolly, that insight – particularly if linked to workers' action – was the way to bring change. He continually pointed to the revolutionary road as the only sure method to take power from the hands of the rich – 'peacefully if possible', but, he added, 'forcibly if necessary'.[36] This clarion call could not be more relevant in Ireland one hundred years later. Talking revolution is no longer some rhetorical flourish to be thrown in at the end of a great speech at the GPO. It is a serious objective whose moment may eventually come. With absolute confidence, Connolly suggested that 'Revolution is never practical – until the hour of the Revolution strikes. Then it alone is practical, and all the efforts of the conservatives and compromisers become the most futile and visionary of human imaginings.'[37]

That confidence is needed even more in Ireland in 2016.

Conclusion

Irish society is shifting to the left. The anti-water charges movement created an explosion of class awareness, because many saw how the political elite answer only to the wealthy. After the demise of the Celtic Tiger, this elite protected privilege while imposing financial burdens on middle- and low-income Ireland. New confrontations on class issues are, therefore, inevitable. When they occur, a layer of activists will search for a language to articulate their grievances and hopes. They may reconnect with a subterranean revolutionary tradition that stretches back to the 1916 Rising.

That insurrection was a blow against empire and an assertion of the right of the Irish people to rule themselves. It should be commemorated as an anti-colonial revolt, as a rejection of imperialist war, and as a demand for a 32-county Ireland. The Rising also helped destroy the Redmondite political caste which had a comfortable niche within the British Empire. Although it is often forgotten, the Irish Parliamentary Party had deep roots in Irish society. They drew their support base from rural Ireland, the Catholic Church and the sectarian bigots of the Ancient Order of Hibernians. They seemed to be a rock of stability, in full control over their population. Yet they were swept away in a revolutionary upsurge caused, ultimately, by a crisis in the imperialist system. It is an illustration of how dramatic political change is possible.

In Ireland in 1916, there was failed insurrection followed by a national and social revolt. In Russia, in 1917, there was a social revolution followed by a successful insurrection. The political awareness of masses of people determined the order of events in both countries. During the Irish revolution of 1918–22, there was a huge swell of popular mobilisation involving strikes, boycotts, workers' occupations and land seizures, as well as an armed struggle involving thousands of fighters. The sheer scale of the revolt has been largely hidden from history and the whole period has been summed up simply as a War of Independence. Yet even though masses of people fought, they did not create organs of dual power that could rule in their name, as occurred in Russia. Instead, they looked to an alternative underground counter-state, known as 'The Republic', but this was a pale imitation of cabinets and government departments found elsewhere.

The Irish revolution was defeated because there was no political force that could combine aspirations for both national and social freedom. The republican leadership saw the armed struggle as the only way forward and regarded the social struggles as an obstacle or diversion. However, once the fight was reduced to a military conflict between the IRA and the British Army, it was contained by the superior forces of the Empire. The failure of the Irish revolution resulted in the Treaty, a Civil War and two deeply conservative sectarian states which were mirror images of each other. It culminated in a counter-revolution where an upper strata of Catholic professionals took control of the Southern state and suppressed all revolutionary aspirations. In the North, a Unionist Party run by landlords and businessmen used the Orange Order to discipline Protestant workers by claiming they were under siege from nationalist hordes.

The long period of reaction that followed resulted in a country with the weakest left in Europe. There was no serious social democratic party that could command the allegiance of the mass of workers and press for reforms. There was little evidence of civil society mobilising for gradual political change. Until very recently, elections in the North were just a sectarian headcount and those in the South were a contest between Tweedledum and Tweedledee, with Labour being available as a support prop for both. But then – just as happened in the early part of the twentieth century – the rock of stability began to crack. The Celtic Tiger's collapse revealed the incompetence and naked class bias of the political elite. As Irish society began to shift leftwards, many leaped over the small puny Labour Party and looked for something far more radical.

This politicisation coincides with the commemoration of the 1916 Rising. The 1916 Rising gave birth to a revolutionary tradition that survived decades of reaction. That tradition was often diffuse and stayed in the minds of people who stood at the back of churches or drank in pubs in Kilburn or joined periodic struggles over workers' rights or against partition. It provided a focal point to critique the abject failures of two societies produced by the counter-revolution of 1923. Sometimes this remained at the level of pure rhetoric: 'Was it for this the men of 1916 died?', pub-house republicans or socialists would ask. At another level, the ideals of the 1916 leaders were understood to stand in marked contrast to the political establishment. The Proclamation claimed the right of the Irish people to the ownership of Ireland and promised to cherish all its children equally. For Pearse as well as Connolly, that meant that the nation had to take control of its natural resources and subordinate private ownership to public control and assent. In an Ireland where the elite periodically give away oil, gas and valuable minerals to multinationals, these statements reverberate like the proverbial ghost of Banquo at a feast of greed. Similarly, the anti-imperialist spirit that animated the Rising stood in sharp contrast to the practice of gesturing towards neutrality but, in reality, supporting America's or Britain's wars. Moreover, the insurrection itself indicated that there are other ways to resolve political issues than by parliamentary majorities.

However, if the Irish revolutionary tradition offered a critique of the current order, it also contained its own ambiguities. It was a mixed tradition that blended elements of militant republicanism and socialism. The twinning of the cultural nationalist, Pearse, with the revolutionary socialist, Connolly, produced that mixture. Connolly's own politics, which sometimes looked for a revolutionary dynamic within republicanism, also helped to cement together the two traditions. Yet there is a fundamental paradox at the heart of modern Irish republicanism. It presents itself as the most determined and disciplined force, capable of destroying partition and imperialist control. Yet in almost every generation, its leaders shift from fighting the system to joining it. There is a pattern whereby the most enthusiastic advocates of armed struggle become the most ardent supporters of compromise. But as the former gunmen turn into respectable politicians, some of their erstwhile comrades split off and look again to the military wing as the saviour of pure principles. This pattern which began with Michael Collins continued with Frank Aiken, Sean McBride and Gerry Adams. The history of Irish republicanism has been a pattern of armed struggle – compromise – split, and then armed struggle – compromise –split.

The reason for this is that the movement is rooted in nationalist politics and has an instrumental attitude to social struggles. Where involvement in fights for workers' rights or resistance to austerity appears to bring the nation forward, republicans will enthusiastically back it. But, equally, when it is believed that US intervention in the peace process or participation in a neoliberal Northern executive moves that nation forward, excuses will be made for these paths. These contradictory impulses mean that republicanism can be a vehicle for articulating a desire for a better Ireland but it lacks the political capacity to actually bring that desire to fruition.

None the less, with all its ambiguities, the Irish revolutionary tradition is a positive asset. It means that the idea of revolution is not as foreign to the body politic as in countries which experienced centuries of gradual, peaceful change. The historic memory of the Rising also provides a reference point for left wingers who seek to popularise their views. The language of socialism normally starts from an understanding of the underlying dynamics of the capitalist system. But this must be related to the specific traditions that shape the consciousness of workers in particular countries. The revolutionary left in Ireland will grow more rapidly if it is able to embrace the anti-colonial spirit that gave rise to the 1916 rebellion.

Moreover, many of the ideas of a key figure of the Rising are of relevance today. James Connolly was a committed Marxist who dedicated most of his life to the overthrow of capitalism. He regarded the working class as the central agent of change because the workers had the power to disrupt the constant search for profit. He did not think workers should confine their demands to economic issues but rather that they should lead a fight against imperialist control and partition. His vision of the Ireland that he wanted was profoundly democratic. He thought that workers were capable of running their own enterprises and could develop an economy that served the needs of people rather than profit. He certainly did not believe that the fate of a whole country should be determined by the investment decisions of a few bankers.

The best way to commemorate the 1916 Rising would be a new revolt to change Ireland – so that it will be, in reality, 'cherishing all the children of the nation equally'.

Notes

Chapter 1   *Ireland Turned Upside Down*

1. 'Scotland shows 1916 Rising a mistake, says John Bruton', *Irish Times*, 18 September 2014.
2. D. Meleady, *John Redmond: The National Leader*, Dublin: Irish Academic Press, 2014, p. 306.
3. R. Foster, *Modern Ireland 1600-1972* Harmondsworth: Penguin, 1988, p. 432.
4. J. Finnan, *John Redmond and Irish Unity 1912–1918*, New York: Syracuse University, 2004, p. 154.
5. P. Walsh, *The Rise and Fall of Imperial Ireland*, Belfast: Athol Book, 2003, p. 462.
6. Ibid., p. 441.
7. Ibid., p. 468.
8. Foster, *Modern Ireland*, p. 331.
9. C. Kinealy, 'Beyond revisionism: Re-assessing the Great Irish Famine', *History Ireland* No. 4, 1995.
10. Noel Kissane, *The Irish Famine: A Documentary History*, Dublin: National Library of Ireland, 1995, p. 51.
11. Ibid.
12. L. Boldeman, *The Cult of the Market: Economic Fundamentalism and its Discontents*, Canberra: Australian National University Press, 2007, p. 25.
13. J. Mitchell, *Jail Journal*, New York: Tinson, 1954, p. 18.
14. J. Connolly, *Labour and Irish History* p. 169. https://www.marxists.org/archive/connolly/1910/lih/.
15. J. Newsinger, *Fenianism in Mid Victorian* Britain, London: Pluto Press, 1994, p. 41.
16. B. Griffin 'Social aspects of Fenianism in Connacht and Leinster', *Eire-Ireland*, Vol. 21, No. 1, Spring 1986, pp. 29–30.
17. P. Bew, *Land and National Question in Ireland, 1858–1882*, Dublin: Gill and Macmillan, 1978, p. 40, emphasis added.
18. E. Purcell, *The Life of Cardinal Manning: Archbishop of Westminster*, New York: Macmillan, 1896, p. 610.
19. Bew, *Land and National Question*, p. 50.

20. Ibid., p. 152.
21. D. Fitzpatrick, 'The Disappearance of the Irish Agricultural Labourer 1841–1912', *Irish Economic and Social History*, 7, 1986, pp. 66–92.
22. D.S. Jones, *Graziers, Land Reform and Political Conflict in Ireland*, Washington, DC: Catholic University of America Press, pp. 42–3.
23. K.B. Anderson, *Marx at the Margins: On Nationalism, Ethnicity and Non-Western Societies*, Chicago, IL: University of Chicago Press, 2010, p. 132.
24. Bew, *Land and National Question*, p. 87.
25. Ibid., p. 126.
26. J.W. Boyle, 'The agricultural labourer: A marginal figure', in S. Clark and J. Donnelly, eds, *Irish Peasants: Violence and Political Unrest, 1780–1914*, Manchester: Manchester University Press, 1983.
27. Bew, *Land and National Question* p. 236.
28. Ibid., p. 237.
29. E. Strauss, *Irish Nationalism and British Democracy*, London: Methuen, 1951, p. 198.
30. P. Bew, *John Redmond*, Dublin: Historical Association of Ireland, 1996, pp. 50–51.
31. L. Kennedy, 'The Roman Catholic Church and economic growth in nineteenth century Ireland', *Economic and Social Review*, Vol. 10, No. 1, 1978, pp. 45–60.
32. Lee, *The Modernisation of Ireland*, p. 17.
33. Strauss, *Irish Nationalism and British Democracy*, p. 210.
34. G. Horgan, 'Changing women's lives in Ireland', *International Socialism Journal*, Vol. 2, No. 91, Summer 2001.
35. J.J. Bergin, *History of the Ancient Order of Hibernians*, Dublin: Ancient Order of Hibernians, 1910, p. 8.
36. J. Connolly, 'John E. Redmond M.P.', *Forward*, 18 March 1911.
37. P. Bew, *Conflict and Conciliation in Ireland 1890–1910*, Oxford: Clarendon Press, 1987, p. 186.
38. W. Welles, *John Redmond: A Biography*, London: Longmans, 1919, p. 134.
39. C. Kennedy, *Genesis of the Rising 1912–1916*, New York: Peter Lang, 2010, p. 27.
40. Ibid., p. 15.
41. S. Paseta, *Before the Revolution: Nationalism, Social Change and Ireland's Catholic Elite 1879–1922*, Cork: Cork University Press, 1999, pp. 63–4.
42. Ibid., p. 67.

43. J. Gray, *City in Revolt: James Larkin & the Belfast Dock Strike of 1907*, Belfast: Blackstaff Press, 1985.

44. J. Newsinger, *Rebel City: Larkin, Connolly and the Dublin Labour Movement*, London: Merlin Press, 2004, p. 4.

45. V. Lenin, *The Irish Question*, Dublin: Repsol, no date, p. 4.

46. J. Connolly, 'Press Poisoners in Ireland', *Forward*, 30 August 1913.

47. J. Hutchinson, *The Dynamics of Cultural Nationalism*, London; Allen and Unwin, 1987, p. 271.

48. Ibid, pp. 178–9.

49. S. Paseta, 'Nationalist responses to two royal visits to Ireland, 1900 and 1903', *Irish Historical Studies*, Vol. 31, No. 134, 1999, pp. 488–504.

50. P. Walsh, *The Rise and Fall of Imperial Ireland*, p. 249.

51. G. Dangerfield, *The Strange Death of Liberal England*, London: Paladin, 1983, p. 100.

52. D.D. Sheehan, *Ireland Since Parnell*, London: Daniel O Connor, 1921, p. 239.

53. A.T.Q. Stewart, *The Ulster Crisis: Resistance to Home Rule 1912–14*, London: Faber, 1969, p. 62.

54. J. Ranelagh, *A Short History of Ireland*, New York: Cambridge University Press, 2012, p. 184.

55. T.P. Coogan, *The Troubles: Ireland's Ordeal and the Search for Peace*, New York: Palgrave, 1996, pp. 16–17.

56. A. Jay, ed., *Lend Me Your Ears: Oxford Dictionary of Political Quotations*, Oxford: Oxford University Press, 2010, p. 36.

57. P. Farrell, *Ireland's English Question*, London: Batsford, 1971, p. 249.

58. Walshe, *The Rise and Fall of Imperial Ireland*, p. 273.

59. Ibid.

60. C. Kennedy, *Genesis of the Rising*, New York: Peter Lang, 2010, p. 38.

61. Sheehan, *Ireland Since Parnell*, p. 216.

62. Walshe, *The Rise and Fall of Imperial Ireland*, p. 295.

63. T. Denman, *Ireland's Unknown Soldiers: The 16th Division*, Dublin: Irish Academic Press, 1992, p. 87.

Chapter 2   1916: Armed Insurrection

1. C. Brennan, 'A TV pageant – The Golden Jubilee of the 1916 Rising', *Irish Story*: http://www.theirishstory.com/2010/11/18/.

2. C.C. O'Brien, *States of Ireland*, London: Pantheon 1972.

3. Quoted in M. McCarthy, *Ireland 1916 Rising – Explorations in History Making, Commemoration, Heritage in Modern Times*, Farnham: Ashgate, 2012, p. 4.

4. P.S. O'Hegarty, *The Victory of Sinn Féin*, Dublin: UCD Press, 1998, p. 3.

5. K. Curtis, *P.S. O'Hegarty (1979–1955) Sinn Féin Fenian*, London: Anthem Press, 2010, p. 100.

6. See T. Garvin, *The Evolution of the Irish Nationalist Politics*, Dublin, 1981, pp. 112–13.

7. J. Newsinger, 'Jim Larkin, syndicalism and the 1913 Dublin lockout', *International Socialism Journal* Vol. 2, No. 25, 1984, pp. 3–36.

8. F. McGarry, *Rebels*, Dublin: Penguin Ireland, 2011, p. 124.

9. M. Wall, 'The background to the Rising from 1914 until the issue of the countermanding order on Easter Saturday 1916', in K.B. Nowlan, ed., *The Making of 1916*, Dublin: Stationary Office, 1969, p. 165.

10. M. Foy and B. Barton, *The Easter Rising*, Stroud: Sutton Publishing, 1999, p. 5.

11. F. X Martin, '1916 – Myth, fact and mystery' *Studia Hibernica* Vol. 7, 1967, p. 7.

12. P. Brendon, *The Decline and Fall of the British Empire*, London: Vintage, 2008, p. 290.

13. D. Macardle, *The Irish Republic*, Dublin: Wolfhound Press, 1999, p. 144.

14. L. O'Broin, *Dublin Castle and the 1916 Rising*, London; Sidgwick and Jackson, 1970, pp. 81–2.

15. Foy and Barton, *The Easter Rising*, p. 155.

16. K. Griffith and T. O'Grady, eds, *Curious Journey: An Oral History of Ireland's Unfinished Revolution*, London: Hutchinson 1982, p. 248.

17. E. Neeson, *Birth of a Republic*, Dublin: Prestige Books, 1998, pp. 175–6.

18. A. Mitchell and P. O'Snodaigh, *Irish Political Documents 1916–19*, Dublin: Irish Academic Press, 1985, p. 25.

19. Ibid., p. 21.

20. C. Kennedy, *Genesis of the Rising 1912–1916*, New York: Peter Lang, 2010, pp. 291–2.

21. Mitchell and O'Snodaigh, *Irish Political Documents*, p. 26.

22. Wall, 'Background to Rising', p. 188.

23. Foy and Barton, *The Easter Rising*, pp. 15–19.

24. William O Brien, 'Introduction', in D. Ryan, ed., *Labour and Easter Week*, Dublin: Sign of Three Candles, 1946, p. 21.

25. C. and A.B. Reeve, *James Connolly in the United States*, Atlantic Highlands, NJ: Humanities Press, 1978, p. 274.

26. Ibid.

27. Foy and Barton, *The Easter Rising*, p. 164.

28. F.A. McKenzie, *The Irish Rebellion: What Happened and Why*, London: C. Arthur Pearson, 1916, pp. 105–6.

29. Foy and Barton, *The Easter Rising*, p. 88.

30. Ibid., p. 103.

31. Kennedy, *Genesis of the Rising*, p. 103.

32. Ibid.

33. Kennedy, *Genesis of the Rising*, p. 95.

34. B. Mac Giolla Choille, *Intelligence Notes*, Dublin: Chief Secretaries Office, 1966, pp. 86–90.

35. P. Callan, 'Recruiting for the British Army in Ireland during the First World War', *Irish Sword*, Vol. XVII, 1987, pp. 42–56.

36. C. Townsend, *Easter 1916: The Irish Rebellion*, London: Penguin, 2006, p. 77.

37. Ibid., p.72.

38. L. O'Broin, *Dublin Castle and the 1916 Rising*, Dublin: Helicon, 1966, p. 53.

39. J. Connolly, 'The returned emigrants', in idem, *The Lost Writings*, London: Pluto Press, 1997, pp. 182–3.

40. Townsend, *Easter 1916*, p. 78.

41. Kennedy, *Genesis of the Rising*, p. 214.

42. F.S.L. Lyons, *John Dillon: A Biography*, London: Routledge and Kegan Paul, 1968, p. 403.

43. Townsend, *Easter 1916*, p. 88.

44. J. Augusteijn, *Patrick Pearse: The Making of a Revolutionary*, London: Palgrave Macmillan, 2010, p. 81.

45. D. Ryan, *Remembering Sion; A Chronicle of Storm and Quiet*, London: A. Barker, 1934, p. 161.

46. L. O'Buachalla, ed., *The Letters of P.H. Pearse*, Gerard's Cross: Colin Smythe, 1980, p. 9.

47. Ibid.

48. R. Dudley Edwards, *Patrick Pearse: The Triumph of Failure*, London, Victor Gollancz, 1977, p. 103.

49. Ibid., p. 29.

50. P. Pearse, 'The murder machine': http://www.ucc.ie/celt/online/ E900007-001/.
51. Dudley Edwards, *Patrick Pearse: The Triumph of Failure*, p. 71.
52. Ibid., p. 159.
53. Augusteijn, *Patrick Pearse: The Making of a Revolutionary*, p. 237.
54. P. Pearse, 'The sovereign people': http://www.ucc.ie/celt/online/ E900007-013/text002.html.
55. Ibid.
56. B. Anderson, *Imagined Communities*, London: Verso, 2006.
57. Pearse, 'The sovereign people'.
58. Dudley Edwards, *Patrick Pearse: The Triumph of Failure*, p. 182.
59. Augusteijn, *Patrick Pearse: The Making of a Revolutionary*, p. 268.
60. Ibid., p. 238.
61. Ibid., p. 183.
62. Pearse, 'The sovereign people'.
63. Ibid.
64. McArdle, *The Irish Republic*, p. 77–8.
65. Augusteijn, *Patrick Pearse: The Making of a* Revolutionary, p. 233.
66. Pearse, 'The coming revolution': http://www.ucc.ie/celt/online/ E900007-003/text001.html.
67. Ibid.
68. D. Nevin, *James Connolly: A Full Life*, Dublin: Gill and Macmillan, 2005, p. 24.
69. C.D. Greaves, *The Life and Times of James Connolly*, London: Lawrence and Wishart, 1976, p. 63.
70. C. Markievicz, *James Connolly and Catholic Doctrine*, Dublin, no date, p. 7, O'Brien Collection, National Library of Ireland.
71. O. Dudley Edwards, *James Connolly: The Mind of an Activist*, Dublin: Gill and Macmillan, 1971, pp. 29–30.
72. J. Connolly, 'Parliamentary democracy', *Workers Republic*, 22 September 1890.
73. J. Connolly. *The New Evangel*, Dublin: New Books, 1972, pp. 27–8.
74. J. Connolly, *Socialism Made Easy*, Chicago, IL: Charles Kerr, 1909: http://www.marxist.net/ireland/connolly/socialism/.
75. J. Connolly, *Labour and Irish History*, London: Bookmarks, 1987, p. 14.
76. D. Ryan, ed., *Socialism and Nationalism*, Dublin: Three Candles, 1948, p. 34.
77. J. Connolly, 'The first hint of partition', *Forward*, 21 March 1914.

78. J. Connolly, 'Sinn Féin, socialism and the nation', *Irish Nation*, 23 January 1909.

79. 'Shannon played vital logistical role in rendition circuits, say researchers', *Irish Times*, 9 December 2014.

80. 'Taoiseach confirms there will be a formal invitation to 1916 Commemorations for Queen Elizabeth', *Irish Independent*, 9 April 2014.

81. 'UK aware of rising sensitivities, Theresa Villiers says', *Irish Times*, 11 February 2015.

82. Heritage Foundation, *Index of Economic Freedom 2014*: http://www.heritage.org/index/.

83. O. Dudley Edwards and B. Ransom, eds, *James Connolly: Selected Writings*, London: Jonathan Cape, 1973, p. 336.

84. S. O'Casey, *The Story of the Irish Citizen Army*, London: Journeyman Press, 1980, p. 27.

85. A. Morgan, *James Connolly: A Political Biography*, Manchester: Manchester University Press, 1989.

86. J. Connolly, 'Our duty in this crisis', *Irish Worker*, 8 August 1914.

87. V. Lenin, 'Ireland's Easter Rising', in J. Riddell, ed., *Lenin's Struggle for a Revolutionary International*, New York, Monad, 1984, p. 377.

88. Greaves, *The Life and Times of James Connolly*, p. 403.

Chapter 3   The Irish Revolution

1. P. Hart, 'Definition: Defining the Irish Revolution', in J. Augusteijn, ed., *The Irish Revolution*, Basingstoke; Palgrave 2002, p. 18.

2. J.A Murphy, *Ireland in the Twentieth Century*, Dublin: Gill and Macmillan, 1975, pp. 20–21.

3. G. Adams, 'The Good Old IRA', *Leargas*, 7 November 2014.

4. Sinn Féin, *The Good Old IRA: Tan War Operations*, Dublin: Sinn Féin Publicity Department, Dublin, 1985, p. 46.

5. C. Townsend, *The Republic: The Fight for Irish Independence*, London: Allen Lane, 2013, p. 98.

6. Ibid., p. 79.

7. B. Farrell, 'The new state and Irish political culture', *Administration* Vol. 16, Autumn 1968, p. 240.

8. Ibid., p. 242.

9. T. Garvin, *1922: The Birth of Irish Nationalism*, Dublin: Gill and Macmillan, 1996, p. 32.

10. Ibid., p. 54.

11. Hart, 'Definition: Defining the Irish Revolution', pp. 26–7.
12. F. Furet and D. Richet, *The French Revolution*, London: Macmillan, 1970.
13. P. Foot, *The Vote: How it was Won and How it was Undermined*, London: Bookmarks, 2012.
14 V. Lenin, *Left Wing Communism – an Infantile Disorder*, in V. Lenin, *Selected Works*, Vol. 3, Moscow: Progress Publishers, 1975, p. 351.
15. F. Engels to E. Bernstein, 27 August 1882, in K. Marx and F. Engels, *Selected Correspondence*, Moscow: Progress Publishers, 1965, p. 364.
16. D. MacArdle, *The Irish Republic,* Dublin: Wolfhound Press, 1999, p. 343.
17. J. Augusteijn, *From Public Defiance to Guerrilla Warfare: The Experience of Ordinary Volunteers in the Irish War of Independence*, Dublin: Irish Academic Press, 1996, p. 111.
18. R. Foster, *Modern Ireland 1600–1972*, Harmondsworth: Penguin, 1989, p. 497.
19. A. Mitchell, *Revolutionary Government in Ireland: Dail Eireann 1919–22*, Dublin: Gill and Macmillan, 1995, p. 128.
20. Ibid., p. 69.
21. Augusteijn, *From Public Defiance*, p. 200.
22. Ibid., p. 202.
23. C. Townsend, *The Republic: The Fight for Irish Independence*, London: Allen Lane, 2013, p. 149.
24. McArdle, *The Irish Republic*, p. 274.
25. D. Fitzpatrick, *Politics and Irish Life*, Dublin: Gill and Macmillan, 1977, p. 178.
26. Mitchell, *Revolutionary Government in Ireland*, p. 145.
27. Ibid., p.142.
28. Fitzpatrick, *Politics and Irish Life*, p. 172.
29. ITUC, *Annual Report*, 1918, p. 38.
30. Ibid., p. 42.
31. C. Kostick, *Revolution in Ireland: Popular Militancy 1917–1923*, Cork: Cork University Press, 2009.
32. J. Kemmy, *The General Strike 1919*: http://www.limerickcity.ie/media/Media,3944,en.pdf.
33. Kostick, *Revolution in Ireland*, p.128.
34. Ibid., p. 131.
35. Ibid., pp. 134–5.
36. Ibid., p. 137.

37. Ibid., p. 143.

38. Ibid.

39. M. Laffan, 'Labour must wait: Ireland's conservative revolution', in P.J. Corish, ed., *Radical, Rebels, and Establishments*, Belfast: Historical Studies, 1985, p. 219.

40. J. Lee, *Ireland 1912–1985: Politics and Society*, Cambridge: Cambridge University Press, 1989, p. 43.

41. D.M. Leeson, *The Black and Tans: British Police and Auxiliaries in the Irish War of Independence*, Oxford: Oxford University Press, 2011, p. 11.

42. McArdle, *The Irish Repu*blic, p. 334.

43. Leeson, *Black and Tans*, Chapter 2.

44. Ibid., p. 44.

45. F. Pakenham, *Peace by Ordeal: The Negotiation of the Anglo-Irish Treaty 1921*, London: Pimlico, 1992, p. 50.

46. Townsend, *The Republic*, p. 159.

47. Kostick, *Revolution in Ireland*, p. 95.

48. Townsend, *The Republic*, p. 163.

49. Ibid.

50. Ibid.

51. M. Farrell, *Arming the Protestants: the Formation of the Ulster Special Constabulary and the Royal Ulster Constabulary 1920–27*, Dingle: Brandon, 1983, p. 314.

52. Ibid., p. 10.

53. M. Hopkinson, *The War of Independence*, Dublin: Gill and Macmillan, 2002, p. 153.

54. Farrell, *Arming the Prote*stants, p. 21.

55. J. MacKay, *Michael Collins*, Edinburgh: Mainstream Publishing, 1996, p. 203.

56. S. Lawlor, *Britain and Ireland, 1914–23*, Dublin: Gill and Macmillan, 1983, p. 60.

57. F. Costello, *The Irish Revolution and its Aftermath 1916–1923*, Dublin: Irish Academic Press, 2003, p. 217.

58. Ibid.

Chapter 4   Republicanism and Counter-revolution

1. B. Maye, *Arthur Griffith*, Dublin: Griffith College Publications, 1997, p. 117.

2. P. Yeates, *Lockout Dublin 1913*, Dublin: Gill and Macmillan, 2000, p. 354.
3. K. Haddick Flynn, 'The Limerick pogrom of 1904', *History Ireland* Vol. 12, No. 2, Summer 2004, p. 32.
4. P.S. O'Hegarty, *The Victory of Sinn Féin*, Dublin; Talbot Press, p. 29.
5. B. Murphy, *Patrick Pearse and the Lost Republican Ideal*, Dublin: James Duffy, 1991, p. 104.
6. D. Figgis, *Recollections of the Irish War*, London: Forgotten Books, 2013, p. 259.
7. Quoted D.R. O'Connor Lysaght, '"Labour Must Wait": The making of a myth', *Saothar* Vol. 26, 2001, p. 61.
8. E. O'Connor, *Syndicalism in Ireland 1917–1923*, Cork: Cork University Press, 1988, p. 148.
9. F. Costello, *The Irish Revolution and its Aftermath 1916–23*, Dublin: Irish Academic Press, 2003, p.163.
10. Democratic Programme of First Dáil: http://www.firstDail.com/wp-content/uploads/2008/12/democraticprogramme.pdf
11. P. Lynch, 'The social revolution that never was', in D. Williams, ed., *The Irish Struggle 1916–1926*, London: Routledge and Kegan Paul, 1966, p. 46.
12. Maye, *Arthur Griffith*, p. 136.
13. E. O'Connor, *Reds and Greens*, Dublin: UCD Press, 2004, p. 15.
14. A. De Blacam, *What Sinn Féin Stands For*, Dublin: Talbot Mellifont Press, 1920, pp. 105–6.
15. O'Connor, *Syndicalism in Ireland*, p. 61.
16. P. Bew, 'Sinn Féin, agrarian radicalism and the War of Independence 1919–1921', in D.G. Boyce, ed., *The Revolution in Ireland, 1919–1923*, Basingstoke: Macmillan, 1988, p. 228.
17. Ibid., p. 229.
18. M. Hopkinson, *Green against Green: The Irish Civil War*, Dublin: Gill and Macmillan, 1988, p. 45.
19. Bew, 'Sinn Féin, agrarian radicalism and the War of Independence', p. 232.
20. Ibid.
21. O'Connor, *Syndicalism in Ireland*, p. 43.
22. Ibid, p. 75.
23. H. Patterson. *The Politics of Illusion: Republicanism and Socialism in Modern Ireland*, London: Hutchinson Radius, 1989, p. 12.

24. Ibid., pp. 119–120.
25. O'Connor, *Syndicalism in Ireland*, pp. 45–6.
26. C. Kostick, *Revolution in Ireland: Popular Militancy 1917–1923*, Cork: Cork University Press, 2009, p. 58.
27. H. Patterson, *The Politics of Illusion: Republicanism and Socialism in Modern Ireland*, London: Hutchinson Radius, 1989, p. 12.
28. J. Connolly, 'Northern notes', *Irish Worker* 22 August 1914.
29. Quoted in A. Mitchell, 'William O'Brien 1881–1968 and the Irish labour movement', *Studies* Autumn–Winter 1971, pp. 311–31.
30. A. Mitchell, 'Tom Johnson 1872–1963: A pioneer labour leader', *Studies* Winter 1969, pp. 396–404.
31. F. Robbins, *Under the Starry Plough*, Dublin: Academy Press, 1978, p. 201.
32. A. Mitchell and P. O'Snodaigh, *Irish Political Documents 1916–1949*, Dublin: Irish Academy Press, 1985, p. 42.
33. Report of Socialist Party of Ireland to the Third International, MS 15674(1) National Library of Ireland.
34. P. O'Donnell, *There will be Another Day*, Dublin: Dolmen Press, 1963, p. 17.
35. Kostick, *Revolution in Ireland: Popular Militancy 1917–1923*, p. 188.
36. A.C. Hepburn, *Ireland 1905–25, Volume 2: Documents and Analysis*, Newtownards: Colourprint Books, 1998, p. 202.
37. M. Laffan, 'Arthur Griffith', *Dictionary of Irish Biography*, Cambridge: Cambridge University Press, 2009, pp. 277–86.
38. P. Hart, *Mick: The Real Michael Collins*, London: Macmillan, 2005, pp. 358–9.
39. Costello, *The Irish Revolution and its Aftermath*, p. 248.
40. G.G. Corone, *The Catholic Church in the Irish Civil War*, Madrid: Cultiva Communicacion, 2009, pp. 22–3.
41. Kostick, *Revolution in Ireland*, p. 208.
42. Costello, *The Irish Revolution and its Aftermath*, p. 278.
43. Hopkinson, *Green against Green*, p. 112.
44. Townsend, *The Republic: the Fight for Irish Independence*, London: Allen Lane, 2013, p. 404.
45. Hopkinson, *Green against Green*, p. 126.
46. J.M. Regan, *The Irish Counter-Revolution 1921–1936*, Dublin: Gill and Macmillan, 2001, p. 72.
47. Ibid., p. 127.

48. Costello, *The Irish Revolution and its Aftermath*, p. 294.
49. Greaves, *Liam Mellows and the Irish Revolution*, London: Lawrence and Wishart, 1971, p. 329.
50. Hopkinson, *Green against Green*, p. 134.
51. Regan, *The Irish Counter Revolution*, p. 87.
52. J. Knirck. *Afterimage of the Revolution: Cumann na nGaedheal and Irish Politics, 1922–1932*, Madison: University of Wisconsin Press, 2014, p. 43.
53. Regan, *The Irish Counter-Revolution*, p. 84.
54. J. McCarthy, *Kevin O'Higgins: Builder of the Irish State*, Dublin: Irish Academic Press, 2006, p. 79.
55. Ibid., p. 82.
56. J. Lee, *Ireland 1912–1985*, Cambridge: Cambridge University Press, 1989, p. 127.
57. Dáil Debates, Vol. 1, No. 2, 11 September 1922.
58. J.J. Walsh, *Recollections of a Rebel*, Tralee: Kerryman Ltd, 1944, p. 63.
59. Knirck, *Afterimage of the Irish Revolution*, p. 67.
60. O'Hegarty, *The Victory of Sinn Féin*, Dublin, p. 105.

Chapter 5   A Most Conservative Country

1. Department of Children and Youth Affairs, *Report of Inter-Departmental Group on Mothers and Babies Homes*, Dublin: Stationery Office, 2014, pp. 10 and 15.
2. Ibid., p. 8.
3. M. Nic Ghiolla Phádraig, 'The power of the Catholic Church in the Republic of Ireland', in P. Clancy, S. Drudy, K. Lynch and L.O. Dowd, eds, *Irish Society: Sociological Perspectives*, Dublin: Institute for Public Administration, 1995, pp. 593–619.
4. S.J. Connolly, *Priests and People in Pre-Famine Ireland*, Dublin: Four Courts Press, 2001, p. 102.
5. J. Whyte, *Church and State in Modern Ireland 1923–1979*, Dublin: Gill and Macmillan, 1980, pp. 45–6.
6. D. Ferriter, *The Transformation of Ireland 1900–2000*, London: Profile Books, 2004, p. 420.
7. J. Cooney, *John Charles McQuaid: Ruler of Catholic Ireland*, Dublin: O'Brien Press, 1999, pp. 70–71.
8. Ibid., p. 94.

9. Ibid., p. 96.
10. M. Curtis, *A Challenge to Democracy: Militant Catholicism in Modern Ireland*, Dublin: The History Press, 2010, p. 183, and Cooney, *John Charles McQuaid*, p. 245.
11. Curtis, *A Challenge to Democracy*, p. 113.
12. T. Garvin, *Preventing the Future; Why Was Ireland So Poor For So Long?* Dublin: Gill and Macmillan, 2004, p. 36.
13. T. Inglis, *Moral Monopoly: The Rise and Fall of the Catholic Church in Modern Ireland*, Dublin: University College Dublin Press, 1998, p. 40.
14. Ibid., p. 48.
15. Cooney, *John Charles McQuaid*, p. 133.
16. De Valera to Papal Nuncio, 9 July 1933, in De Valera Papers, File 1280/1, UCD archives.
17. *Quadragesimo Anno*: http://w2.vatican.va/content/pius-xi/en/encyclicals/documents/hf_p-xi_enc_19310515_quadragesimo-anno.html.
18. J. Lee, *Ireland 1912–1985: Politics and Society*, Cambridge: Cambridge University Press, 1989, p. 281.
19. Cooney, *John Charles McQuaid*, p. 258.
20. N. Browne, *Against the Tide*, Dublin: Gill and Macmillan, 1986, p. 190.
21. Minutes of Central Council, CIU, 26 October 1951.
22. Cooney, *John Charles McQuaid*, p. 229.
23. M. Manning, *Irish Political Parties*, Dublin: Gill and Macmillan, 1972, p. 60.
24. K. Boland, *Up Dev*, Dublin: Boland, 1978, p. 26.
25. Dáil Debates, Vol. 25, Col. 478, 12 July 1928.
26. *The Nation*, 2 April 1927.
27. Fianna Fáil, *Coiriu Fianna Fáil*, Dublin: Fianna Fáil, no date.
28. H. Patterson, *The Politics of Illusion: Republicanism and Socialism in Modern Ireland*, London: Hutchinson Radius, 1989, pp. 30–43.
29. *The Nation*, 16 April 1927.
30. *Irish Times*, 2 February 1931.
31. Dáil Debates, Vol. 22, Col. 1651, 22 March 1928.
32. Fianna Fáil, *Founding Document*, Dublin: Fianna Fáil archive.
33. T. Dooley, 'Land and politics in independent Ireland 1923–1948: The case for a re-appraisal', *Irish Historical Studies* Vol. 34, No. 134, 2004, pp. 175–97.
34. Ibid.

35. R. Barrington, *Health, Medicine and Politics in Ireland 1900–1970*, Dublin: Institute of Public Administration, 1987, p. 124.

36. J.A. Murphy, *Ireland in the Twentieth Century*, Dublin: Gill and Macmillan, 1976, p. 86.

37. ITGWU, *Annual Report and Conference Proceedings (1948)*, Dublin: ITGWU, 1948, p. 14.

38. National Economic and Social Council, *A Review of Industrial Policy (Telesis Report)*, Dublin: NESC, 1982, pp. 187–8.

39. 'Orange Order to develop interpretive centres', Press release, EU Special Programmes Body, 31 October 2012.

40. M. Elliot, *The Catholics of Ulster*, London: Allen Lane, 2000, p. 380.

41. P. Gibbon, 'The Dialectic of Religion and Class in Ulster', *New Left Review* Vol. 1, No. 55, 1969, pp. 20–42.

42. G. Bell, *The Protestants of Ulster*, London: Pluto, 1978, p. 100.

43. Ibid., p. 104.

44. Ibid., p. 40.

45. B. Probert, *Beyond Orange and Green: The Northern Ireland Crisis in a New Perspective*, Dublin: Academy Press, 1978, p. 57.

46. Ibid., pp. 58–9.

47. Elliot, *The Catholics of Ulster*, p. 386.

48. Probert, *Beyond Orange and Green*, p. 59.

49. Ibid., p. 61.

50. Elliot, *The Catholics of Ulster*, p. 391.

51. 'Northern Irish workers: Huge wage divide compared to British peers doing the same job', *Belfast Telegraph*, 16 June 2014.

52. R. Sales, *Women Divided: Gender, Religion and Politics in Northern Ireland*, London: Routledge, 1997, p. 36.

53. E. McCann, *War and an Irish Town*, London: Pluto Press, 1993, p. 68.

54. Ibid.

55. B. Hanley, 'Oh, Here's to Adolf Hitler? … The IRA and the Nazis', *History Ireland* Vol. 13, No. 3, May/June 2005.

56. Patterson, *The Politics of Illusion*, p. 75.

57. B. Behan, *The Borstal Boy*, London: Corgi Books, 1967, p. 86.

58. 'Short film focuses zealot Sean South's campaign against Hollywood', *Limerick Leader*, 11 January 2015.

59. M. Milotte, *Communism in Modern Ireland: The Pursuit of the Workers Republic since 1916*, Dublin: Gill and Macmillan, 1984, p. 150.

60. G. Gilmore, *The Republican Congress*, Cork: Cork Workers Club, 1978, p. 35.
61. Ibid., p. 36.
62. Ibid.
63. Milotte, *Communism in Ireland*, p. 153.
64. Ibid., p. 153–4.
65. *Republican Congress*, 13 October 1934.

Chapter 6   The Rise and Fall of Radical Republicanism

1. P. Bishop and E. Mallie, *The Provisional IRA*, London: Heineman, 1987, p. 31.
2. Ibid.
3. K. Marx and F. Engels, *The Communist Manifesto*, Moscow: Progress Publishers, 1969, p. 15.
4. R. Rose, *Governing without Consensus: An Irish Perspective*, London: Faber and Faber, 1971, p. 465.
5. Bishop and Mallie, *The Provisional IRA*, p. 45.
6. D. McKittrick and D. McVea, *Making Sense of the Troubles*, Belfast: Blackstaff Press, 2000, p. 51.
7. E. McCann, *War in an Irish Town*, London: Pluto Press, 1993, p. 272.
8. B. Hanley and S. Millar, *The Lost Revolution*, Dublin: Penguin Ireland, 2010, p. 37.
9. Ibid., pp. 132–3.
10. Interview, 'Discussion on strategy of People Democracy', *New Left Review* Vol. 1, No. 55, May–June 1969, pp. 4–19.
11. P. Arthur, *The People's Democracy 1968–1973*, Belfast: Blackstaff, 1974, p. 55.
12. People's Democracy, *Fascism and the Six Counties*: Belfast: Peoples Democracy, n.d., p. 8.
13. B. O'Brien, *The Long War: The IRA and Sinn Féin*, Dublin: O'Brien Press, 1995, p. 401.
14. B. Anderson, *Joe Cahill: A Life in the IRA*, Dublin: O'Brien Press, 2002, p. 191.
15. E. McCann, 'Open for the Provos', in idem, *War and Peace in Northern Ireland*, Dublin: Hot Press Books, 1998, p. 66.
16. G. Bradley and B. Fenny, *Insider: Gerry Bradley's Life in the IRA*, Dublin: O Brien Press, 2009, p. 64.

17. E. Moloney, *Voices from the Grave: Two Men's War in Ireland*, London: Faber and Faber, 2010, p. 68.

18. J. Boyer Bell, *The Secret Army: The IRA 1916–1979*, Dublin: The Academy Press, 1979, pp. 368–9.

19. R. White, *Provisional Irish Republicans: An Oral and Interpretive History*, Westport, CT: Greenwood, 1993, p. 35.

20. K. Kelley, *The Longest War: Northern Ireland and the IRA*, London: Zed Books, 1988, p. 129.

21. Bishop and Mallie, *The Provisional IRA*, p. 147.

22. K. Kelley, *The Longest War*, p. 201.

23. Ibid., p. 210.

24. Ibid., p. 225.

25. P. Bew and G. Gillespie, *Northern Ireland: A Chronology of the Troubles*, Dublin: Gill and Macmillan, 1999, p. 100.

26. P. Dixon, *Northern Ireland: The Politics of War and Peace*, London: Palgrave Macmillan, 2008, p. 162.

27. E. Moloney, *A Secret History of the IRA*, London: Penguin, 2007, p. 170.

28. Sinn Féin, *Peace With Justice*, Dublin: Sinn Féin, 1972, p. 3.

29. G. Adams, *The Politics of Irish Freedom*, Dingle: Brandon, 1986, p. 91.

30. 'Bodenstown Oration', *Republican News*, 18 June 1977, p. 7.

31. Moloney, *A Secret History of the IRA*, p. 187.

32. Ibid., p. 188.

33. L. O'Ruairc, *A History of the Provos*: ttps://theirishrevolution. wordpress.com/2011/08/17/a-history-of-the-provos-part-two.

34. 'Peter King, 'IRA supporter and enthusiastic counter-terrorism advocate', *Washington Post*, 5 March 2011.

35. G. Adams, *Free Ireland: Towards a Lasting peace*, Dingle: Brandon, 1986, p. 51.

36. Ibid., p. 201.

37. 'We will never be slaves again', *An Pophlacht*, 28 June 1984, p. 7.

38. B. Campbell, *Nor Meekly Serve My Time: H Block Struggle 1976–1981*, Belfast: Beyond the Pale, 1994, pp. 263–4.

39. K. Bean, *The New Politics of Sinn Féin* , Liverpool: Liverpool University Press, 2007, p. 186.

40. Ibid., p. 183.

41. Moloney, *A Secret History of the IRA*, p. 269.

42. The TUAS Document: http://cain.ulst.ac.uk/othelem/organ/ira/tuas94.htm.

43. Ibid.

44. The Northern Ireland Peace Agreement: http://www.taoiseach.gov.ie/attached_files/Pdf%20files/NIPeaceAgreement.pdf.

45 A. McIntyre, *Good Friday: The Death of Irish Republicanism*, New York: Ausubo Press, 2008, p. 207.

46. Sinn Féin, *Towards a New Republic*, Dublin: Sinn Féin, 2014, p. 3.

47. E. O'Broin, *Sinn Féin and the Politics of Left Republicanism*, London: Pluto Press, 2009, p. 307.

48. A. Maillot, *New Sinn Féin*, New York Routledge, 2005, p. 60.

49. M.G. Backus, '"A most curious state of affairs": An interview with Eamonn McCann on Northern Ireland and the Good Friday Agreement', *Re-Thinking Marxism* Vol. 13, No. 1, 2010, pp. 83–97.

50. 'Adams predicts a united Ireland', *BBC News*, 14 January 2000: http://news.bbc.co.uk/2/hi/uk_news/northern_ireland/601115.stm

51. Quoted in K. Bean and M. Hayes, 'Sinn Féin and the new republicanism in Ireland: Electoral progress, political stasis, and ideological failure', *Radical History Review* No. 104, Spring 2009, pp. 126–42.

52. Portland Trust, *Economics in Peacemaking: Lessons from Northern Ireland*, London: Portland Trust, 2007, p. 15.

53. 'A new kind of trouble', *The Economist*, 24 January 2015.

54. Northern Ireland Executive, *Northern Ireland Budget 2014–2015*, p. 8: http://www.northernireland.gov.uk/draft-budget-2015-2016.pdf.

55. PWC, *Northern Ireland Economic Outlook 2015*, Belfast: PWC, 2015, p. 9.

56. Ibid., p. 23.

57. Northern Ireland Executive, *Economic Strategies for Sustainable Growth and Prosperity*, Belfast: NIE, 2015 p. 71.

58. R. Murphy, *Pot of Gold or Fool's Gold*, Dublin: ICTU, 2010.

59. P. Mac Flynn, *Public Sector Employment in Northern Ireland*, Belfast: NERI, 2015, p. 3.

60. C. Gormley-Heenan and R. MacGinty, 'Ethnic outbidding and party modernization: Understanding the Democratic Unionist Party's electoral success in the post Agreement environment', *Ethnopolitics* Vol. 7, No. 1, 2008, pp. 43–61.

61. B. Murtagh and P. Shirlow, 'Devolution and the politics of development in Northern Ireland', *Environment and Planning* Vol. 30, 2012, pp. 46–61.

Chapter 7   From the Ashes a Phoenix is Born

1. '30 days in September: An oral history of the bank guarantee', *The Journal.ie*, 17 December 2014.
2. Ibid.
3. Ibid.
4. 'Cantillon: Banking inquiry becomes Night of the Differing Memories', *Irish Times*, 2 May 2015.
5. 'Patrick Honohan – Clarification of evidence previously given to the committee', at Committee of Inquiry into the Banking Crisis Hearings: https://inquiries.oireachtas.ie/banking/hearings/patrick-hono-han-clarification-of-evidence-previously-given-to-the-committee/.
6. Memorandum from Merrill Lynch, 28 September 2009, p. 9.
7. Public Accounts Committee Documents – Transcript of handwritten note of meeting between Goldman Sachs and Department of Finance, Central Bank and Financial Regulator, 21 September 2008.
8. 'Enda Kenny unveils Irish cabinet for "new phase of recovery"', *BBC News*, 11 July 2014.
9. 'McCann corners Ireland's asset-covered bond market', *The Lawyer.com*, 24 April 2004.
10. Deutsche Bank, *Covered Bond Market Set for Further Structural Changes*, London: Deutsche Bank, 2011, p. 85.
11. '30 days in September'.
12. Davy Stockbrokers, *Housing: The Past, Present and Future*, Dublin: Davy, 2014, and 'Global property bubble fears mount as prices and yields spike', *Financial Times* , 16 April 2015.
13. 'Banks write off over €300m in three deals with Denis O'Brien', *Irish Times*, 13 June 2014.
14. T. Boland, 'Why don't the Irish protest', *South Eastern Sociology*, 7 November 2011.
15. N. Klein, *The Shock Doctrine*, London: Allen Lane, 2007.
16. 'Political stability helps drive Irish recovery', *Financial Times*, 27 January 2012.
17. R. Hearne, *The Irish Water War, Austerity and the 'Risen People'*, Maynooth: Department of Geography, NUIM, 2015.
18. P. Mair, *Ruling the Void: The Hollowing Out of Western Democracy*, London: Verso, 2013.

19. M. Gallagher and M. Marsh, *How Ireland Voted 2007: The Full Story of Ireland's General Election*, Basingstoke: Palgrave Macmillan, 2007.

20. 'Did you hear the one about Sinn Féin's sectarian leaflet', *Irish Times*, 7 May 2015.

21. 'Greece's new prime minister reckons Sinn Féin will win the election next year', *The Journal.ie*, 26 January 2016.

22. Personal notes taken at conference.

23. E. Laclau and C. Mouffe, *Hegemony and Socialist Strategy*, London: Verso, 2001.

24. L. Stobbart, 'Understanding Podemos: Radical Populism', *Left Flank*, 14 November 2014: http://left-flank.org/2014/11/14/understanding-podemos-23-radical-populism/.

25. I. Errejon, 'Obituary to Ernest Laclau, Theorist of Hegemony': http://www.versobooks.com/blogs/1578-ernesto-laclau-theorist-of-hegemony.

26. I. Errejon, 'Spain's Podemos: Inside view of a radical left sensation', *Revolting Europe*, 15 July 2014: revolting-europe.com/2014/07/15/spains-podemos-inside-view-of-a-radical-left-sensation/.

27. 'Spiegel Interview with Greek Prime Minister Tsipras: "We Don't Want to Go on Borrowing Forever"', *Spiegel*, 7 March 2015.

28. J. Connolly, *Workshop Talks*, Chicago, IL: Charles Kerr, 1909: https://www.marxists.org/archive/connolly/1909/talks/shoptlks.htm.

29. Ibid.

30. Ibid.

31. Ibid.

32. Ibid.

33. J. Connolly, 'Industrial Unionism and Constructive Socialism', in idem, *Socialism Made Easy*, Chicago, IL: Charles Kerr, 1908: https://www.marxists.org/archive/connolly/1908/sme/inconsoc.htm.

34. Connolly, *Workshop Talks*.

35. Ibid.

36. Ibid.

37. Ibid.

Select Bibliography

Anderson, B. *Joe Cahill: A Life in the IRA*, Dublin: O Brien Press, 2002.

Arthur, P. *The People's Democracy 1968-1973*, Belfast: Blackstaff, 1974.

Augusteijn, J. *The Irish Revolution*, Basingstoke; Palgrave 2002.

———. *From Public Defiance to Guerrilla Warfare: The experience of ordinary volunteers in the Irish War of Independence*, Dublin: Irish Academic Press, 1996.

———. *Patrick Pearse: The Making of a Revolutionary*, London: Palgrave, 2010.

Bean, K. *The New Politics of Sinn Fein*, Liverpool: Liverpool University Press, 2007.

Bell, G. *The Protestants of Ulster*, London: Pluto, 1978.

Bew, P. *Conflict and Conciliation in Ireland 1890–1910*. Oxford Clarendon Press, 1987.

———. *John Redmond*, Dublin: Historical Association of Ireland, 1996.

———. *Land and National Question in Ireland, 1858–1882*, Dublin: Gill and Macmillan, 1978.

Bishop, P. and E. Mallie, *The Provisional IRA*, London: Heineman, 1987.

Boyer Bell, J. *The Secret Army: The IRA 1916–1979*, Dublin: The Academy Press, 1979.

Brendon, P. *The Decline and Fall of the British Empire*, London: Vintage, 2008.

Browne, N. *Against the Tide*, Dublin: Gill and Macmillan, 1986.

Connolly, J. *Socialism Made Easy*, Chicago, IL: Charles Kerr, 1908.

———. *The Lost Writings*, London: Pluto Press, 1997.

Connolly, S.J. *Priests and People in Pre-Famine Ireland*, Dublin: Four Courts Press, 2001.

Cooney, J. *John Charles McQuaid: Ruler of Catholic Ireland*, Dublin: O'Brien Press, 1999.

Costello, F. *The Irish Revolution and its Aftermath 1916–23*, Dublin: Irish Academic Press, 2003.

Curtis, M. *A Challenge to Democracy: Militant Catholicism in Modern Ireland*, Dublin: The History Press, 2010.

Dudley Edwards, R. *Patrick Pearse: The Triumph of Failure*, London, Victor Gollancz, 1977.

Elliot, M. *The Catholics of Ulster*, London: Allen Lane, 2000.

Farrell, M. *Arming the Protestants: the Formation of the Ulster Special Constabulary and the Royal Ulster Constabulary 1920–27*, Dingle: Brandon, 1983.

Ferriter, D. *The Transformation of Ireland 1900–2000*, London: Profile Books, 2004.

Figgis, D. *Recollections of the Irish War*, London: Forgotten Books, 2013.

Finnan, J. *John Redmond and Irish Unity 1912–1918*, New York: Syracuse University, 2004.

Fitzpatrick, D. *Politics and Irish Life*, Dublin: Gill and Macmillan, 1977.

——. 'The Disappearance of the Irish Agricultural labourer 1841–1912', *Irish Economic and Social History*, 7, 1986, pp. 66–92.

Foster, R. *Modern Ireland 1600–1972*, Harmondsworth: Penguin, 1988.

Foy, M. and B. Barton. *The Easter Rising*, Stroud: Sutton Publishing, 1999.

Garvin, T. *1922: The Birth of Irish Nationalism*, Dublin: Gill and Macmillan, 1996.

——. *The Evolution of the Irish Nationalist Politics*, Dublin, 1981.

Gray, J. *City in Revolt: James Larkin & the Belfast Dock Strike of 1907*, Belfast: Blackstaff Press, 1985.

Hanley, B. and S.Millar, *The Lost Revolution*, Dublin: Penguin Ireland, 2010.

Hart, P. *Mick: The Real Michael Collins*, London: Macmillan, 2005.

Hopkinson, M. *Green against Green: The Irish Civil War*, Dublin: Gill and Macmillan, 1988.

——. *The War of Independence*, Dublin: Gill and Macmillan, 2002.

Inglis, T. *Moral Monopoly: The Rise and Fall of the Catholic Church in Modern Ireland*, Dublin: University College Dublin Press, 1998.

Kelley, K. *The Longest War: Northern Ireland and the IRA*, London: Zed Books, 1988.

Kennedy, C. *Genesis of the Rising 1912–1916*, New York: Peter Lang, 2010.

Kennedy, L. 'The Roman Catholic Church and Economic Growth in Nineteenth Century Ireland', *Economic and Social Review*, Vol. 10, No. 1, 1978, pp. 45–60.

Kinealy, C. 'Beyond Revisionism: Re-Assessing the Great Irish Famine', *History Ireland*, No. 4, 1995.

Knirck, J. *Afterimage of the revolution: Cumann na nGaedheal and Irish Politics, 1922–1932*, Madison: University of Wisconsin Press, 2014.

Kostick, C. *Revolution in Ireland: Popular Militancy 1917–1923*, Cork: Cork University Press, 2009.

Lee, J. *Ireland 1912–1985: Politics and Society*, Cambridge: Cambridge University Press, 1989.

Leeson, D.M. *The Black and Tans: British Police and Auxiliaries in the Irish War of Independence*, Oxford: Oxford University Press, 2011.

Lynch, P. 'The social revolution that never was', in D. Williams, ed., *The Irish Struggle 1916–1926*, London: Routledge and Kegan Paul, 1966.

Macardle, D. *The Irish Republic*, Dublin: Wolfhound Press, 1999.

McCann, E. *War and an Irish Town*, London: Pluto Press, 1993.

McCarthy, J. *Kevin O'Higgins: Builder of the Irish State*, Dublin: Irish Academic Press, 2006.

McGarry, F. *Rebels*, Dublin: Penguin Ireland, 2011.

MacKay, J. *Michael Collins*, Edinburgh: Mainstream Publishing, 1996.

McKittrick, D. and D. McVea, *Making Sense of the Troubles*, Belfast: Blackstaff Press, 2000.

Maye, B. *Arthur Griffith*, Dublin: Griffith College Publications, 1997.

Meleady, D. *John Redmond: The National Leader*, Dublin: Irish Academic Press, 2014.

Milotte, M. *Communism in Modern Ireland: The Pursuit of the Workers Republic since 1916*, Dublin: Gill and Macmillan, 1984.

Mitchell, A. *Revolutionary Government in Ireland: Dail Eireann 1919–22*, Dublin: Gill and Macmillan, 1995.

Moloney, E. *A Secret History of the IRA*, London: Penguin, 2007.

——. *Voices from the Grave: Two Men's War in Ireland*, London: Faber and Faber, 2010.

Murphy, B. *Patrick Pearse and the Lost Republican Ideal*, Dublin: James Duffy, 1991.

Murphy, J.A. *Ireland in the Twentieth Century*, Dublin: Gill and Macmillan, 1975.

Neeson, E. *Birth of a Republic*, Dublin: Prestige Books, 1998.

Newsinger, J. *Fenianism in Mid Victorian Britain*, London: Pluto Press.

O'Brien, B. *The Long War: The IRA and Sinn Fein*, Dublin: O'Brien Press, 1995.

O'Broin, L. *Dublin Castle and the 1916 Rising*, London: Sidgwick and Jackson, 1970.

O'Buachalla, L., ed. *The Letters of P.H. Pearse*, Gerard's Cross: Colin Smythe, 1980.

O'Connor, E. *Syndicalism in Ireland 1917–1923*, Cork: Cork University Press, 1988.

O'Donnell, P. *There will be Another Day*, Dublin: Dolmen Press, 1963.

O'Hegarty, P.S. *The Victory of Sinn Fein*, Dublin: UCD Press, 1998.

Pakenham, F. *Peace by Ordeal: The Negotiation of the Anglo-Irish Treaty 1921*, London: Pimlico, 1992.

Patterson, H. *The Politics of Illusion: Republicanism and Socialism in Modern Ireland*, London: Hutchinson Radius, 1989.

Pearse, P. *Collected Works of P.H. Pearse*, Political Writings and Speeches, Dublin: Phoenix, 1916.

Paseta, S. *Before the Revolution, Nationalism, Social Change and Ireland's Catholic Elite 1879-1922*, Cork: Cork University Press, 1999.

Probert, B. *Beyond Orange and Green: The Northern Ireland Crisis in a New Perspective*, Dublin: Academy Press, 1978.

Reeve, C. and A.B. *James Connolly in United States*, Atlantic HIghlands, NJ: Humanities Press, 1978.

Regan, J.M. *The Irish Counter-Revolution 1921–1936*, Dublin: Gill and Macmillan, 2001.

Robbins, F. *Under the Starry Plough*, Dublin: Academy Press, 1978.

Strauss, E. *Irish Nationalism and British Democracy*, London: Methuen, 1951.

Townsend, C. *The Republic: The Fight for Irish Independence*, London: Allen Lane, 2013.

Wall, M. 'The background to the Rising from 1914 until the issue of the countermanding order on Easter Saturday 1916', in K. B. Nowlan, ed., *The Making of 1916*, Dublin: Stationery Office, 1969.

Walsh, P. *The Rise and Fall of Imperial Ireland*, Belfast: Athol Book, 2003.

Whyte, J. *Church and State in Modern Ireland 1923–1979*, Dublin: Gill and Macmillan, 1980.

Yeates, P. *Lockout Dublin 1913*, Dublin: Gill and Macmillan, 2000.

Index